THE ARTS & ENTERTAINMENT IN LONDON

In association with London Transport

FRANCESCA COLLIN

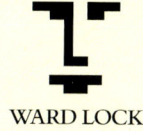

WARD LOCK

To Simon, who makes things possible

A WARD LOCK BOOK
First published in the UK 1997 by Ward Lock
Wellington House, 125 Strand
LONDON WC2R 0BB

A Cassell Imprint
Copyright
© Text Francesca Collin 1997
© Posters and advertisements London Transport Museum 1997
© Volume Ward Lock 1997

Distributed in the United States
by Sterling Publishing Co., Inc.
387 Park Avenue South, New York, NY 10016–8810

A British Library Cataloguing in Publication Data block for this
book may be obtained from the British Library
ISBN 0 7063 7513 0

Project Editor Jane Birch
Designed by Richard Carr
Printed and bound in Spain

CONTENTS

About London Transport 4
Introduction 6
Symbols Used in This Book 7

VISUAL ARTS 9
1 FINE ARTS 10
2 DECORATIVE ARTS 34
3 SPECIAL INTEREST MUSEUMS 47
4 HISTORIC HOUSES AND BUILDINGS 84

PERFORMING ARTS 107
5 THEATRE 108
6 MUSIC 139
7 BALLET, DANCE AND OPERA 154
8 CINEMA 165
9 COMEDY 180
10 OUTDOOR ENTERTAINMENT 184
11 THE ENTERTAINMENT YEAR 190

Additional Information 200
Index 202
Acknowledgements 208

❖

ABOUT LONDON TRANSPORT

THE UNDERGROUND

With trains running every few minutes on most lines, the Underground provides a frequent and reliable service, 20 hours a day. Once you are armed with a copy of the Tube Map (on the inside front cover of this book and also available free from ticket offices and Travel Information Centres), finding your way around the Tube is straightforward.

Tickets have to be purchased before you travel on the Tube, otherwise you are liable to a penalty fare of £10. Tickets can be purchased through ticket machines in the stations or from the station's booking office. Fares are based on a zonal system; further details are available from all ticket offices.

Most central London stations now have automatic exit and entry ticket gates. Put your ticket into the automatic gate, then take it out at the top, at which point the gate will open and you can walk through. If you have completed your journey the machine will keep the ticket, but valid travelcards will be returned by the machine on the automatic gate.

THE BUSES

London's famous buses now come in all shapes and sizes. Many are still red but other companies run buses in their own colours for London Transport. The London Transport Service symbol on the front of those buses that are not red tells you that Travelcards are accepted.

There are two types of bus stop: Compulsory (white background) and Request (red background). Buses will stop automatically to pick up at Compulsory stops unless the bus is full. Buses will only stop at Request stops if you signal to the bus driver by putting your arm out, or if you ring the bell while on the bus.

NIGHT BUSES

If you stay out late you can always get home by using one of the special night buses. These are identified by letter N before the number. Many of the night buses follow daytime routes, but others have their own routes. All night buses (except N31) pass through Trafalgar Square to the popular entertainment areas. But remember that One-Day Travelcards and Weekend Travelcards are not accepted on night buses and fares are higher than during the day. All bus stops become Request stops at night.

TRAVELCARDS AND SEASON TICKETS

You can purchase Travelcards valid for one or seven days, but One-Day Travelcards can be subject to early morning rush hour restrictions. Travelcards are accepted on all London Transport buses, Underground lines, Docklands Light Railway and most trains, within the zones you have paid for. Period Travelcards, which do not have rush hour restrictions, are valid for one week, one month or any period up to a year.

The Family Travelcard is a One-Day ticket for the family with all the benefits of the One-Day Travelcard, but which saves you even more money. You can use the Tube, buses (not night buses) displaying the London Transport buses sign, Docklands Light Railway and any rail service within the travel zones selected.

The Weekend Travelcard is valid for the two days of the weekend or two consecutive days during a weekend with a public holiday. It has the same validity as the Family Travelcard.

The Carnet is a book of ten tickets for Zone 1 only. It saves money if you are travelling solely within Zone 1, and is available for adults and children.

TRAVEL INFORMATION

London Transport Travel Information Centres (TICs) offer a wide range of services, including maps, phone cards, souvenirs and sightseeing tours. They can be found at:

RAIL STATIONS

Euston, Victoria

BUS STATIONS

Hammersmith, West Croydon

HEATHROW AIRPORT TERMINALS

Terminal 1, 2 and 4 Arrivals

UNDERGROUND STATIONS

Heathrow 1, 2, 3, King's Cross, Liverpool Street, Oxford Circus, Piccadilly Circus, St James's Park

LT TRAVEL INFORMATION CALL CENTRE

You can telephone 0171 222 1234 twenty-four hours a day (except Christmas Day) for up-to-the-minute information on all aspects of public transport within the Greater London area.

RAIL

Those travelling from outside London can reach the city by rail and many of the services connect with the Underground network. While you are more dependent on timetables with rail, there are fewer stops so distances are covered more quickly. The main stations in London are: Charing Cross, Euston, King's Cross, Liverpool Street, Paddington, St Pancras, Victoria and Waterloo, which now gives you access to Europe through the Channel Tunnel.

INTRODUCTION

T HE ARTS HAVE long played a major role in London life and are, I feel, even more important today than at any other time. As the pressures of living in this busy city get ever greater, the wealth of culture, arts and entertainment available here assumes an increasing significance as a vital antidote. In this book I have brought together the best of what London offers with something to interest all ages and tastes.

WHEN did you last see your Picassos?

You are the owner of millions of pounds' worth of paintings by the great masters, not and new, displayed for your enjoyment in London's art galleries and museums. Some of your pictures this year are watching the International Picasso exhibition at the Tate Gallery from 6 July to 18 September

Undesigned by Westminster Bus-line 739 (Sundays), 94. Admission to the Picasso exhibition 2/-

Fine art (paintings and sculpture) are superbly represented in London's major galleries. You don't need to be an art historian to enjoy spending an afternoon wandering around the Tate, the National or the National Portrait Gallery. These important institutions house the nation's collections of art and give a fascinating visual history of western art from the Renaissance to the present day. Just about everyone agrees that these are among the finest major galleries in the world – so take advantage of them.

Although these major galleries are an excellent starting point for anyone interested in art, they are by no means the only places to visit. Smaller galleries, often built up by private collectors, such as the delightful Dulwich Picture Gallery in south London, the peaceful Serpentine Gallery in Hyde Park or the avant-garde Saatchi Gallery in St John's Wood, show the full breadth of the definition of art. Don't forget the commercial galleries either – they are excellent places to see (and buy) works of art.

The decorative arts (everything in art that is not a picture or sculpture) can be found in many museums across London, but the best in this field is the wonderful Victoria & Albert Museum in South Kensington. Two more of London's best-loved museums – the Science Museum and the Natural History Museum – are also in South Kensington. All three were established with the profits made from the Great Exhibition of 1851 held in nearby Hyde Park.

Museums threw off their stuffy image long ago and today are great places to have fun as well as to learn. However, some museums are purely for entertainment: the popularity of Madame Tussaud's never wanes and the Rock Circus – a hall of fame for rock stars – is proving equally successful.

If you want to see your favourite pop stars in the flesh, London offers live music seven days a week, from spectacular shows at Wembley to lively gigs in local pubs.

Classical music also plays an important role in the performing arts world. Both the London Symphony and the Philharmonic orchestras are based here and there are always plenty of concerts to choose from. Perhaps one of the most delightful ways to spend a Sunday morning is to go to a concert at the Wigmore Hall, or, if you are after pomp and ceremony, don't miss the high point of the classical music year, the last night of the Proms in September.

London's theatre scene is among the most dynamic and exciting in the world. Every type of theatre is performed, from popular West End shows to repertory productions and mime theatre. Dance and opera can be found throughout London too. Watching a performance at the Royal Opera House is a memorable experience, but I have also included less well-known and less expensive venues.

Live comedy has taken off in recent years and London offers an excellent platform for comics. The Comedy Store has produced many of today's best-known artists and is always packed, but it is fun to check out some smaller clubs too and, perhaps, even heckle the comedians who don't make the grade!

Entertainment is not just an indoor activity. Each summer a season of outdoor theatre and concerts takes place across London – there's no more relaxed way to spend a warm evening – and all through the year you will find street entertainment from jugglers to dancers in Covent Garden's piazza. In the Entertainment Year section I have included the best of what's on regularly each year – enough to keep even the most active person busy.

London is the nation's treasure house for the arts – both visual and performing. They are there for you to enjoy. Get out and have some fun!

Francesca Collin

Symbols Used in This Book

⊖	Underground station	∿		Boat
▣	Railway station	P		Parking available
DLR	Docklands Light Railway station	♿		Wheelchair access
🚌	Buses (where several buses serve a particular place, only the major ones are given)	£		Small charge – less than £6
		££		Moderate charge – £6 and above

Overleaf: 'Bacchus and Ariadne' by Titian. The National Gallery

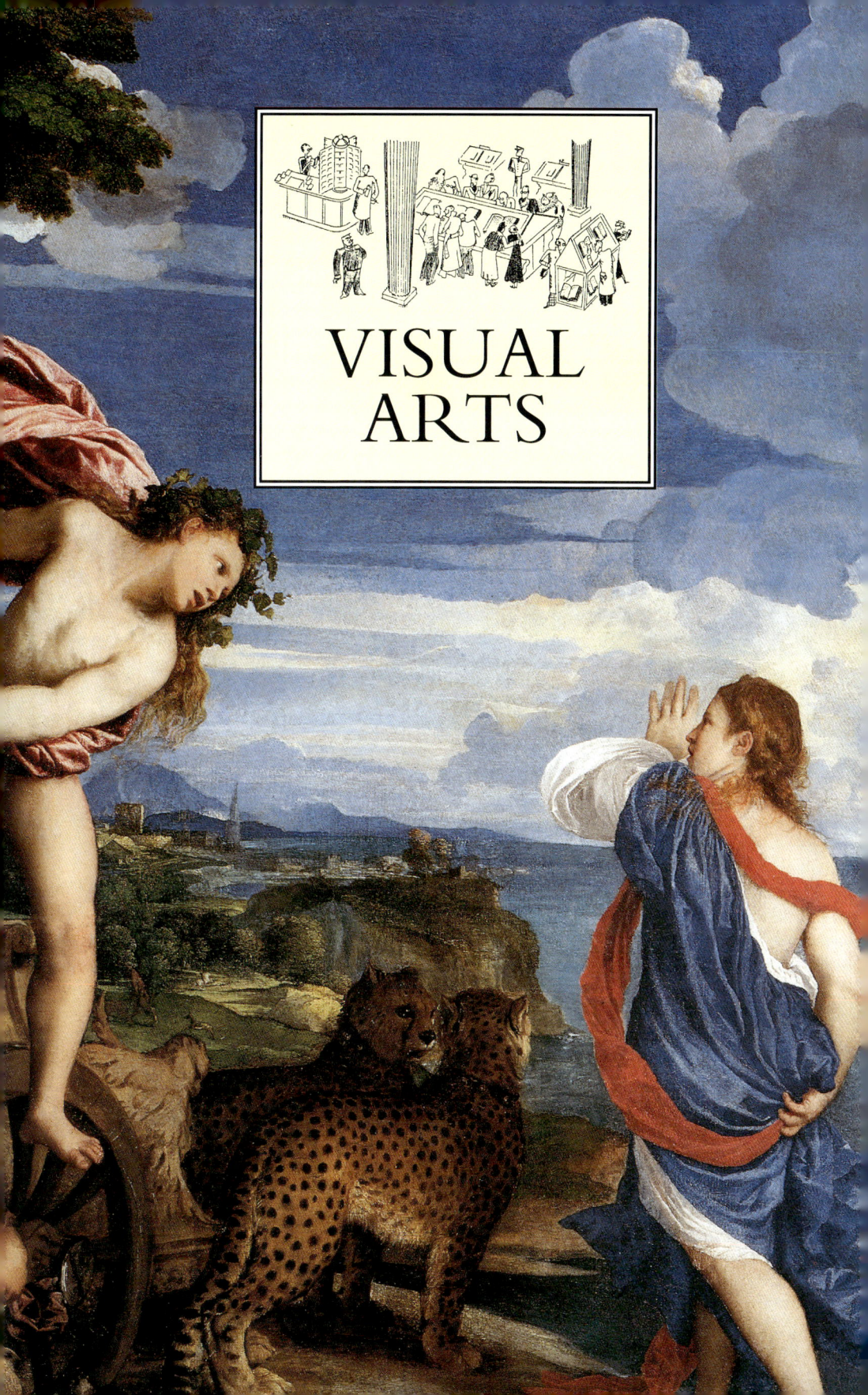

VISUAL
ARTS

1
FINE ARTS

NATIONAL COLLECTIONS

L ONDON'S THREE MAJOR galleries span the history of art from medieval to modern, with some of the best works of art in the world. They house the nation's collections of pictures, paintings, drawings and sculpture that form the core of London's art world.

See also the British Museum (page 34), the Imperial War Museum (page 61), the National Maritime Museum (page 62) and the Victoria & Albert Museum (page 37).

The National Gallery
Trafalgar Square, WC2 (0171 839 3321; 0171 777 2885: information)
Two factors in particular make the National Gallery one of the most important and enjoyable galleries in the world. First, unlike many major galleries in other countries, its collection is international rather than national, housing one of the world's finest collections of western European paintings from 1260 to 1920 and offering a fascinating journey through the history of western art. Second, it is almost unique in having all the paintings in its collection on display, except those on loan and those being reframed or treated in the Conservation Department.

Room 41 of the National Gallery

The National Gallery was founded in 1824 when Parliament voted £57,000 for the purchase of thirty-eight pictures from the collection of John Julius Angerstein (1735–1823), a City banker. His paintings included Titian's 'Venus and Adonis', Rubens' 'Rape of the Sabine Women', Rembrandt's 'Woman taken in Adultery' and the 'Adoration of the Shepherds'. Originally the collection was hung in his house at 100 Pall Mall but it was moved to its present site in 1838, when the National Gallery building was completed. On the site of the former Royal Mews, the building was intended as an architectural climax to Trafalgar Square. It has never been entirely popular, however, and the Sainsbury Wing added in 1991 was even more controversial, especially after HRH the Prince of Wales described it as a 'monstrous carbuncle'. Nevertheless, the National still remains a hugely popular gallery with over four million visitors each year and now houses over 2,300 pictures. New acquisitions are made for the collection too, and are referred to as 'having been bought for the Nation'. Recent purchases include Holbein's 'Lady with a Squirrel and a Starling'.

Among the best-known works in the National Gallery are 'The Arnolfini Marriage' by Jan van Eyck, 'The Baptism of Christ' by Piero della Francesca, 'The Virgin and Child with Saint Anne and Saint John the Baptist' by Leonardo da Vinci, 'Bacchus and Ariadne' by Titian, 'The Chapeau de Paille' by Rubens, 'The Haywain' by Constable, 'The Water-lily Pond' by Monet and 'Sunflowers' by Van Gogh.

Each Wing of the gallery contains paintings from a different period. The oldest paintings, dating from 1260 to 1510 and including van Eyck, Piero della Francesca, Botticelli, Leonardo da Vinci, Bellini and Raphael, are hung in the Sainsbury Wing. The West Wing contains paintings from 1510 to 1600, including Cranach, Michelangelo, Holbein, Titian, Veronese and El Greco. The North Wing contains paintings from 1600 to 1700, including Rubens, Poussin, Velázquez, Van Dyck, Claude, Rembrandt and Vermeer. The East Wing contains paintings from 1700 to 1920, including Gainsborough, Turner, Constable, Cézanne, Monet, Van Gogh, Seurat and Picasso. The remainder of the collection is displayed in the lower-floor galleries.

Temporary exhibitions are frequently held to complement the permanent collection, usually in the Sainsbury Wing exhibition galleries.

The Associate Artist scheme began in 1990 with Paula Rego as the participating artist, followed by Ken Kiff in 1992. Exhibitions of works produced during the association are shown at the gallery at the end of the period.

An innovation introduced in 1991 is the Micro Gallery, where you can see any painting in the collection by working a user-friendly touch-screen computer. This enables you to explore your individual area of interest, whether it is a particular painting, artist, period, subject matter or genre, and is free of charge.

An excellent way to look round the National Gallery is to use the gallery guide soundtrack, available for hire from the distribution desks at the main entrance and at the Sainsbury Wing entrance. You can select commentaries on pictures of your choice in any order you wish and these will provide information on the subject matter, history, technique, artists, and the gallery in which a particular picture is hung.

Tours are available twice daily from Monday to Saturday. There are lectures at 1.00 p.m. (Tuesday–Friday; 12 noon on Saturday) at most times of the year and films about artists or schools of painting at 1.00 p.m. on Monday. Facilities include a restaurant, a café and a bookshop.

☻ Charing Cross, Leicester Square, Embankment, Piccadilly Circus

🚌 11, 12, 15, 24, 29, 77A

♿ Orange Street, Sainsbury Wing

Open: Gallery Monday–Saturday, 10.00 a.m.–6.00 p.m.; Sunday 12 noon–6.00 p.m.; Wednesday 10.00 a.m.–8.00 p.m.Micro Gallery Monday–Saturday 10.00 a.m.–5.30 p.m., Sunday 12 noon–5.30 p.m. (closed 1 January, Good Friday, May Day holiday, and 24–26 December); Library (by appointment only)

Free

National Portrait Gallery

St Martin's Place, WC2 (0171 306 0055)

Founded in 1856 to collect paintings of royal and political characters, the National Portrait Gallery brings history to life through its hundreds of portraits of Britain's most influential and famous figures.

The exhibits are arranged chronologically starting from the top of the building, where you will find medieval and Tudor pictures – portraits in the modern sense were not produced in the Middle Ages. Among the earliest works that is on display is a portrait of Margaret Beaufort, mother of Henry VII, which was painted on a panel *c.*1485.

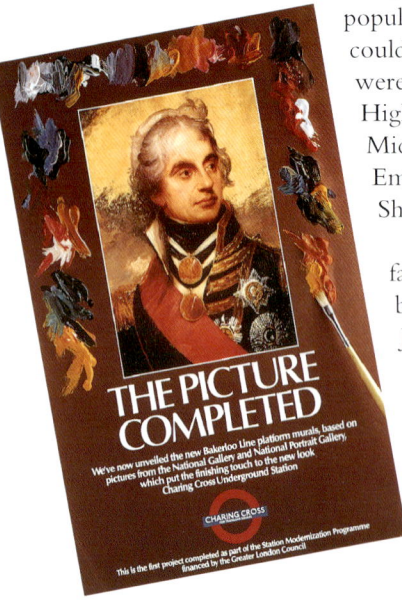

By Tudor times, portraits of monarchs were more popular. By this time, it was realized how useful they could be for purposes of state and propaganda and they were distributed by means of copies and engravings. Highlights from this period include 'Henry VII' by Michael Sittow, painted in 1505 for the Holy Roman Emperor, and the only known portrait of William Shakespeare.

From the seventeenth century there are the famous 'Kit-Cat' portraits. These were painted between 1700 and 1720 by Sir Godfrey Kneller for Jacob Tonson, a well-known publisher. The portraits took their name from the Kit-Cat club that met at a tavern near Temple Bar in London, kept by Christopher Cat. The tavern was renowned for its mutton pies, known as Kit-Cats.

Portraits of Lord Nelson and the Duke of Wellington record the Napoleonic periods and there is a wonderful series of paintings of the great romantic poets: Wordsworth, Coleridge, Keats, Shelley and Byron.

Among the Victorians displayed are splendid portraits of Queen Victoria, Prince Albert and many of the great politicians, scientists and explorers of the era. Victorian artists and writers are recalled in portraits which range from the remarkable study of the Brontë sisters by their brother, Branwell, to works by G.F. Watts and John Singer Sargent.

The Early Twentieth-Century Galleries cover the period from 1914 to 1945. The display includes First World War portraits, as well as paintings of politicians, scientists and major stars of stage and screen. A substantial collection of portraits of the Bloomsbury Group of writers and artists includes Duncan Grant's portrait of Vanessa Bell.

The Later Twentieth-Century Galleries feature contemporary portraits from 1945 to the present day. The exhibition space includes the Porter Gallery for newly acquired and commissioned works and the Emmanuel Kaye Gallery for portraits of scientists, technologists and business tycoons. The Photography Gallery features both works from the Gallery's photographic collection and loan exhibitions from contemporary photographers.

Among the permanent collection of the Twentieth-Century Gallery you will find a host of well-known personalities, including such writers as Iris Murdoch and T.S. Eliot and such artists as David Hockney, Lucian Freud and Graham Sutherland. Sports figures include footballer Bobby Charlton and cricketer Ian Botham, while from the world of pop music there is Paul McCartney and Elton John. Portraits of Her Majesty the Queen and the present royal family are on display on the mezzanine landing.

The National Portrait Gallery has a regular programme of free lunch-time lectures, room talks, videos and musical and dramatic events. Details about these are available from the Information Desk. There is also a bookshop.

⊖ Charing Cross, Leicester Square

▣ Charing Cross

🚌 11, 12, 15, 24, 29, 77A

♿ through Orange Street entrance

Open: Gallery Monday–Saturday, 10.00 a.m.–6.00 p.m.; Sunday, 12 noon–6.00 p.m. (closed 1 January, Good Friday, May Day bank holiday, and 24–26 December); Heinz Archive and Library (in Orange Street) by appointment, Tuesday–Saturday, 10.00 a.m.–5.00 p.m.

Free (£ for some exhibitions)

Tate Gallery

Millbank, SW1 (0171 887 8000)

Set in a majestic nineteenth-century building on the site of the old Millbank Prison and facing south across the Thames, the Tate Gallery ranks with the National Gallery, the British Museum and the Victoria & Albert Museum as one of the great museums of Britain.

The Tate Gallery has a dual role as the museum of British art and international twentieth-century art. It was set up in 1897 as the National Gallery of British Art to house the collection of nineteenth-century painting and sculpture given to the nation by Sir Henry Tate, together with some paintings transferred from the National Gallery in Trafalgar Square. Its responsibilities were specifically for modern British art, then defined as work by artists born after 1790.

In 1917, following a bequest of modern paintings from the collection of Sir Hugh Lane, the Tate Gallery was formally constituted as the National Gallery of Modern Foreign Art. At the same time, its responsibilities for British art were extended to artists born before 1790. In 1939, at the outbreak of the Second

World War, the gallery was closed and the collection dispersed to places of safety. It reopened in 1945 having sustained extensive war damage.

The spacious and well-lit main galleries are built around a central hall. As with many of the world's great art museums, the Tate Gallery has not nearly enough space to show its entire collection at once. For this reason, the Tate's displays now change each year and some also change at intervals throughout the year. This programme is called 'New Displays' and provides different ways of looking at the Collection, offering changing contexts and readings and suggesting connections between the arts of the past and present. Each room has a closely defined theme, explained in an introductory wall text, with extended captions providing further information about individual works of art.

One of the best ways to enjoy the gallery is to head for Duveen Sculpture Galleries which offer the main route into the gallery. From Room 1, you can trace the story of British paintings until Impressionism in the nineteenth century and then the inter-relationship of British and foreign art in the twentieth century. Within the sequence, particular schools of artists are represented in depth, such as eighteenth-century landscape painting, the Pre-Raphaelites and the London Avant-Garde, 1910–20. A free plan available at the Information desk gives locations of all current displays. It is worth hiring a personal audio guide, known as Tate Inform, from the Rotunda which will guide you through the maze of painters and works.

Since the Tate building was first opened in 1897, new gallery space has been added. One of the main developments was the Clore Gallery for the Turner Collection which opened in 1987. This houses the most comprehensive display of Turner's work in the world.

One of the Tate's most famous initiatives is the Turner Prize, awarded each year to a British artist under fifty years of age for an outstanding presentation of

Turner Collection

Joseph Mallord William Turner (1775–1851) is perhaps the best-loved British artist. One of the greatest (and most prolific) landscape artists, Turner produced over 300 major oil paintings and 20,000 drawings and watercolours. On his death he left his works to the nation and today they are housed in the Clore Gallery at the Tate. All the major oil paintings, such as 'Steamboat in a Snowstorm' and 'Approach to Venice', are on view in the main or reserve gallery and his drawings and watercolours are shown in temporary exhibitions.

their work in the past year (see also page 198). Always controversial, but never dull, the choice of prize winner is purposely intended to promote public discussion on new developments in British contemporary art. Previous winners include Damien Hirst, best known for works belonging to his 'Natural History' series, in which dead animals are presented, preserved in formaldehyde.

In addition to an established base in London, the Tate has also spread its wings to other parts of England. The Tate Gallery Liverpool opened in 1988, in the Albert Docks complex of dockland warehouses, while the Tate Gallery in St Ives, Cornwall opened in summer 1993 and was built to show changing displays from the Tate Gallery's collection of work by artists associated with St Ives. Some of the works not currently on show are on loan to the Tate Gallery Liverpool and to other regional museums and galleries through touring exhibitions.

A good selection of events and talks are held regularly in conjunction with current exhibitions and displays. Free guided tours are also given every day, each one on a different theme, while on Saturday you can go on a general tour. There is a café and restaurant. Friends of the Tate Gallery can enjoy free admission to exhibitions with a guest, a discount in the shop and a special events programme.

⊖ Pimlico

🚌 2, C10, 36, 77A, 88, 185

♿ via Clore Gallery

Open: Monday–Saturday, 10.00 a.m.–5.50 p.m.; Sunday, 2.00 p.m.–5.50 p.m.

Free (special exhibitions £)

PERMANENT COLLECTIONS

The galleries featured below house permanent collections of art, although some of them occasionally hold temporary exhibitions too. They are grouped alphabetically within geographical areas.

CENTRAL

Architectural Association

School of Architecture, 34–36 Bedford Square, WC1
(0171 636 0974)

The Architectural Association was founded in 1874 in opposition to a system of education controlled by the Crown. The school continues today and the association offers a forum available to members, visitors and students to discuss architecture.

Access to the slide library with over 120,000 slides is possible for researchers. Already the largest of its kind in Europe, the collection continues to grow as more new and important buildings are documented. There is also a library with over 25,000 volumes on the history of architecture of all countries and periods. Evening lectures and temporary exhibitions

are open to the public and provide a platform for both influential contemporary projects and neglected areas of architectural history.

⊖ Tottenham Court Road

🚌 7, 10, 24, 29, 73, 134

Limited ♿

Open: Monday–Friday, 9.30 a.m.–8.00 p.m.; Saturday, 10.00 a.m.–3.00 p.m.

(School opening times may vary)

Free

British Council Collection

Visual Arts Department, 11 Portland Place, W1 (0171 389 3049)

The British Council was formed in 1934 to promote cultural, educational and technical co-operation between Britain and other countries and has a large collection of twentieth-century British art. Artists represented include David Hockney, Barbara Hepworth and Graham Sutherland. Many of these paintings and works of art are circulated in exhibitions overseas, but there is always plenty to see in London too.

⊖ Oxford Circus

🚌 C2, 6, 8, 15, 25, 135, 98, 159

♿

Open: by appointment only for research

Free

Courtauld Gallery

Courtauld Institute of Art, Somerset House, Strand WC2 (0171 873 2526)

The Courtauld Gallery is the museum of the University of London. It holds an important collection of European paintings from the Renaissance to the twentieth century, and is one of the finest collections of Impressionist and Post-Impressionist paintings in the world.

The Gallery's Collection is made up of eleven bequests. The most important is Samuel Courtauld's founding collection of paintings, including Van Gogh's

'Nevermore' by Paul Gauguin. The Courtauld Gallery

'Self-Portrait with a Bandaged Ear', Manet's 'Bar at the Folies Bergère', Cézanne's 'Montagne Sainte-Victoire' and Renoir's 'La Loge'. Other collections are the Princes Gate collection, bequeathed in 1978 by Count Antoine Seilern, which includes paintings by Rubens, Tiepolo and Impressionists, and the Lee collection bequeathed by Lord Lee of Farnham, which includes paintings by Botticelli, Gainsborough and Goya.

The Gallery also holds a collection of Old Master prints and drawings. Three temporary exhibitions from the collection of 7,000 drawings and 27,000 prints are held each year in a special exhibition space in Somerset House.

⊖ Covent Garden, Temple

🚌 4, 6, 11, 15, 23, 26, 68, 76, 171, 188

Open: Monday–Saturday, 10.00 a.m.–6.00 p.m.; Sunday, 2.00 p.m.–6.00 p.m. (last admission 5.15 p.m.)

£ (free after 5.00 p.m.)

Queen's Gallery

Buckingham Palace Road, SW1 (0171 799 2331: recorded information)

The Royal Collection of pictures and works of art is impressively large (over 190,000 items). Permanent displays from the collection can be seen in several London galleries and museums, including Hampton Court (see page 97), Buckingham Palace (see page 85) and other properties in the country managed by the Historic Palaces Agency, Royal Collection Enterprises and English Heritage. The Queen's Gallery plays host to temporary exhibitions which examine themes from the Royal Collection. Artists represented include Van Dyck, Canaletto, Stubbs and Gainsborough, as well as Michelangelo, Holbein and more recent artists such as Stanley Spencer and Augustus John. Loans from the Royal Collection are regularly staged in other institutions in Britain and overseas.

The Queen's Gallery lies next to Buckingham Palace on the site of a conservatory built to the design of John Nash in 1831. The conservatory was converted into a chapel for Queen Victoria in 1843 but was destroyed in the Second World War during an air raid. In 1962 it was reconstructed, partly as the private chapel of Buckingham Palace and partly as an art gallery open to the public.

⊖/🚆 Victoria

🚌 2, 8, 16, 36, 38, 52

No ♿

Open: daily, 9.30 a.m.–4.30 p.m.

£

Royal Institute of British Architects

66 Portland Place, W1 (0171 580 5533)

The British Architectural Library in Portman Square holds a fascinating and wide-ranging collection of drawings, books, photographs and manuscripts. The drawing collection is the largest and most important collection of British architectural drawings in the world from the Renaissance to the present day and is a graphic record of the work of architects and designers.

The 500,000 drawings also contain important work by international architects and include many of Andrea Palladio's surviving drawings, seventeenth- and eighteenth-century Italian and French stage designs, an Indian collection and drawings by Frank Lloyd Wright, Le Corbusier and Mies van der Rohe. Among the work of British architects are Inigo Jones's architectural drawings, Sir Christopher Wren's City churches and drawings by such major twentieth-century architects as Lutyens and Sir Norman Foster.

As well as drawings of buildings, there are designs for gardens, furniture, metalwork, textiles and other decorative arts, and also topographical drawings, models, drawing instruments, furniture, medals and portraits. Although many of these items are locked away in RIBA's library, there are regular exhibitions that draw on the material in the collection at the RIBA Heinz Gallery at 21 Portman Square. A full list of exhibitions, catalogues and details of slide sets of exhibitions are available on request.

The British Architectural Library also holds over 400,000 photographs from 1850 to the present day. This collection comprises the work of architectural photographers, including Bedford Lemere, John Maltby and Henk Snoek. Architecture is interpreted in its widest sense and the collection includes images of related topics, such as interior design, landscape architecture, topography and construction.

The library's collection of books and periodicals contains over 135,000 books, 20,000 pamphlets and 2,000 serial titles. The library collects material on architecture – contemporary and historical – from all over the world, with an emphasis on the architecture of Great Britain. Publications about related subjects, such as civil and structural engineering, landscape architecture, interior design, town and country planning, and construction law are also collected for their contribution to the study, practice and history of architecture.

The manuscript and archives section of the library offers a fascinating insight into the minds of history's greatest architects. The oldest document is an account for the repair of Richmond Palace supervised by Inigo Jones in 1622, while from the twentieth century there is a series of letters from the architect Sir Edwin Lutyens to his wife.

⊖ Bond Street, Marble Arch

🚌 2, 12, 25, 30, 113, 176

♿

Open: British Architectural Library, by appointment only, Tuesday–Thursday, 10.00 a.m.–1.00 p.m., 2.00 p.m.–5.00 p.m. Monday, 1.30–5.00 p.m., Tuesday, 10.00 a.m.–8.00 p.m., Wednesday–Friday, 10 a.m.–5.00 p.m., Saturday, 10 a.m.–1.30 p.m. (closed August); Heinz Gallery (entrance in Gloucester Place), during exhibitions, Monday–Friday, 11.00 a.m.–5.00 p.m.; Saturday, 10.00 a.m.–1.00 p.m. (closed August)

££ (Heinz Gallery free)

University College Art Collection

Strang Print Room, University College, Gower Street, WC1 (0171 387 7050)
University College, part of London University, has a large collection of art including drawings, paintings and European and Japanese prints in the Strang Print Room. Temporary exhibitions are held during termtime. The plaster casts of the work of the English sculptor, John Flaxman (1755–1826) are displayed in the gallery upstairs.

⊖ Euston, Euston Square, Warren Street
▣ Euston
🚌 7, 10, 24, 29, 73, 134
♿ (phone first)
Open: Strang Print Room termtime by appointment only, exhibitions,
Wednesday–Thursday, 1.00–5.00 p.m.; Flaxman Gallery Monday–Friday,
9.00 a.m.–5.00 p.m.
Free

Wallace Collection

Hertford House, Manchester Square, W1 (0171 935 0687)

Acquired principally in the nineteenth century by the 3rd and 4th Marquesses of
Hertford and Sir Richard Wallace, the illegitimate son of the 4th Marquess, the
Wallace Collection was bequeathed to the nation by Sir Richard's widow in 1897
and is displayed on the ground and first floors of Hertford House, the family's
main London home.

Among the superb works of art on view, there are outstanding collections of
French eighteenth-century paintings, furniture and porcelain, together with Old
Master paintings by Titian, Canaletto, Rembrandt, Hals, Rubens, Velázquez and

The Wallace Collection

Gainsborough. The finest collection of arms and armour in England outside the Tower of London is shown in four galleries and there are further displays of gold boxes, miniatures, French and Italian sculpture, and medieval and Renaissance works of art, including Limoges enamels, maiolica, glass, silver, cuttings from illuminated manuscripts, and carvings in ivory, rock crystal and boxwood.

The paintings were largely acquired by the 3rd Marquess of Hertford (1777–1842) who had a fondness for Dutch pictures of the seventeenth century, and the 4th Marquess (1800–1870), who spent most of his life in Paris and was an avid collector. He added many more Dutch and Flemish pictures, as well as masterpieces of the seventeenth-century French and Spanish schools. It is also thanks to the 4th Marquess that the Wallace has its splendid display of eighteenth-century French paintings, by Watteau, Boucher and Fragonard in particular, and its important collection of pictures by French and English artists of the early nineteenth century, including Delacroix and Bonington.

The miniature collection of over 300 works was largely built up by Sir Richard Wallace (1818–90). He also acquired an important collection of Renaissance glass, maiolica, French and Italian bronzes and Limoges enamels, as well as early Italian paintings and a collection of illuminated manuscript cuttings.

There is also an excellent collection of eighteenth-century Sèvres porcelain. Particularly well represented are the splendid examples decorated with coloured grounds, including pieces once owned by Louis XV and his mistress Madame de Pompadour.

Public lectures on aspects of the Collection are given on weekdays and week-ends, and tours and study days can also be arranged.

⊖ Bond Street, Marble Arch

🚌 2, 12, 25, 30, 113, 176

♿

Open: Monday–Friday, 10.00 a.m.–5.00 p.m.; Sunday, 2.00 p.m.–5.00 p.m.
(closed 24–26 December, New Year's Day)

Free

The Grand Tour

Many of London's most important collectors, such as Sir Richard Wallace and Sir John Soane, built up their collections by buying art and antiques while travelling abroad in European centres of art, including Rome, Florence and Paris. These cultural journeys were known as the Grand Tour, and were an important part of a young gentleman's education in the arts in the eighteenth century. Classical art and architecture were greatly admired at this time and these wealthy young men were able to bring home Roman and Greek antiquities or the eighteenth-century versions bought from contemporary European artists – the first souvenirs. Many important artists flourished at this time, including Canaletto, Batoni and Piranesi, commissioned by the culture-hungry aristocrats.

Corporation of London Permanent Collection

Guildhall Library and Art Gallery, Aldermanbury, EC2 (0171 606 3030)

The Corporation of London Collection comprises a range of works of art relating to London, including nineteenth-century paintings and drawings, topographical pictures and Pre-Raphaelite works. A selection of works from its modern art collection can be seen at the Barbican Art Gallery (see page 47).

⊖ Bank, Barbican, Moorgate, St Paul's

🚌 4, 8, 22B, 25, 56, 133, 172

♿ (library only)

Open: by appointment only, Monday–Friday

Free

NORTH

Harrow School Old Speech Room Gallery

Church Hill, Harrow-on-the-Hill, Middlesex
(0181 869 1205)

One of the oldest public schools in the country, Harrow is also well-known for its collection of art and antiquities donated by old boys. Among the paintings are modern British paintings and etchings and English watercolours. There is also a collection of Greek, Egyptian and Etruscan antiquities, a natural history collection and school memorabilia.

Guided tours available.

⊖ Harrow-on-the-Hill

🚌 H10, H17, 258

No ♿

Open: termtime, daily except Wednesday, 2.30 p.m.–5.00 p.m.

Free

Royal College of Physicians

11 St Andrew's Place, Regent's Park, NW1 (0171 935 1174 ext. 374)

Trace the history of scholarship in the medical world through the portraits, busts and miniatures of the world's leading doctors and scientists from the sixteenth to the twentieth century.

⊖ Great Portland Street, Regent's Park

🚇 Euston

🚌 C2, 18, 27, 30, 135

Limited ♿

Open: by appointment only, Monday–Friday, 10.00 a.m.–5.00 p.m.

Free

Dulwich Picture Gallery

College Road, Dulwich, SE21 (0181 693 5254)
Designed by Sir John Soane (1754–1837) and opened in 1817, Dulwich was the
first purpose-built art gallery in England. In the heart of Dulwich village, it is an
ideal place to visit as part of a trip to this pretty corner of London. Take in the art
first and then wander round the pretty eighteenth-century village and end up for
refreshment in the nearby Crown and Greyhound pub.

With its outstanding collection of Old Master paintings, Dulwich is one of the
most beautiful galleries in England. The pictures are mostly by seventeenth- and
eighteenth-century artists, including Rembrandt, Poussin, Claude, Rubens, Van
Dyck, Watteau, Gainsborough, Reynolds, Tiepolo and Canaletto. Among the
highlights are 'Rinaldo and Armida' by Nicolas Poussin, Murillo's 'Flower Girl'
and Rembrandt's 'Girl at a Window'.

The collection owes its existence to Stanislaus Augustus II, king of Poland and
lover of Catherine the Great. He commissioned Noel Desenfans, a London art
dealer, to acquire paintings for a national collection in Poland. But the king was
forced to abdicate in 1795, leaving the pictures unpaid for. Desenfans' proposal to
the British government for a National Gallery was rejected and his heir, Sir Francis
Bourgeois, found a home for the collection in Dulwich where it could be viewed
by the public.

The gallery is divided into twelve rooms and a curious mausoleum (with
sarcophagi of Sir Francis Bourgeois and the gallery's founders, Mr and Mrs
Desenfans).

🚇 Herne Hill, North Dulwich, West Dulwich
🚌 68, 68A, 115, 196, 322
♿

Open: Tuesday–Friday, 10.00 a.m.–5.00 p.m.; Saturday, 11.00 a.m.–5.00 p.m.;
Sunday, 2.00 p.m.–5.00 p.m.
£

WEST

Marianne North Gallery

Royal Botanic Gardens, Kew, Surrey (0181 332 5000: recorded information)
This gallery in the heart of London's most famous gardens contains a wonderful
collection of flower paintings by the nineteenth-century artist, Marianne North.
She was born in Sussex in 1830, the daughter of an MP. At an early age she
revealed a talent for drawing and after the death of her father in 1869 devoted the
remainder of her life to flower painting. She travelled widely, visiting every
continent and often enduring considerable hardship and discomfort.

Although she received no formal training in drawing or painting, her work
achieved a high level of artistic competence. She painted quickly, often
completing a picture in a day. Her output was enormous; for instance, during one
fifteen-month stay in India she produced over 200 paintings. After her first exhibition in a London gallery in 1879, Marianne North thought of presenting the

pictures to the Royal Botanic Gardens at Kew. She also generously offered to provide a suitable building in which to display them.

🚇 Kew Gardens
🚉 Kew Bridge, Kew Gardens
🚌 65, 391
♿

Open: daily, from 9.30 a.m., closing time varies throughout year

Free to visitors to the Royal Botanic Gardens (£)

Orleans House Gallery

Riverside, Twickenham, Middlesex (0181 892 0221)

Built in 1710, Orleans House was, sadly, demolished in 1926 and only the Octagon, added in 1720, has survived. Located on an attractive stretch of riverside in a picturesque woodland garden, the gallery was built by James Gibbs *c.*1720 as a garden pavilion. Inside, it is richly decorated with ornamental mouldings and gilding. Medallion portraits incorporated within the decoration probably represent Louis Philippe, George II and his Queen, Caroline of Ansbach.

Today, the gallery houses a fine collection of art. The Ionides Collection, bequeathed by Mrs Basil Ionides in 1962, comprises the bulk of the work displayed and includes paintings by Samuel Scott, George Hilditch, Peter de Wint and Augustin Heckel. The Paton Collection, mostly consisting of eighteenth- and nineteenth-century views of Richmond, is also kept here and items from the borough art collections are frequently included in the changing exhibition programme.

Orleans Gallery holds changing exhibitions of works covering a variety of themes, including craft, local history, art, photography and cartoons. Concerts and lectures often accompany exhibitions and workshops take place in the stables during the summer.

🚉 Twickenham
🚌 H22, 33, R68, R70, 90, 290
♿ to ground floor

Open: April–September, Tuesday–Saturday, 1.00 p.m.–5.30 p.m., Sunday, 2.00–5.30 p.m.; October–March, Tuesday–Saturday, 1.00 p.m.–4.30 p.m., Sunday 2.00–4.30 p.m., also Bank Holiday Monday 2.00–5.30 p.m.

Free

Royal College of Music

Department of Portraits, Prince Consort Road, South Kensington, SW7·
(0171 589 3643)

The Royal College of Music has a remarkable collection of portraits of famous musicians, composers and singers, including Mozart, Beethoven and Bach. It also holds the largest archive of concert programmes in the country.

🚇 South Kensington
🚌 9, 10, 14, 49, 52, 70, 74
Limited ♿

Open: by appointment only, Monday–Friday, 10.00 a.m.–5.00 p.m.

Free

PUBLIC GALLERIES AND EXHIBITION SPACES

Throughout London there are dozens of mostly small public galleries and exhibition spaces which display a wide cross-section of art. Some comprise works from the collection of an individual art lover, such as the Saatchi Gallery which houses the collection of Charles Saatchi, while others are from such institutions as the Royal Watercolour Society. All the galleries featured below (alphabetically within geographical areas) hold regular temporary exhibitions and sometimes works of art are for sale.

CENTRAL

Architecture Foundation

30 Bury Street, St James's, SW1 (0171 839 9389)
At the foot of the modern Economist tower building is the Architecture Foundation dedicated to the display and discussion of contemporary architecture and the built environment. As well as a wide-ranging series of exhibitions, the Foundation holds open forums on architectural and urban planning questions led by architects of today.
⊖ Green Park
🚌 8, 9, 14, 19, 22, 38
Limited ♿
Open: Tuesday–Sunday, 12 noon–6.00 p.m.
Free

Ben Uri Art Gallery

21 Dean Street, W1 (0171 437 2852)
The Ben Uri Art Society was founded in 1915 in the East End of London and named after Bezalel Ben Uri, who is named in Exodus 31 in the Bible as the craftsman-builder of the Tabernacle. For over eighty years the Ben Uri Society has been at the heart of the artistic and cultural life of Anglo Jewry. Its aim is to promote Jewish art as part of the Jewish cultural heritage. The society has built up an important collection of over 700 paintings, drawings and sculpture by Jewish artists. The collection includes works by the most important Anglo-Jewish artists of this century, including David Bomberg, Mark Gertler, Jacob Epstein, Leon Kossoff, Frank Auerbach and R.B. Kitaj.

The gallery provides a showcase for exhibitions of contemporary art as well as its permanent collection. The exhibition offers art for sale and in recent years has included work by Solomon J. Solomon, Claude Rogers, Leonard Baskin, Abram Games and Bernard Cohen.
⊖ Oxford Circus, Tottenham Court Road
🚌 7, 10, 25, 73, 98, 176
♿

Open: Monday–Thursday, 10.00 a.m.–5.00 p.m.; selected Sundays, 2.00 p.m.–5.00 p.m. (phone first)
Free

ICA Gallery

Institute of Contemporary Arts, Nash House, The Mall, SW1 (0171 930 3647: box office; 0171 930 0493: membership enquiries; 0171 930 6393: recorded information)
See also pages 125, 147 and 154

Opposite St James's Park at the Trafalgar Square end of the Mall is this multi-arts centre for art, film, music and talks. Avant-garde work is shown throughout the year in two galleries and features artists from Britain and overseas. There is also an excellent arts bookshop and a café.

ICA talks feature some of the world's most significant artists and thinkers in conversation and it is possible to buy specially recorded talks on audio cassette so you can listen to them again at home.

⊖ Charing Cross, Embankment, Piccadilly Circus
▣ Charing Cross
🚌 11, 12, 15, 22, 109, 176
♿

Open: Gallery daily, 12 noon–7.30 p.m. (Friday 9.00 p.m.)
£ (free to members)

Photographers' Gallery

5–8 Great Newport Street, WC2
(0171 831 1772)

The gallery aims to promote the role of photography in contemporary culture on both a national and international level. The gallery offers four exhibition spaces, a print sales room, an excellent bookshop and a café serving inexpensive home-cooked food.

It is worthwhile planning your visit to coincide with one of the talks. Phone in advance for times.

⊖ Leicester Square
🚌 14, 19, 24, 29, 38, 176
♿

Open: Monday–Saturday, 11.00 a.m.–6.00 p.m.
Free

Go to the pictures by Tube
The Photographers' Gallery, 5 Great Newport Street, WC2
Nearest station Leicester Square

Royal Academy of Arts

Burlington House, Piccadilly, W1 (0171 439 7438)

Set in a magnificent eighteenth-century building in Burlington Gardens, the Royal Academy has played a major role in British artistic life for over 200 years. It was founded in 1768 to provide a school of art to promising young students and to give more experienced artists the opportunity of buying and selling their work. Each of the eighty elected members, called Royal Academicians, has to give an example of their work to the Academy before they receive their Diploma which is signed by the Queen.

❖

The most popular exhibition is the Summer Exhibition, held between June and August every year since 1769. Over 1,500 pictures by living artists are displayed for sale and any artist can submit up to three works.

Exhibitions always draw huge numbers of visitors, so it is often best to book in advance for tickets or try and visit early in the morning. Stay for lunch though as the restaurant is excellent. Membership of the Friends of the Royal Academy means you can also retreat to the Friends' room and relax on cosy sofas while enjoying the pictures by prominent Royal Academicians on view around you. You are also allowed to use the library, which contains a huge number of books, some dating back to the seventeenth century, which were given or bequeathed to the library by Royal Academicians. In the shop, as well as souvenirs from current exhibitions, you will find a huge selection of postcards, posters and gifts.

Fine art picture framing and gilding are also undertaken by the Academy Framing department, which is situated in the vaults of Burlington House and is best approached via the Royal Academy Schools Gate in Burlington Gardens. The Schools hold two shows, which are worth visiting too, one for finalists in July and another in February.

Θ Green Park, Piccadilly

🚌 8, 9, 14, 19, 22, 38

♿

Open: daily, 10.00 a.m.–6.00 p.m.; Library (by arrangement only for Friends) Monday–Friday, 2.00 p.m.–5.00 p.m.; Academy Framing Department Monday–Friday, 10.00 a.m.–5.00 p.m. and by appointment on Saturday mornings

£ (free to members)

The Royal Academy of Arts

St John's

Smith Square, SW1 (0171 222 1061: box office)

As well as being an important venue for classical concerts (see page 142), St John's holds regular art exhibitions in the restaurant. Entrance to the exhibitions is possible during the day, but you may want to enjoy the exhibition and attend an evening concert on the same visit.

⊖ St James's Park, Westminster

🚌 3, C10, 77A, 88, 159, 507

♿ (phone first)

Open: Box office and gallery Monday–Friday, 10.00 a.m.–5.00 p.m.

Free

EAST

Barbican Art Gallery

Gallery Floor (level 3), Barbican Centre, Silk Street, EC2 (0171 638 4141 ext 7105; 0171 588 9023: recorded information)

See also page 109, page 141 and page 171

Since opening in 1982, Barbican Art Gallery has established an international reputation for holding an exciting programme of innovative temporary exhibitions. The gallery particularly specializes in photography exhibitions featuring, for example, Bill Brandt and Eve Arnold, and in the re-assessment of late nineteenth- and twentieth-century art, often covering areas previously unexamined, such as Impressionism in Britain.

⊖ Barbican, Moorgate

🚌 4, 43, 56, 141, 172, 214

♿

Open: daily, 10.00 a.m.–6.45 p.m.; Tuesday 10.00 a.m.–5.45 p.m.; Sunday and public holidays 12 noon–6.45 p.m. (Last admission 15 minutes before closing)

£(££ season ticket)

National Museum of Cartoon Art

Baird House, 15–17 St Cross Street, EC1 (0171 405 4717)

Exhibitions of the best of British and international cartoons, caricatures and comic strips.

⊖ Chancery Lane, Farringdon

🚆 Farringdon

🚌 45, 55, 63, 243, 259, 505

♿

Open: Monday–Friday, 12 noon–6.00 p.m.

Free

The Showroom

44 Bonner Roads, Bethnal Green, E2 (0181 983 4115)

This gallery has a changing programme of about six or seven exhibitions each year and promotes innovative commissioned works by established and new artists.

In presenting visual and live art works that deal with both formal and conceptual concerns, the gallery aims to present and commission works which engage with both the cultural and social climate in which they are made.

⊖ Bethnal Green
▣ Cambridge Heath
🚌 D6, 8, 48, 106, 253, 309
Limited ♿

Open: Wednesday–Sunday, 1.00 p.m.–6 p.m.
Free

Whitechapel Gallery

80 Whitechapel High Street, E1
(0171 522 7888)

The gallery was built in 1899 (opened in 1901) by the social reformer, Canon Augustus Samuel Barnett (1844–1919), as a way of bringing the visual arts into the East End of London. Together with his wife, Barnett instigated enormous social improvements in this area, clearing the slums and bringing in music, culture and art. The Art Nouveau gallery was designed by the architect C.H. Townsend and today it is one of the most lively contemporary galleries in London, as well as a meeting place and information centre. Talks, workshops and films are also held and there is a good bookshop and café.

⊖ Aldgate East
🚌 15, 25, 67, 253
♿

Open: Tuesday–Sunday, 11.00 a.m.–5.00 p.m. (Wednesday to 8.00 p.m.)
Free (£ for annual exhibition)

NORTH

Camden Arts Centre

Arkwright Road (corner of Finchley Road), NW3 (0171 435 2643)

Located in a Victorian building, this arts centre features regular exhibitions of international contemporary artists.

The centre also has a strong awareness of community needs and offers a range of daytime evening and weekend classes for children and adults, including ceramics, painting, drawing and sculpture. Classes are run by practising artists, each with a distinct approach. No previous experience is necessary.

❖

⊖ Finchley Road
▣ Finchley Road and Frognal
🚌 C11, C12, 13, 82, 113, 268
No ♿

Open: Tuesday–Thursday, 12 noon–8 p.m.; Friday–Sunday, 12 noon–6.00 p.m.
Free

Lauderdale House Community Arts Centre
Waterlow Park, Highgate Hill, N6 (0181 348 8716)
Lauderdale House is a Grade I listed building which was partially gutted by fire in 1963. Some of the building has been restored and it now houses an art gallery which holds regular exhibitions. There is also a café serving homemade food with an Italian flavour.
⊖ Archway
🚌 4, W5, C11, 143, 210, 271
♿ (ground floor only)
Open: Tuesday–Friday, 11.00 a.m.–4.00 p.m.
Free, but donations welcome

Saatchi Gallery
98a Boundary Road, NW8 (0171 624 8299: recorded information)
Charles Saatchi has become one of the foremost collectors of contemporary art in Britain since the 1970s. His collection comprises over 1,000 works and the gallery now focuses on young British artists such as Damien Hirst, Marc Quinn, Rachel Whiteread, Richard Wilson, Jenny Saville and John Frankland. A selection from

'Campbell's Soup Can' by Andy Warhol. Saatchi Gallery

the collection is shown on a rotating basis and changes about every two months. There are also guest exhibitions.

⊖ Swiss Cottage

🚌 13, 46, 82, 113, 139

No ♿

Open: Thursday–Sunday, 12 noon–6.00 p.m.

£ (free on Thursday)

SOUTH

Bankside Gallery

48 Hopton Street, SE1 (0171 928 7521)

More than a commercial gallery, Bankside offers a chance to view some of the best contemporary watercolours and prints available. The gallery is host to two prestigious art societies: the Royal Watercolour Society and the Royal Society of Painter-Printmakers. The work of these two societies forms the basis of its varied exhibition programme, which is supplemented by exhibitions of 'guest' artists.

The Royal Watercolour Society is the oldest society of its type in the world. Founded in 1804 by a group of young artists determined to secure watercolour's rightful place in the face of contemporary indifference from the art establishment, early members included such masters as Samuel Palmer and David Cox. The Royal Society of Painter-Printmakers was founded in 1880 and its function was to provide an annual exhibition for artists who were making original etchings and engravings. Originally known as the Royal Society of Painters, Etchers and Engravers, in recent years the society changed its name to Painter-Printmakers to reflect the wider range of printing techniques available.

Other facilities at Bankside include educational courses led by eminent members of each society and researchers can also make use of a slide library, a databank and general library covering the history of the societies and artist members past and present.

⊖ Blackfriars, then bus

Buses: D1, P11, 45, 63, 149, 172

♿

Open: during exhibitions only, Tuesday, 10.00 a.m.–8 p.m., Wednesday–Friday, 10 a.m.–5.00 p.m.; Sunday, 1.00 p.m.–5.00 p.m.; also last Saturday of each exhibition, 1.00 p.m.–5.00 p.m.

£

Battersea Arts Centre

Lavender Hill, SW11 0171 223 2223

See also page 128

This multi-arts centre is home for art exhibitions, plays and performances.

🚉 Clapham Junction

🚌 49, 77, 77A, 337, 344, 345

♿

Open: Monday–Saturday, 10.00 a.m.–10.00 p.m. (Monday to 6.00 p.m.); Sunday, 12 noon–8 p.m.

Free (but £ for plays and performances)

Hayward Gallery on the South Bank

South Bank Centre, Belvedere Road, SE1 (0171 928 3144; 0171 261 0127: recorded information)

The Hayward is one of two galleries in London funded by the Arts Council of Great Britain – the other is the Serpentine, see page 33. The one drawback to the Hayward is the difficulty in finding it – it is very easy to get lost in the maze of steps and paths around the South Bank Centre – but once there you will find an important venue for exhibitions of both modern and historical art. Recent shows include a retrospective of the Impressionist artist Pierre Bonnard; 'Art and Power', a view of architecture in Europe from 1932 to 1945; and 'Spellbound', and exhibition on art and film in Britain. Each show lasts about three months and the gallery is closed for about a month in between shows to allow for the changeover.

Θ/🚍 Waterloo

🚌 26, 68, 171, 171A, 176, 188

♿

Open: during exhibitions Thursday–Monday, 10 a.m.–6.00 p.m.; Tuesday and Wednesday, 10 a.m.–8 p.m.

£

South London Art Gallery

65 Peckham Road, SE5 (0171 703 6120)

Aimed at making contemporary art accessible to everyone, this gallery holds about six temporary exhibitions every year. For children there are also occasional special activities.

Θ Elephant and Castle, Oval

🚌 P3, 12, 36, 171, 345

No ♿

Open: Tuesday, Wednesday and Friday, 11 a.m.–6.00 p.m.; Thursday, 11 a.m.–7.00 p.m.; Saturday and Sunday, 2.00 p.m.–6.00 p.m.

Free

WEST

Goethe Institute

50 Princes Gate, Exhibition Road, SW7 (0171 411 3400)

The official cultural arm of the German government in London, the Goethe Institute offers a range of activities, from language courses to film showings, musical performances, talks and exhibitions. The exhibitions focus on all types of German art, from historical to modern. Amenities include a café.

Θ South Kensington

🚌 9, 10, 52

No ♿

Open: Library and teachers' centre Monday–Thursday, 10.00 a.m.–8.00 p.m.; Saturday, 10.00 a.m.–1.00 p.m. (lending service only); Language courses personal callers Monday–Thursday, 2.30 p.m.–6.00 p.m.

Exhibitions free (£ for some events)

Kew Gardens Gallery

*Royal Botanic Gardens, Kew, Surrey
(0181 332 5618)*

This gallery offers a lively programme of exhibitions featuring work with a botanic theme (see also the Marianne North Gallery, page 32).

⊖ Kew Gardens
🚃 Kew Bridge, Kew Gardens
🚌 65, 391
♿

Open: daily from 9.30 a.m., closing time varies throughout year
Free to visitors to the Royal Botanic Gardens (£)

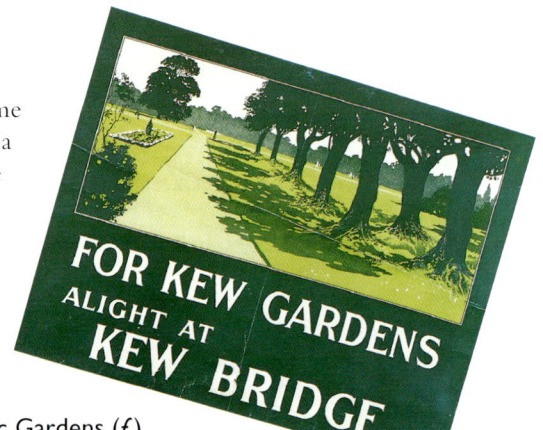

Narwhal Inuit Art Gallery

55 Linden Gardens, Chiswick, W4 (0181 747 1575)

What is Narwhal Inuit Art and what is it doing in Chiswick? Actually, it is the art of the Inuit people, also known as Eskimos. The gallery was founded by a couple who acquired a passion for this art while living and working in Calgary in Canada.

Art in Action

It is always fun to watch artists at work and at the Glasshouse in Islington and the London Glass Blowing Workshop near London Bridge you can see delicate glass items being blown and moulded. Both workshops have a gallery with artefacts for sale too.

Glasshouse

21 St Alban's Place, Islington, N1 (0171 359 8162)
⊖ Angel
🚌 4, 19, 30, 38, 43, 73
Limited ♿ (not workshop)
Open: Tuesday–Saturday, 10.00 a.m.–6.00 p.m. (gallery only, Saturday)
Free

London Glass Blowing Workshop

7 Leather Market, Weston Street, SE1 (0171 403 2800)
⊖ Borough, London Bridge
🚃 London Bridge
🚌 P3, P11, 21, 35, 40, 47, 133
Limited ♿ (phone first)
Open: Monday–Friday, 10.00 a.m.–5.00 p.m.
Free

Their collection continues to grow and now numbers over 300 items, from stone and bone carvings to wall hangings and prints. Art is seen from a different perspective by the Inuit. An Inuit artist expresses it like this: 'A white man, if he is going to buy a carving, buys it purely by the appearance. The white people do not consider the meaning of a carving, simply the appearance.'

⛵ Turnham Green

🚌 E3, 27, H40, 237, 267, 391

No ♿

Open: by appointment only

Free

Serpentine Gallery

Kensington Gardens, W2 (0171 723 9072: recorded information)

Set in the heart of a London park and built in 1934 as a teahouse, the Serpentine Gallery makes an attractive setting for its exhibitions of post-war British art and sculpture. The gallery's image has changed a good deal since it first opened as a gallery in 1970. For the first three years a shoestring budget allowed it to operate only in the summer months when no heating was required. Today, it is so well-respected that major international figures such as Andy Warhol have exhibited here. Works by established artists such as Henry Moore, Anthony Caro and Richard Hamilton have also been shown here.

The Serpentine is also an important showcase for young artists: Damien Hirst, Richard Wentworth and Rachel Whiteread are among those who exhibited at the gallery in the early stages of their career. The lawn outside the gallery is also used as an exhibition space for sculpture.

For those wanting to find out more about a particular exhibition, the education department publishes explanatory brochures alongside exhibition catalogues. It also arranges free talks in the gallery every Sunday afternoon and holds workshops for schoolchildren.

⛵ Knightsbridge, Lancaster Gate, South Kensington

🚌 9, 10, 12, 14, 48, 52, 94

♿

Open: daily, 10.00 a.m.–6.00 p.m. during exhibitions

Free

2
DECORATIVE ARTS

MAJOR MUSEUMS

TODAY, MUSEUMS HAVE shaken off the stuffy image once associated with them and are exciting centres of discovery. The big ones in London are the British Museum, which traces the history of the world through its art and culture, and the South Kensington museums, comprising the Natural History Museum (see page 47), the Science Museum (see page 49) and the Victoria & Albert Museum (see page 37) with its wonderful collection of decorative arts.

British Museum
Great Russell Street, WC1 (0171 636 1555)
In 1753 Parliament agreed that a public lottery should be held for the specific purpose of establishing a national museum. With the grand sum of £95,194 8s 2d raised, the British Museum came into being and its doors opened to the public in 1759. One of the great landmarks of London, the imposing buildings of the British Museum are home to the country's finest cultural treasures. The museum is always busy, so it is a good idea to plan in advance what you would like to see. Since the collection is so vast, it is wise to concentrate on only one section on each visit.

The British Museum

The collection of coins and medals is one of the largest in the world, with over 600,000 coins, medals, banknotes, tokens and badges. Among the earliest coins on display are pieces from seventh-century Asia Minor.

The largest and most comprehensive collection of Egyptian antiquities outside Cairo illustrates every aspect of Ancient Egyptian culture from the Predynastic period (*c.*4000 BC) to the Coptic (Christian) period (AD twelfth century) and includes a large amount of material from Nubia and the Sudan. The most popular Egyptian items are the mummies and mummy cases, but also look out for the tomb painting from Thebes. Dating from *c.*1400 BC it depicts a nobleman hunting in the marshes by the Nile, with his wife, daughter and cat. Other items of particular interest include the painted sandstone head of Mentuhotep II from *c.*2025 BC and a bronze calf with gold nose ring and earrings from the Roman period, after 30 BC.

In the seventh century the Assyrian Empire stretched across Asia. In the rooms containing Assyrian antiquities you can see magnificent low reliefs of the Assyrian Army in battle.

The British Library receives a copy of every book published in Britain. Its famous circular Reading Room has been used by many scholars, notably Karl Marx who wrote *Das Kapital* here. The library currently takes up forty per cent of the museum's floor space and is to move to a new building at St Pancras. It is only open to academic staff, as well as researchers after they have exhausted all other resources.

The Greek world from the beginning of the Bronze Age, Italy and Rome from the Bronze Age and the whole of the Roman Empire apart from Britain until the Edict of Milan (AD 313) are covered in the rooms devoted to Greek and Roman antiquities. One of the most comprehensive collections of classical antiquities in the world, it is particularly notable for Greek architectural sculpture, ancient jewellery and bronzes, Greek vases and Roman silver.

Elsewhere the Japanese decorative arts are represented in a series of temporary exhibitions, a collection which is among Europe's finest, while the Japanese paintings form the most comprehensive collection in Europe.

The collection of medieval and later antiquities covers the period from the Edict of Milan in AD 313 to the present day in Europe. The collections also embrace the art and archaeology of other Christian and Jewish cultures, including Byzantium, Nubia, Anatolia and the Caucasus region.

❖

Another section of the museum features paintings and prints from all areas of the Orient, apart from the Near East and Japan. The sculpture collections from India are the most comprehensive in the West and the museum also holds the richest collections of Chinese antiquities, paintings and porcelain in Europe and the best Islamic pottery. Highlights here include T'ang horses and camels, guardian figures, Yuan blue and white porcelain and the Sambas Treasure of Buddhist images.

The collections of prehistoric and Romano-British antiquities are drawn from the Palaeothic and Mesolithic periods throughout the world, from the Neolithic, Bronze and Iron Ages of Europe and from Roman Britain. From prehistoric days (10500–1600 BC), there are cave paintings, household and farm implements, flint axes and pottery. Later European prehistory is represented by Celtic jewellery, pre-Roman metalwork and shields. Roman life in Britain (AD first–fourth centuries) is portrayed through everyday objects and events. Of particular interest is some wonderful jewellery and goldwork.

The collection of prints covers the development of printmaking from its beginnings in the fifteenth century up to modern times and includes many rare, as well as artistically and historically outstanding works. The drawings collection similarly features many of the works of the highest quality by most of the leading artists of European schools from the fifteenth century onwards.

The art and antiquities of the near East are also represented with bronze figurines, funereal monuments, pottery, head-dresses, gold goblets, a silver lyre and arms and armour.

If you are short of time, then just aim to see the following highlights. They are well signposted and many stand on their own podiums away from the other displays.

On the ground floor: the Assyrian lion hunt reliefs dating from the reigns of King Ashurbanipal (668–627 BC) and his grandfather Sennacherib (704–681 BC) at Nineveh; the Indian bronze sculpture of 'Shiva' c.AD 950; the Lindisfarne Gospels, English illuminated manuscripts produced at the monastery of Lindisfarne in the seventh century; and two of the four originals of the Magna Carta.

❖

On the upper floor: the Egyptian mummies; the walrus ivory chessmen found on the island of Lewis in 1831; the Lindow Man – the twisted and tortured-looking remains of a ritually slaughtered ancient Briton preserved in a peat bog for over 2,000 years; the Mildenhall Treasure – a set of Roman silver tableware found in Suffolk in the 1940s; the Portland Vase – a cameo glass production, with the top layer carved to reveal the blue underneath; and the Sutton Hoo treasure – (seventh-century Anglo-Saxon burial ship found in Suffolk in 1939).

Amenities include a shop, café and restaurant.

⊖ Holborn, Goodge Street, Russell Square, Tottenham Court Road

🚌 10, 24, 29, 73, 131, 171

♿

Open: Monday–Saturday, 10.00 a.m.–5.00 p.m.; Sunday, 2.30 p.m.–6.00 p.m.
Free, but donations welcome

South Kensington museums

The museums at South Kensington owe their existence to the enormous success of the Great Exhibition of 1851. A showcase for Victorian design, invention and achievement, the exhibition was opened in nearby Hyde Park in the Crystal Palace, an enormous glass and iron exhibition hall. Later the Crystal Palace was dismantled and taken to Sydenham in south London (where it sadly burnt down many years later). When Prince Albert suggested that the profits should be used to found a centre for education and culture in South Kensington, 34 hectares (85 acres) of land were bought and on them were built the Natural History Museum (see page 47), the Science Museum (see page 49) and the Victoria & Albert Museum, as well as such colleges as the Royal College of Music and the Royal College of Art. These funds also enabled the Royal Albert Hall (see page 140) to be built.

The Victoria & Albert Museum

South Kensington, SW7 (0171 938 8500)

A precious jewel in London's cultural heritage, the Victoria & Albert Museum, better known as the V & A, is home to the world's greatest collection of decorative art and design. Its galleries reflect centuries of achievement in such varied fields as ceramics, sculpture, furniture, jewellery, metalwork, textiles and dresses, from Europe, the Far East, South Asia and the Islamic world. The V & A also contains

The Victoria & Albert Museum

the National Collection of watercolours, portrait miniatures and the art of photography, as well as the National Art Library.

In 1837 a school of design was founded at Somerset House under the auspices of the Board of Trade. The movement grew and other schools were instituted, not only in London but also in Birmingham, Manchester and other large cities. The Great Exhibition in 1851 gave it an impetus and a selection of items were chosen from the exhibition to form the Museum of Manufacturers which opened at Marlborough House in 1852. Five years later, the collection was moved to South Kensington and a building called the South Kensington Museum was opened in 1857 by Queen Victoria & Prince Albert (then known as the Prince Consort). The building was finally named the Victoria & Albert Museum in 1899.

The collections are now displayed in two types of gallery. In the Art and Design Galleries (mostly on Level A) objects are displayed alongside items from a similar period, movement or country, while in the Materials and Techniques Galleries you will find objects of one material or type showing developments in form, function or technique. There are large, colour-coded banners hanging throughout the museum to guide you: red banners direct you north; yellow, east; green, south; and blue, west.

The highlights on Level A include: the Raphael Cartoons – seven designs for tapestries to be hung on special occasions on the walls of the Sistine Chapel in Rome, painted 1515–16; Tippoo's Tiger – a wooden effigy of a tiger attacking a British soldier, made in the late eighteenth century for Sultan Tipu, the ruler of Mysore in India, and containing a miniature organ which simulates the tiger's roar and the groans of pain of its victim; the Ardabil Carpet – often referred to as the most beautiful carpet ever made, this exquisite item was made in Persia in the sixteenth century and brought to England in the 1880s; and the Dress Collection – spanning four centuries of fashion, this gallery chronologically traces the development of European fashion and style.

The highlights on Level B include: the twentieth-century gallery – devoted to the design classics of this century; the Great Bed of Ware – measuring 3.04 x 3.04 metres (10 x 10 feet), this enormous Elizabethan bed is thought to have been made at the end of the sixteenth century for the White Hart Inn at Ware in Hertfordshire – 26 butchers and their wives are said to have slept in it on 13 February 1689!; the Devonshire Hunting Tapestries – illustrating courtly hunts in the fifteenth century, these tapestries once belonged to the Dukes of Devonshire; and over 800 objects from the Middle Ages to the twentieth century are displayed in the Ironwork Gallery, showing the history and beauty of iron.

In the Glass Gallery on Level C over 7,000 pieces from the Middle East, Europe and the western world span the history of glass, from the second millennium BC to the present day.

The Jazz Brunch served in the New Restaurant on Sunday between 11.00 a.m. and 3.00 p.m. is a popular feature. There is also a café as well as tempting shops.

The V & A also administers the Bethnal Green Museum of Childhood (see page 45), the Wellington Museum at Apsley House (see page 84) and the Theatre Museum in Covent Garden (see page 73).

⊖ South Kensington

🚌 C1, 9, 14, 49, 52, 74, 345

♿

Open: Museum Monday, 12 noon–5.50 p.m., Tuesday–Sunday, 10.00 a.m.–5.50 p.m.; Picture Library Monday, 2.00 p.m.–5.00 p.m., Tuesday–Friday, 10.00 a.m.–1.00 p.m. and 2.00 p.m.–5.00 p.m.; National Art Library research services 10.00 a.m.–5.00 p.m.

£

SPECIALIST DECORATIVE ARTS MUSEUMS

In this section the museums are grouped alphabetically within subject areas.

ARCHAEOLOGY

All Hallows-by-the-Tower Undercroft Museum

Byward Street, EC3 (0171 481 2928)

Originally built as a church in the seventh century over Roman foundations, All-Hallows-by-the-Tower has a small museum where displays include Saxon stonework, part of a Roman pavement and a model of Roman London. The baptism record of William Penn, founder of Pennsylvania, and the marriage lines of John Quincy Adams, sixth president of the United States, are also in the museum.

⊖ Tower Hill

🚌 15, 100

No ♿

Open: Monday–Saturday, 10.00 a.m.–4.30 p.m.; Sunday, 1.00 p.m.–4.30 p.m.

£ (including audio guide)

Petrie Museum of Egyptian Archaeology

University College London, Gower Street, WC1
(0171 387 7050)

William Matthew Flinders Petrie, known as the father of Egyptian archaeology, was born in 1853 and began his career in Egyptology in 1880. Over the next forty years, he developed a unique collection of Egyptian artefacts. At the Petrie Museum his wealth of archaeological material, dating from prehistoric to Roman times is gathered together, and makes a fascinating place to visit for anyone with an interest in Ancient Egypt. The museum has a shop.

⊖ Euston, Euston Square, Goodge Street, Russell Square

🚌 10, 24, 29, 73, 134

No ♿

Open: Monday–Friday, 10.00 a.m.–12 noon, 1.15 p.m.–5.00 p.m., and selected Saturday mornings during termtime (closed for a week at both Christmas and Easter and for four weeks during the summer)

Free

St Bride's Crypt Exhibition

St Bride's Church, Fleet Street, EC4 (0171 353 1301)

St Bride's was bombed in the Second World War and during restoration after the war, the site was excavated by archaeologists. As a result of this dig, nearly 1,000 years were added to St Bride's known history. A second-century AD Roman pavement was found and it was proved that there has been a church on this site since the sixth century. Other remains were found, including a Roman ditch.

There is a display of items about St Bride's history and the discovery of these items in the crypt, along with a historical display of the development of printing and the City of London.

⊖/🖵 Blackfriars

🚌 4, 11, 15, 23, 26, 45, 63, 76

No ♿

Open: daily, 8.30 a.m.–5.00 p.m.

Free

ARCHITECTURE

The Brooking Collection

University of Greenwich, Dartford Campus, Oakfield Lane, Dartford, Kent (0181 331 9897)

The Charles Brooking Collection of Architectural Detail is the work of a living collector who is fascinated with the minutiae of building construction and design. His aim is to create a systematic material record of not only the more obvious collectable architectural fragments, such as doors, windows and fireplaces, but also of staircase sections and balustrades, rainwater heads and bootscrapers. There is even a section of architraves, skirtings, sash boxes and glazing bars.

Architecturally, the collection's sweep is from the grandest private homes to commercial buildings and urban terraced houses from the early sixteenth to the late twentieth centuries. Many items come from London, but also from other parts of Britain.

🖵 Dartford

🚌 476

♿

Open: by appointment only with Julie Wakefield, the Keeper

Free

COINS AND BANKING

Bank of England Museum

Bartholomew Lane, EC2 (0171 601 5545)

Sir John Soane designed the Bank of England, but sadly only his elegant exterior remains. The rest was rather foolishly torn down in the inter-war years to allow for an enlargement of the premises. The museum offers a fascinating glimpse into the world of money, charting the history of the bank from its Royal Charter in 1694 to the present day. Exhibits include Roman gold bars and coins, a collection of banknotes, the re-creation of Sir John Soane's Stock Office and an interactive video which allows you to watch happenings on the dealing floor. There is also a shop.

⊖ Bank

🚌 8, 11, 22B, 26, 133

♿ by prior arrangement

Open: Monday–Friday, 10.00 a.m.–5.00 p.m.

Free

Diocesan Treasury in the Crypt of St Paul's Cathedral

Chapter House, St Paul's Churchyard, EC4 (0171 248 2705)

Built by Sir Christopher Wren between 1675 and 1709, this magnificent cathedral is full of works of art. In the crypt you can see church plate and cathedral textiles and treasures, but the building itself is perhaps the greatest work of art here.

⊖ St Paul's

🚌 8, 11, 15, 22B, 26, 56

&

Open: Monday–Saturday, 9.00 a.m.–4.00 p.m. (by prior arrangement).

£

The Fan Museum

12 Crooms Hill, Greenwich, SE10 (0181 858 7879: recorded information 0181 305 1441)

At one time, it was *de rigeur* for a lady of wealth to carry a fan with her to the theatre or parties. They are out of fashion today, but remain beautiful items with a fascinating history. The Fan Museum is the only museum in the world devoted to all aspects of these appealing works of art.

Set in two elegant Georgian town houses, the museum has a permanent exhibition of the history, materials used and types and sources of fans. There are regular exhibitions illustrating a variety of themes and, for hands-on involvement, you can join a craft workshop for fan-making, conservation and restoration. There is also a shop.

🚋 Greenwich

🚌 177, 180, 188, 199, 286

&

Open: Tuesday–Saturday, 11.00 a.m.–4.30 p.m.; Sunday, 12 noon–4.30 p.m.

£ (free on Tuesday, 2.00 p.m.–4.30 p.m., for Senior Citizens and disabled people)

CRAFTS

Crafts Council

44a Pentonville Road, Islington, N1 (0171 278 7700)

The Crafts Council houses Britain's largest contemporary crafts gallery. There is a continuous programme of major craft exhibitions, some of which tour nationally and internationally. Other amenities include a gallery shop selling books and crafts, a reference library, a picture library as well as a programme of educational events which correspond to the current exhibition.

☉ Angel

🚌 19, 30, 38, 73, 171A, 214

♿

Open: Tuesday–Saturday, 11.00 a.m.–6.00 p.m.; Sunday, 2.00 p.m.–6.00 p.m.
Free

DESIGN

Design Museum

Shad Thames, SE1 (0171 403 6933; 0171 378 6055: exhibition hotline)

The Design Museum is located within the Butlers Wharf conservation area. The brainchild of Britain's most famous designer, Sir Terence Conran, the museum traces the history of classic design for the past 100 years, as well as displaying state-of-the-art innovations from around the world.

Temporary exhibitions are also held and there is an excellent shop where you can buy the latest design gadgets and gizmos.

☉ Tower Hill

🚉 London Bridge

DLR: Tower Gateway

🚌 P11, 42, 47, 78, 188

♿

Open: Monday–Friday, 11.30 a.m.–6.00 p.m.; Saturday and Sunday, 12 noon–6.00 p.m.
£

DOMESTIC INTERIORS

Geffrye Museum

Kingsland Road, Shoreditch, E2 (0171 739 9893; 0171 739 8543: recorded information)

The Geffrye Museum is a fascinating collection of almshouses and a chapel depicting the changing style of English domestic interiors through a series of small rooms arranged in chronological order from 1600 to the present day.

There is always a lively atmosphere here, with regular events, talks and other activities, including craft workshops. It is informal and relaxed: you are even able to sit down and browse through some of the museum's books and magazines on view. The historic herb garden is an attractive

Period rooms and Furniture
L.C.C. GEFFRYE MUSEUM
KINGSLAND ROAD, SHOREDITCH, E2
Weekdays 10-5 ☉ Sundays 2-6 · Free
☉   BY TRAM : 43 · 47 · 49 · 31 · 55 · 57
BY BUS : 22 · 35 · 69 · 6 · 6ᴬ · 47 · 78

❖

setting for other events arranged by the museum. There is also a comprehensive reference library and furniture trade archive for detailed research. Facilities include a shop and a café too.

🚇 Dalston Kingsland

🚌 22A, 22B, 67, 149

♿

Open: Tuesday–Saturday, 10.00 a.m.–5.00 p.m.; Sunday and bank holiday Monday, 2.00 p.m.–5.00 p.m.

Free

POTTERY AND PORCELAIN

Martinware Pottery Collection

Southall Library, Osterley Park Road, Southall, Middlesex (0181 574 3412)

Southall potters, the three Martin brothers, Charles, Edwin and Wallace, produced an unusual selection of saltglazed stoneware from 1873 to 1923. Known as Martinware, items ranged from floor tiles to teapots. Probably the best single collection of Martinware can be seen at Southall Library which owns over 200 items reflecting the full scope of the Martin brothers' work.

Among the highlights are quirky-looking 'Wally-Bird' jars for which the Martin brothers were most famous, along with everyday items such as eggcups.

🚇 Southall

🚌 E2, H32, 105, 120, 195, 207

No ♿

Open: Tuesday, Thursday and Friday, 9.30 a.m.–7.45 p.m.; Wednesday and Saturday, 9.00 a.m.–5.00 p.m.

Free

The Percival David Foundation of Chinese Art

University of London, School of Oriental and African Studies, 53 Gordon Square, WC1 (0171 387 3909)

The Foundation houses the finest collection of Chinese ceramics outside China as well as a library of East Asian and western books relating to Chinese art and culture. Presented to the University of London in 1950 by the late Sir Percival David, the Foundation exists to promote the appreciation, study and teaching of the art and culture of China and the surrounding regions.

The ceramic collection is a remarkable archive of Chinese workmanship from the tenth to the eighteenth century. A number of items were once in the possession of Chinese emperors and inscriptions added on the orders of the Emperor Qianlong (1736–95) appear on several pieces.

The stoneware collection includes items from the Song (960–1279) and Yuan (1279–1368) dynasties, with examples of the rare Ru and Guan wares.

🚇 Euston Square, Russell Square

🚌 10, 30, 68, 73, 91, 168, 188

No ♿

Open: Monday–Friday, 10.30 a.m.–5.00 p.m.

Free, but donations welcome

Bethnal Green Museum of Childhood

Cambridge Heath Road, Bethnal Green, E2 (0181 980 2415: recorded information)

The Museum of Childhood is part of the Victoria & Albert Museum (see page 37) and houses one of the largest toy collections in the world, with unique exhibits including dolls, dolls' houses, teddy bears, trains, games and puppets. The museum also has a range of children's costume and nursery furniture in three displays: Birth and Infancy, the Early Years and Breaking Away.

During school holidays there are activities and events for children, as well as free art workshops most Saturdays. The museum has a shop and café.

⊖ Bethnal Green

🚌 8, 106, 253

Limited ♿

Open: Monday–Thursday and Saturday, 10.00 a.m.–5.50 p.m.; Sunday 2.30 p.m.–5.50 p.m.

Free

The London Toy and Model Museum

21–23 Craven Hill, Bayswater, W2 (0171 402 5222: recorded information)

Tucked away in a quiet corner of Bayswater is a museum for children of all ages. A large Georgian town house has been converted into a rabbit warren of fascinating rooms, full to bursting with all sorts of toys, dolls and games.

The museum has a pleasant, intimate feel and there are plenty of buttons for small hands to push that activate working models, slot machines and toys. Tracing the history of toys, displays range from an Ancient Roman gladiator doll to prototype toys for the twenty-first century in the 'Whatever Next' gallery.

In the garden there is a miniature electric railway, complete with ride-on trains for small passengers and a cheery café in the conservatory wing.

⊖ Bayswater, Lancaster Gate, Queensway

🚌 12, 94

Limited ♿

Open: Monday–Saturday, 10.00 a.m.–5.30 p.m.; Sunday and bank holiday, 11.00 a.m.–5.30 p.m. (last admission 4.30 p.m.)

£

Pollock's Toy Museum

1 Scala Street, W1 (0171 636 3452)

Tucked away behind Charlotte Street in an area of London known as Fitzrovia is a marvellous old curiosity shop housing the Pollock's Toy Museum. In fact the museum covers two small houses that have been joined together. Inside, you can wander up and down winding staircases through tiny rooms packed with goodies.

This is definitely a museum that will appeal to children. There are displays of toys dating back for several hundred years, including wax and composition dolls, folk toys, board games, teddy bears and toy soldiers.

The main feature of the museum, however, are the toy theatres. The museum is named after one of the leading publishers of juvenile drama, Benjamin Pollock (1856–1937). A furrier by trade, he took over his father-in-law's publishing business on his death and proceeded to publish large numbers of play reprints, as well as toy theatres and figures.

⊖ Goodge Street

🚌 10, 24, 29, 73, 134

No ♿

Open: daily, except Sunday and bank holiday, 10.00 a.m.–5.00 p.m.

£

Juvenile drama

Before the advent of cinema and television, the theatre was the most popular form of inexpensive public entertainment, with dozens of new plays performed in Europe's major cities every year from the eighteenth century onwards.

English toy theatres quickly developed independently from the rest of Europe and became closely associated with current London stage productions. By the early nineteenth century publishers and printers were producing sheets of figures and dialogue for children to re-create plays at home. The sheets were sold as 'penny plain' or 'tuppence coloured' and the whole genre became known as 'juvenile drama'.

3
SPECIAL INTEREST MUSEUMS

WHILE THE Natural History Museum and the Science Museum are undoubtedly the major special interest museums in London, there are many others covering almost every subject area from tea to transport.

The most interesting museums are detailed below, grouped alphabetically in the various subject areas. They are all closed on 25 and 26 December.

London White Card

One of the best ways to see many of the better known museums and galleries is to buy a 'London White Card'. This is a three-day or seven-day pass which is validated at the first venue you visit and offers unlimited access for families to the following venues: Barbican Art Gallery; Courtauld Institute; Design Museum; Hayward Gallery; Imperial War Museum; London Transport Museum; Museum of London; Museum of the Moving Image (MOMI); National Maritime Museum; Old Royal Observatory and Queen's House; Natural History Museum; Royal Academy of Arts; Science Museum; and Victoria & Albert Museum (except certain temporary exhibitions).

Cards may be purchased at all London Underground Information Centres, Victoria Tourist Information Centre, London Visitor Centre at Waterloo International Terminal, Stoll Moss Theatre, tour operators, airlines and from hotel concierges.

MAJOR MUSEUMS

Natural History Museum

Cromwell Road, SW7 (0171 938 9123)

A blend of Victorian curiosities and specimens, giant dinosaurs and modern research, the Natural History Museum offers a fascinating glimpse into the natural world and the development of our understanding of it. The museum was built in 1881, at the height of Victorian thirst for knowledge about themselves. Even the façade of the building is decorated with animal figures (both living and extinct), while in the grounds outside stands a replica of a *Stegosaurus*.

On entering the museum you come face to face with a life-sized plaster-cast skeleton of another dinosaur, the 135-million-year-old *Diplodocus*. The museum

Diplodocus *and* Triceratops *skeletons at the Natural History Museum*

is divided into two parts: the Life Galleries and the Earth Galleries. The Life Galleries include the Bird Gallery, Creepy Crawlies and, within 'Discovering Mammals', there are whales (look up at the huge model of the blue whale above you here), dolphins, elephants and hippos. The Earth Galleries have been transformed into the most advanced and exciting Earth Science galleries in the world. Covering three floors, the exhibition offers a fascinating glimpse into the earth's core and visitors can even walk underneath a volcano to see how it erupts and experience an earthquake in a Japanese supermarket.

On the first floor there is the 'Origins of Species' exhibition with some stuffed animals. Above the Central Hall is an exhibition on 'Our Place in Evolution'. The Minerals Gallery displays gemstones and crystals. Down in the basement is the Discovery Centre. Here there is plenty for inquisitive hands and eyes to explore, from 'feelie' boxes to put your hands in and see what's inside to microscopes to investigate. Don't forget the Human Biology on the ground floor too. The displays here explain how the body works.

Outside is a wildlife garden, specially created to encourage wildflowers, frogs and other animals to thrive.

⊖ South Kensington

🚌 C1, 9, 14, 49, 52, 74, 345

♿

Open: Monday–Saturday, 10.00 a.m.–5.50 p.m., Sunday, 11.00 a.m.–5.50 p.m. (closed 23–26 December)

£

Science Museum

Exhibition Road, SW7 (0171 938 8080; 0171 938 8008: recorded information)

As the largest museum of this kind in the world, the Science Museum houses over 200,000 exhibits, covering almost every imaginable sector of science, technology, industry and medicine. Particularly interesting exhibits include some of the oldest trains, planes and automobiles in the world, some of the very earliest veterinary and medical instruments, clocks and time measurement devices throughout the ages, and the first computers.

Nearly 2,000 of the exhibits are interactive, so visitors can explore and discover science and technology for themselves. 'Launch Pad', 'Things and the Garden', 'Flight Lab' and 'On Air' are all hands-on galleries designed especially for children of all ages.

⊖ South Kensington

🚌 C1, 9, 14, 49, 52, 74, 345

♿

Open: Daily, 10.00 a.m.–6.00 p.m.

£

The Science Museum

GARDENS

Museum of Garden History

St Mary-at-Lambeth, Lambeth Road, SE1 (0171 261 1891; 0171 633 9701)

This museum provides a fascinating insight into the history of gardening through a permanent exhibition and regular lectures.

Outside is the Tradescant Garden, which only contains plants grown by the Tradescant family and other plants from the seventeenth century. The Tradescants, father and son, were gardeners, successively, to the 1st Lord Salisbury, the Duke of Buckingham and then Charles I and Henrietta. They brought back from their travels in Europe and America many of the flowers, shrubs and trees we take for granted today.

The Tradescants are buried in the churchyard at St Mary-at-Lambeth, next to the tomb of Admiral Bligh of HMS *Bounty*. The church was closed in 1972, but a public appeal to save it was launched in 1977 and the work of restoration has continued steadily.

⊖ Lambeth North, Waterloo, Westminster

🚇 Waterloo

🚌 3, C10, 77, 344

♿

Open: April–October, Monday–Friday, 10.30 a.m.–4.00 p.m.;
Sunday 10.30 a.m.–5.00 p.m.

Free, but donations welcome (£ for special exhibitions)

HERITAGE

Westminster Abbey Museum

Westminster Abbey, SW1
(0171 222 5152)

Effigies of such monarchs as Charles II, Elizabeth I, William III and important dignitaries are on display in this museum. Modelled from death masks, they give a realistic image of what these people really looked like.

The museum also houses a collection of Romanesque carvings, a set of replica Coronation regalia, drawings by Sir Christopher Wren and several pieces of silvergilt plate.

⊖ St James's Park, Westminster

🚇 Victoria

🚌 3, 11, 12, 24, 77A, 211

♿

Open: daily, 10.30 a.m.–4.00 p.m.

£ (includes Chapter House)

EAST

Hackney Museum

Central Hall, Mare Street (opposite Hackney Town Hall), E8 (0181 986 6914)
In addition to an exhibition recording the history of Hackney, this museum has a fascinating collection, with many items donated by local people, reflecting the lives of the different communities that have made Hackney their home.

'Hackney Voices' is a new multi-media computer program that allows you to listen to local people from some of Hackney's many communities talking about their experiences and memories of settling in Hackney.

A lively programme of activities for children includes a Saturday Museum Club, games and quizzes.

⊖ Bethnal Green, then bus

🚇 Hackney Central

🚌 D6, 26, 48, 55, 106, 253

♿

Open: Tuesday–Friday, 10.00 a.m.–12.30 p.m., 1.30 p.m.–5.00 p.m.;
Saturday, 1.30 p.m.–5.00 p.m.

Free

Valence House Museum

Becontree Avenue, Dagenham, Essex (0181 595 8404)
Parts of Valence House date back to the fifteenth century and it is the only remaining manor house in Dagenham. Home of the borough's local history museum and art gallery, various items illustrating the history of the area are on display. Fishing was one of the most important industries in Barking from the fourteenth to the nineteenth centuries. Major fishing fleets operated out of the mouth of Barking Creek and many relics from this period are on display.

The jewel in the crown of the museum's collection is undoubtedly the Fanshawe Family Portraits and Archive. In addition, the O'Leary Gallery houses temporary exhibitions throughout the year and the history of the Becontree Estate which covers most of the borough is charted in the Becontree Room. The museum has a shop. There is an attractive herb garden where you can sit.

⊖ Becontree

🚇 Chadwell Heath

🚌 5, 87, 129, 145, 364, 368

Limited ♿ (ground floor only)

Open: Tuesday–Friday, 9.30 a.m.–1.00 p.m., 2.00 p.m.–4.30 p.m.;
Saturday, 10.00 a.m.–4.00 p.m.

Free

Vestry House Museum

Vestry Road, Walthamstow, E17 (0181 509 1917)
Set in the attractive old village of Walthamstow, the museum is housed in what was once a workhouse. Built in 1730 as a home for local paupers and a meeting

place for the Vestry (a parish council), it became a police station in the nineteenth century and one of the old police cells can still be seen. After various other uses the building was converted to a museum in 1930. The museum now serves as a centre for the collection, preservation and interpretation of the past and present story of the people of Waltham Forest.

In the 'Hearth and Home' gallery, the story of local domestic life over the past 100 years is told through original domestic equipment and implements such as mangles and flat irons. Other exhibits illustrate themes from local industry and fashion to childhood and leisure. The star attraction for many visitors is one of the claimants to being the oldest British manufactured car in existence, built by Frederick Bremner in 1892–4.

If you are interested in researching more about the history of this area, a good place to begin is the archives and local history library here. The archives range from medieval manorial court records to parish registers and school log books. There is a shop.

⊖/🚆 Walthamstow Central

🚌 20, 34, 48, 58, 69, 212

Limited ♿

Open: Monday–Saturday, 10.00 a.m.–1.00 p.m., 2.00 p.m.–5.30 p.m. (5.00 p.m., Saturday)

Free

NORTH

Grange Museum of Community History

Neasden Roundabout, Neasden Lane, NW10 (0181 452 8311)

Neasden Roundabout is an unexpected place to find a museum, but the Grange is an unusual and fascinating place. Once a farm, the museum now houses an exhibition of Brent history, and a community gallery. Local photographers and artists can display their work here and children can take part in art and craft workshops too. There is also a large garden, with a Victorian herb garden and a conservatory. Touring exhibitions organized by the Grange Museum are also on display at Brent Town Hall, local libraries and the Willesden Green Library Centre.

⊖ Neasden

🚌 16, 182, 226, 297, 302

Limited ♿ (downstairs only)

Open: Summer, Tuesday–Friday, 11.00 a.m.–5.00 p.m.; Saturday, 11.00 a.m.–5.00 p.m., Sunday, 2.00 p.m.–5.00 p.m.; Winter, Monday–Friday, 11.00 a.m.–5.00 p.m.; Saturday, 10.00 a.m.–5.00 p.m.

Free

Hampstead Museum

Burgh House, New End Square, NW3 (0171 431 0144)

This handsome Queen Anne house in the heart of Hampstead is now a community arts centre with art exhibitions, concerts, lectures and other regular events. It is also the home of the Hampstead Museum of local history and a collection of paintings by the popular Victorian artist Helen Allingham, who was resident in Hampstead at one time.

The house is of interest too, with its original panelled rooms, staircase and magnificent wrought-iron gates. There is a café.

θ Hampstead

🚌 46, 210, 268

Limited ♿

Open: Wednesday–Sunday, 12 noon–5.00 p.m.; bank holiday Monday, 2.00 p.m.–5.00 p.m.

Free

Haringey Museum and Archive Service

Lordship Lane, Haringey, N17 (0181 808 8772)

Haringey Museum is housed in Bruce Castle, one of only a handful of Grade I listed buildings in the borough. Once the manor house of Tottenham, it dates from the late sixteenth century. Since then, the building has been modified several times. In 1827 the Hill family bought the building and set up a progressive school for boys. It opened as a museum in 1906.

Displays include a Roman kiln, Victorian costume and domestic equipment, a postal collection, a reconstructed 1930s office and examples of local paintings, photographs and prints. The archive is a treasure house for researchers, with local maps, newspapers, street directories and photographs.

As well as the permanent exhibitions, the museum holds regular talks on local history and workshops for children.

θ Wood Green, Turnpike Lane, then bus

🚉 Bruce Grove

🚌 123, 149, 171A, 259, 279

Limited ♿

Open: Wednesday–Sunday, 1.00 p.m.–5.00 p.m.

Free

SOUTH

Bexley Museum

Hall Place, Bourne Road, Bexley, Kent (01322 526574)

This historic mansion is set in beautiful gardens beside the River Cray in south-east London. The northern half of the house dates from *c*.1540; the south side was added about a century later. Now owned by Bexley Council, it serves as a museum and is also the home of the Local Studies Centre.

Some rooms are open to the public, including the great hall in which stands the eighteenth-century chamber organ built by George England. Hall Place also houses a permanent display of local history and stages special exhibitions on a wide range of subjects. Concerts and lectures are held here too.

🚉 Bexley, Crayford

🚌 96, 132, 229, 269

No ♿

Open: Monday–Saturday, 10.00 a.m.–5.00 p.m.; also April–October, Sunday, 2.00 p.m.–6.00 p.m. (museum only)

Free

Bromley Museum

Church Hill, Orpington, Kent (01689 873826)

Historical celebrities, prehistoric tools and twentieth-century collectables are all featured in the Bromley Museum. The collection of John Lubbock, the 1st Lord Avebury, a nineteenth-century banker, is an important part of the displays. An avid anthropologist, archaeologist, botanist, geologist, zoologist and writer, he collected a wealth of material. A lively temporary exhibition programme includes paintings and crafts by local people and work by school children. The museum also runs a free education service for all schools in the borough and teachers can borrow objects to help with their lessons. Contact the museum for information on the nearby Crofton Roman Villa.

🚆 Orpington

🚌 51, 61, 208

Limited ♿

Open: Monday–Wednesday, Friday and Saturday, 9.00 a.m.–5.00 p.m.

(subject to alteration)

Free

The Courthouse

Garratt Lane, Wandsworth, SW18 (0181 871 7074)

A local history museum telling the story of the borough of Wandsworth from prehistoric times to the present day. Separate displays look at each of the local villages of Balham, Battersea, Putney, Roehampton, Tooting and Wandsworth.

Regular events and activities are held for children and there is a community gallery, a temporary exhibition gallery and a shop.

⊖ East Putney

🚆 Wandsworth Town

🚌 28, 37, 44, 77A, 156, 220

♿

Open: Tuesday–Saturday, 10.00 a.m.–5.00 p.m.; Sunday, 2.00 p.m.–5.00 p.m.

Free

The Cuming Museum

155–157 Walworth Road, Southwark, SE17 (0171 701 1342)

The unusual collections of the Cuming Museum are based on a large donation from the Cuming family. Richard Cuming was born in Walworth Road in 1777 and began collecting historical and scientific objects at the age of five. Together with his son, Henry, he built up a vast and wide-ranging collection of over 30,000 objects. They collected everything from local toys and souvenirs to exotic objects from all over the world. When Henry Cuming died in 1902, he left his collections to Southwark and the Cuming Museum was opened in 1906.

The museum shows the history of Southwark from its importance as a Roman crossroads 2,000 years ago to a busy London borough today. Special exhibitions feature themes from all over the world and show aspects of Southwark's recent past too. Two outstanding exhibits are part of a 2,000-year-old boat rescued from an inlet near the Thames and stone sculptures found down a well at Southwark Cathedral. In the seventeenth century Bermondsey was a centre for the manufacture of leather goods and English Delftware; examples of work from this period are on display as well as aspects of Victorian life.

⊖ Elephant & Castle

🚌 12, 35, 40, 45, 68, 171

No ♿

Open: Tuesday–Saturday, 10.00 a.m.–5.00 10.00 p.m.

Free

Greenwich Borough Museum

232 Plumstead High Street, Greenwich, SE18 (0181 855 3240)

Discover the archaeology, social history and natural history of Greenwich, Woolwich, Eltham, Deptford, Charlton, Plumstead and Thamesmead. The museum also holds a programme of temporary exhibitions, holiday activities and a Saturday Club.

🚆 Plumstead

🚌 96, 99, 180, 272, 422, 469

No ♿

Open: Monday, 2.00 p.m.–7.00 p.m.; Tuesday and Thursday–Saturday,
10.00 a.m.–1.00 p.m.; 2.00 p.m.–5.00 p.m.

Free

The Pumphouse Educational Museum (Rotherhithe Heritage Museum)

Lavender Pond and Nature Park, Lavender Road, Rotherhithe, SE16 (0171 231 2976)

The story of Rotherhithe and its people is told by a unique collection of objects found on the Thames foreshore. This fascinating collection is the result of over ten years' intensive beachcombing by a local resident, Mr Ron Goode. The museum is in the Lavender Pond Pumphouse which originally housed dock machinery and is surrounded by a nature park and pond.

⊖ Rotherhithe, Surrey Quays

🚌 P11

♿

Open: Monday–Friday, 9.30 a.m.–3.00 p.m.

Free, but donations welcome

Wandle Industrial Museum

Vestry Hall Annexe, London Road, Mitcham, Surrey (0181 648 0127)

The Wandle Industrial Museum was established in 1983 by local people with the main aim of creating a riverside museum that would reflect the rich heritage of the Wandle Valley in south-west London.

Its exhibition concentrates on two of the Wandle's better-known industries: snuff and tobacco, and textiles. Particular homage is paid to the area's most famous entrepreneurs, the designer William Morris and the retailer Arthur Liberty.

🚆 Mitcham (closed Sunday)

Buses: 118, 280

Limited ♿

Open: Wednesday, 1.00 p.m.–4.00 p.m.; first Sunday of each month, 2.00 p.m.–5.00 p.m.

£

Kingston Museum

Wheatfield Way, Kingston-upon-Thames, Surrey (0181 546 5386)

Built in 1904, the museum is a Grade II listed building which has recently been renovated and contains permanent displays, an art gallery and a shop.

The museum holds a fine collection of Martinware pottery collected by a local businessman, as well as other historical items from local areas, ranging from Stone Age relics to twentieth-century vacuum cleaners. The gallery is used for a variety of national, regional and local exhibitions of art, craft and photography.

🚋 Kingston-upon-Thames

🚌 65, 71, 216, 218, 406, 411

♿

Open: daily except Wednesday and Sunday, 10.00 a.m.–5.00 p.m.

Free

Museum of Richmond

Old Town Hall, Whittaker Avenue, Richmond, Surrey (0181 332 1141)

Housed in the Old Town Hall and overlooking the Thames, the Museum of Richmond covers the history of Richmond, Kew, Petersham and Ham. For a hands-on exploration of local history here, check out the times of local guided walks at the Tourist Information Centre (0181 940 9125) at the Old Town Hall too.

🚇 Richmond

🚌 H22, 33, 65, R68, 90, 290

Limited ♿

Open: Tuesday–Saturday, 11.00 a.m.–5.00 p.m.; also May–October, Sunday, 2.00 p.m.–5.00 p.m.

£

MEDICAL SCIENCE

Alexander Fleming Laboratory Museum

St Mary's Hospital, Praed Street, Paddington, W2 (0171 725 6528)

See for yourself the spot on which Alexander Fleming discovered penicillin in 1928 at this reconstruction of Fleming's laboratory. Displays and a video tell the remarkable story of Fleming and the discovery of penicillin, which was destined to play a crucial role in the fight against bacterial disease. Guided tours are conducted by volunteers, many of whom knew Fleming and have personal tales to tell of the impact of penicillin when it was first introduced in the 1940s.

⊖/🚃 Paddington

🚌 7, 15, 23, 27, 36

No ♿

Open: Monday–Thursday, 10.00 a.m.–1.00 p.m.; by arrangement at other times

£

Florence Nightingale Museum

St Thomas's Hospital (at car park level), 2 Lambeth Palace Road, SE1 (0171 620 0374)
'The Lady with the Lamp' as she is fondly known, Florence Nightingale (1820–1910) was a remarkable Victorian achiever. Her campaigning for army health reform and humanitarian causes first brought her to public attention during the Crimean War (1853–56). Here, she applied the principles of 'sanitary science' to improve the hygiene of the hospital buildings and used her managerial skill to reorganize the laundry and kitchens and to improve the supply of bedding, linen and other hospital necessities. Furthermore, she became a friend to all the soldiers she looked after, writing home on their behalf, acting as banker and lessening their suffering.

But perhaps her greatest achievement was to raise nursing to the level of a respectable profession for women. In 1860 she established the Nightingale Training School for nurses at St Thomas's Hospital. In 1860 she published *Notes on Nursing* which set down the principles of nursing and is still in print today. In 1883 Queen Victoria awarded Florence Nightingale the Royal Red Cross and in 1907 she became the first woman to be awarded the Order of Merit.

The museum traces her life through personal artefacts, letters, diaries and pictures creating a fascinating story of one of the nineteenth century's greatest figures.

⊖/🚃 Waterloo

🚌 P11, 12, 53, 77, 109, 171A

♿

Open: Tuesday–Sunday and bank holiday Monday, 10.00 a.m.–5.00 p.m.

(last admission 4.00 p.m.)

£

Freud Museum

20 Maresfield Gardens, Hampstead, NW3 (0171 435 2002/5167)
This was the home of the founder of psychoanalysis, Sigmund Freud, after the family had escaped the Nazi annexation of Austria in 1938. It remained the family home until Anna Freud, the youngest daughter, died in 1982.

The centrepiece of the museum is Freud's library and study, complete with patients' couch, preserved just as it was during his lifetime. The famous couch looks rather comfortable and is covered with a luxurious Persian carpet and chenille cushions. This room also contains Freud's remarkable collection of antiquities: Egyptian, Greek, Roman and Oriental.

The Freud family was fortunate enough to be able to bring to London all their furniture and household items, including tables, cupboards, nineteenth-century Austrian painted country furniture and Biedermeier chests, which are displayed in the house.

The museum is not simply a shrine to psychoanalaysis; it organizes active programmes of research and publication.

⊖ Finchley Road
🚌 13, 46, 82, 113
Limited ♿

Open: Wednesday–Sunday, 12 noon–5.00 p.m.
£

Michael Faraday's Laboratory and Museum

The Royal Institution of Great Britain, 21 Albemarle Street, W1 (0171 409 2992)
The museum houses a unique collection of original apparatus, manuscripts, pictures and personal memorabilia showing Faraday as man and scientist. Faraday, the son of a blacksmith and apprenticed to a bookbinder, became the father of electricity. His work on electricity and magnetism, and in particular his discovery of electro-magnetic induction, laid the foundations for today's electrical industries. He produced the first electric motor, the first transformer, the first dynamo, the first condenser, discovered the laws of electrolysis and carried out the experiments that led to the formulation of the electro-magnetic theory of light.

The Magnetic Laboratory, where many of Faraday's important discoveries were made, has been restored to how it looked in 1845.

⊖ Green Park
🚌 4, 8, 9, 14, 19, 22, 38
♿

Open: Monday–Friday, 10.00 a.m.–4.00 p.m.
£

The Old Operating Theatre, Museum and Herb Garret

9a St Thomas's Street, SE1 (0171 955 4791)
One of the more unusual museums in London, it displays the history of surgery, herbal medicine and nursing at two of London's major hospitals, Guy's and St Thomas's, and is set in the 'herb garret' of a church built by Sir Christopher Wren's master mason.

The oldest surviving operating theatre in the country (built in 1822), it was available for women only and has now been fully restored. In the centre of the theatre is an ominous-looking nineteenth-century operating table. Before anaesthetics were discovered in December 1846 operations must have been terrifying – surgeons had to work fast and only amputations could be carried out as it was too dangerous to perform internal operations.

A good time to visit is on the afternoon of the first Sunday of each month, when a special lecture about the museum is held at 2.30 p.m.

⊖/🚊 London Bridge
🚌 P11, 21, 35, 40, 47, 133
No ♿

Open: Tuesday–Sunday, 10.00 a.m.–4.00 p.m.
£

Science Museum

See page 49

Wellcome Trust

183 Euston Road, NW1 (0171 611 7211: recorded information; 0171 611 8298: advance bookings for large parties, 'Science for Life')

The Wellcome Trust was set up under the will of Sir Henry Wellcome to support research in medicine and allied subjects. At its headquarters in a refurbished 1930s building and in the new 210 Gallery at 210 Euston Road several exhibitions are open to the public. 'Science for Life' is both an explanation and a celebration of biomedical science. It explores the mysteries of the human body, the nature of scientific discovery and the artistry of the scientist. Aimed at the general layman, the exhibition makes biomedics accessible to the ordinary person, with interactive models so you can see your body through the eyes of a doctor and a walk-through cell magnified a million times.

The Wellcome Institute for the History of Medicine is based primarily on the outstanding collection of the Wellcome Institute Library and presents a lively programme of thematic exhibitions on various aspects of the history of medicine.

⊖ Euston, Euston Square, Warren Street

▣ Euston, King's Cross, St Pancras

🚌 10, 24, 29, 30, 73, 134

Limited ♿

Open: Monday–Friday, 9.45 a.m.–5.00 p.m.; Saturday, 9.30 a.m.–1.00 p.m.

Free

MILITARY & MARITIME

Cutty Sark

King William Walk, SE10 (0181 858 3445)

Queen of the tea clippers, the *Cutty Sark* was launched in 1869 at Dumbarton in Scotland. From 1870 to 1877 she worked as a tea clipper and it is through this that she became best known, achieving the fastest voyage from China to England in 1871, completed in 107 days with a crew of twenty-eight. In the latter part of the nineteenth century she was employed in the Australian wool trade. Since 1954 she has been in dry dock and is both a wonderful historical relic and a museum with hundreds of nautical artefacts, including brass instruments, paintings and figureheads.

▣ Greenwich

DLR: Island Gardens, then foot tunnel to Greenwich

🚌 188, 199

No ♿

Open: April–September, Monday–Saturday, 10.00 a.m.–6.00 p.m., Sunday, 12 noon–6.00 p.m.; October–March, Monday–Saturday, 10.00 a.m.–5.00 p.m., Sunday, 12 noon– 5.00 p.m.

£

The Cutty Sark

The Guards Museum
Wellington Barracks, Birdcage Walk, SW1 (0171 414 3271)
Situated close to Buckingham Palace near the entrance to the elegant William IV listed Wellington Barracks, this museum offers a fascinating history of Her Majesty's Foot Guards. As well as uniforms and weapons, there are personal mementoes, such as letters and diaries from individual officers and men which tell the human story behind the pomp and ceremony. The museum has a shop.

⊖ St James's Park

🚌 3, 11, 12, 24, 53, 211

♿

Open: daily, 10.00 a.m.–4.00 p.m.

£

HMS Belfast

Hay's Galleria, Vine Lane, Tooley Street, SE1 (0171 407 6434)

The *Belfast* (11,500 tons) was a Second World War cruiser that saw service with the Arctic convoys and on D-day. Today, visitors can enjoy exploring the ship from the quarterdeck up to the top of her bridge and all the way down through seven decks to her massive boiler and engine rooms, well below the ship's waterline.

On the way, it is possible to see inside her triple 15-centimetre (6-inch) gun turrets, operate her light anti-aircraft guns, explore the heavily armoured shell room and magazines and experience what life was like for her crew by visiting the cramped mess decks, officers' cabins, galley and sick bay.

⊖/🚉 London Bridge

🚌 17, 21, 35, 40, 47, 133

No ♿

Open: March–October, daily, 10.00 a.m.–6.00 p.m.; November–February, daily, 10.00 a.m.–5.00 p.m.

£

Imperial War Museum

Lambeth Road, SE1 (0171 416 5000)

You know you've arrived at the right place when you see the two imposing naval guns at the entrance of this museum. A history of all the military campaigns fought by Britain and the Commonwealth since the First World War is told here through a series of lively and realistic displays, such as the Trench Experience, with a dug-out and first aid post, and an authentic reconstruction of a London street in 1940, evoking the era of the Blitz during the Second World War.

In addition, there are dozens of tanks, guns and models to stimulate the imagination. You can also go on a simulated fighter plane ride with Operation Jericho on a secret mission.

Temporary exhibitions, history evenings, films and holiday events for children all add to the variety of activities offered here.

⊖ Elephant & Castle, Lambeth North

🚉 Waterloo

🚌 1, 12, 45, 53, 63, 68

♿ (please phone to give 48 hours' notice)

Open: daily, 10.00 a.m.–6.00 p.m. (free after 4.30 p.m.)

£

National Army Museum

Royal Hospital Road, Chelsea, SW3 (0171 730 0717)

This museum tells the soldier's story of the British Army from the formation of the Yeomen of the Guard by Henry VII at the Battle of Bosworth Field in 1485 to the United Nations' peacekeeping force of the present day. There are reconstructions, models and videos of the major events in the army's history, as well as personal mementoes and diaries.

In the Uniform Gallery you can see displays of uniform. The Art Gallery contains portraits by Romney, Gainsborough and Reynolds of Britain's military leaders.

⊖ Sloane Square
🚌 11, 22, 211, 137
♿

Open: daily, 10.00 a.m.–5.30 p.m. (closed Good Friday, first bank holiday in May and 25–26 December)
Free

National Maritime Museum and Royal Observatory

Park Row Greenwich, SE10 (0181 858 4422)

Founded in 1934, the Maritime Museum promotes an understanding of the history and future of Britain and the sea, the story of time, astronomy and navigation as well as of the historic buildings at Greenwich.

The museum is housed in the seventeenth-century Queen's House by Inigo Jones, the first Palladian villa to be built in England. It was begun in 1616 for Anne of Denmark as a palace by the river and completed for Henrietta Maria, wife of Charles I, in 1638. The house was restored in the 1980s and opened to the public again in 1990. The furniture and fittings include some historic items, but most are newly made of original materials, patterns and techniques.

In the West Wing there are galleries which trace Britain's marine history from Captain Cook's exploration of the Pacific to Nelson's battles with the French in contemporary paintings, along with guns, maps, navigational instruments, models and a large collection of decorated chinaware. Other galleries are 'All Hands', a children's interaction gallery and a twentieth-century sea power gallery.

The Royal Old Observatory was built in 1675 by Sir Christopher Wren on the orders of Charles II. Since 1884 the world has set its clocks according to the time of day on the Meridian at Greenwich, Longitude 0°.

Charles II appointed John Flamsteed as his first Astronomer Royal in 1675 to begin research on how to calculate time at sea – an essential requirement for the exploration and mapping of the globe. The Observatory was completed in 1676 and extended with later buildings. Today, it has been completely renovated and contains Sir Christopher Wren's Octagon Room and the apartments of the Astronomers Royal. The displays tell the story of time and astronomy and of the Observatory itself.

Outside, you can stand astride the Greenwich Meridian which runs through the courtyard. There is also a café and a shop.

🚉 Greenwich
🚌 177, 180, 199, 286
Limited ♿

Open: daily, 10.00 a.m.–5.00 p.m.
£

RAF Museum

Graham Park Way, Hendon, NW9 (0181 205 2266)
The RAF Museum houses one of the world's finest collections of historic aircraft and associated aeronautica, illustrating the story of flight from before the Wright brothers to the present day. Sited on 6 hectares (15 acres) of the former historic airfield at Hendon, the main aircraft hall occupies two hangars dating from the First World War. The complex also includes the Bomber Hall and 'The Battle of Britain Experience', as well as extensive display galleries.

Over seventy aircraft are displayed under cover, including the legendary Spitfire and Lancaster, German and American aircraft, as well as more recent fighter planes such as the Harrier and Tornado.

Other attractions include the Tornado Flight Simulator, the 'Touch & Try' Jet Provost cockpit where visitors can try out the controls for themselves, and the RAF 2000 exhibition with a three-screen panoramic 'Eurofighter' display, as well as a shop and a café.

⊖ Colindale
🚉 Mill Hill Broadway
🚌 204, 303
♿

Open: daily, 10.00 a.m.–6.00 p.m.
£

Black Cultural Archives and Museum

378 Coldharbour Lane, Brixton, SW9 (0171 738 4591)

This museum holds temporary exhibitions from collections of black culture, including African artefacts, slave papers, photographs and art. The archives have an unparalleled collection of material on black culture and are an important source for research into this field.

⊖ Brixton

🚌 35, 37, 45, 118, 196, 322

Limited ♿

Open: Museum Monday–Saturday, 10.00 a.m.–6.00 p.m.; Archives by appointment only, 10.00 a.m.–4.00 p.m.

Free

Horniman Museum

100 London Road, Forest Hill, SE23 (0181 699 1872)

The museum was set up by Frederick John Horniman MP, a Victorian tea magnate and anthropology enthusiast, who donated the surrounding park and museum to the public in 1902. The museum contains displays on the cultures, traditions and changing living conditions of the peoples of the world and origins and customs of different religious beliefs.

Equally renowned are the musical instruments from all parts of the world and from all musical traditions. In the Music Room Gallery you can experience the instruments yourself and the music they create by using the specially provided headphones. There is also a video that explores the making, playing and physics of the French horn. Handling sessions using instruments are arranged in the central activity area.

The magnificent Victorian conservatory once stood in the Horniman family home at Coombe Cliff in Croydon and was rebuilt here in 1989 by English Heritage. Today, it is regularly used for concerts and exhibitions. The museum holds regular workshops for children and adults. There is a café and souvenir shops.

🚇 Forest Hill

🚌 P4, 63, 176, 185, 312

♿

Open: Monday–Friday, 10.30 a.m.–5.30 p.m.; Sundays, 2.00 p.m.–5.30 p.m.

Free

The Jewish Museum

Raymond Burton House, 129–131 Albert Street, Camden Town, NW1
(0171 284 1997) and 80 East End Road, Finchley, N3 (0181 349 1143)

The Jewish Museum opens a window on to the history and religious life of the

Jewish community in Britain and beyond. Founded in 1932, the museum has one of the world's finest collections of Jewish ceremonial art. It has amalgamated with the former London Museum of Jewish Life on a two-site basis and the combined museum represents an important new educational and cultural resource for London.

Its history gallery traces the story of the Jewish community in Britain from the Norman Conquest to recent times. Highlights include medieval notched wooden tax receipts, eighteenth-century portraits, a Queen Anne silver tray and loving cups presented to the Lord Mayors of London by the Spanish and Portuguese Synagogue. Through an interactive map, visitors can plot changes over the centuries. The ceremonial art gallery aims to illustrate and explain Jewish religious practice with objects of rarity and beauty. These include Italian synagogue art and cradle charms, the oldest English-made Chanucah lamp, embroidered textiles and illuminated marriage certificates.

There is also a temporary exhibition gallery to accommodate an exciting programme of changing exhibitions designed to illustrate different facets of Jewish history and culture in Britain and overseas.

The Finchley location houses the museum's social history collection. These include an Oral History Archive with some 400 tape-recorded memories, a photographic archive and a wide range of documents and artefacts. The museum has also expanded its permanent exhibition on the history of Jewish people in London.

Camden Town location

⊖ Camden Town
🚊 Camden Road
🚌 C2, 24, 27, 29, 168, 274
♿

Open: Sunday–Thursday, 10.00 a.m.–4.00 p.m. (closed Friday, Saturday, Jewish Festivals and public holidays)
£

Finchley location
⊖ Finchley Central
🚌 143
♿

Open: Monday–Thursday, 10.30 a.m.–5.00 p.m.; Sunday, 10.30 a.m.–4.30 p.m. (closed Friday, Saturday, Jewish festivals and public holidays)
£

Museum of London

London Wall, EC2 (0171 600 3699; 0171 600 0807: recorded information)

The Museum of London is the largest and most comprehensive city museum in the world. It is dedicated to the story of London and its people. Throughout its history, London has attracted people from all parts of the world. The collections on display in the museum's permanent galleries reflect the influences that have made London the cosmopolitan city it is today. Almost every kind of object that illustrates society and culture in the past and present is represented, from excavated artefacts, paintings, costume and textiles, to street signs, ceramics and metalwork.

A whole range of special events and exhibitions are also offered, including film festivals, workshops, gallery talks and walks around London, as well as a shop and a café. The museum also runs evening classes and study days throughout the academic year.

⊖ Bank, Barbican, St Paul's

▣ City Thameslink, Liverpool Street, Moorgate

🚍 8, 22B, 56

♿

Open: Tuesday–Saturday, 10.00 a.m.–5.50 p.m.; Sunday, 12 noon–5.50 p.m.

£ (free from 4.30 p.m.)

Museum of Mankind

Ethnography Department of the British Museum, 6 Burlington Gardens, W1 (0171 437 2224; 0171 323 8043: information desk; 0171 323 8031: readers' tickets for library)

The Museum of Mankind presents a series of changing exhibitions illustrating the variety of non-western societies and cultures.

Its collections come from the indigenous peoples of Africa, Australia and the Pacific Islands, North and South America, and parts of Asia and Europe, and include some ancient as well as recent and contemporary cultures.

Research services include access to the reserve collections, photographs and opinions (not valuations) on visitors' objects (in the Students' Room, Monday–Friday, 1.00 p.m.–4.45 p.m.). The library is open for reference to everyone. There is a café and a bookshop.

⊖ Green Park, Piccadilly Circus

🚍 3, 9, 14, 19, 22, 38

♿

Open: Monday–Saturday, 10.00 a.m.–5.00 p.m.; Sunday, 2.30 p.m.–6.00 p.m.

Free (£ for some exhibitions)

The Polish Institute and Sikorski Museum

20 Princes Gate, South Kensington, SW7 (0171 589 9249)

In the heart of London's South Kensington you will find memories of Poland. The institute is a cultural centre for the Polish community here and also presents a glimpse of the history and tradition of Poland, one of central Europe's oldest nation states.

The General Sikorksi Collection comprises personal items and papers relating to the Polish General, who was Prime Minister of Poland and Supreme Commander-in-Chief from 1939 to 1943. The museum also has a superb collection of militaria, comprising over 10,000 items. Highlights include regimental colours, badges and uniforms. There are also showcases with impressive displays of weapons, from cavalry sabres and infantry rifles to ceremonial swords and daggers.

Other items on display include unique photographs, and china and cutlery from the mess rooms of eminent pre-Second World War regiments.

⊖ South Kensington

🚌 9, 10, 52

No ♿

Open: Museum Monday–Friday, 2.00 p.m.–4.00 p.m., also first Saturday of each month, 10.00 a.m.–4.00 p.m.; Archives Tuesday–Friday, 9.30 a.m.–4.00 p.m.

Free, but donations welcome

PEOPLE, POLITICS & RELIGION

Cabinet War Rooms

Clive Steps, King Charles Street, SW1 (0171 930 6961)

Enter the Cabinet War Rooms tucked away in a corner of Whitehall at the centre of British government and you feel as if you have stepped back through history to the dark days of the Second World War. The Cabinet War Rooms were moved here for safety in 1939 and it was here that Churchill worked and lived with his ministers and war workers while planning the British strategy for winning the war against Germany.

In the Cabinet Room the clocks are set at 16.58 and the tables have been prepared as they were for a Cabinet meeting, while in the floor below are the dormitories where the workers slept. Other rooms include the Transatlantic Telephone Room, adapted in 1943, that housed a direct telephone link between Churchill and the American President, Franklin Roosevelt; a Map Room; Room 60A, a typing area which provided a 24-hour service and Room 60 Left which held BBC Radio transmitting equipment. Churchill broadcast four major speeches from his office-bedroom further along the corridor which were then relayed from Room 60 Left to the outside world.

⊖ Westminster

🚌 3, 11, 24, 77A, 109, 211

Limited ♿

Open: daily, 10.00 a.m.–6.00 p.m. (1 April–30 September, from 9.30 a.m.)

£

Dickens House

48 Doughty Street, WC1 (0171 405 2127)

Although Charles Dickens (1812–70) only lived at 48 Doughty Street for two years, from 1837 to 1839, it was while he was here that he established his reputation as one of Britain's greatest writers. It was here he finished *Pickwick Papers* and worked on *Oliver Twist*, *Nicholas Nickleby*, *Barnaby Rudge*, *Sketches of Young Gentlemen* and *The Lamplighter*.

In this house Dickens also entertained fellow writers such as Leigh Hunt in his drawing room which has been carefully reconstructed from this period. Also of interest are Dickens's manuscripts, letters, first editions of his books and even the desk he used for public readings of his works. There is a shop.

Θ Chancery Lane, Holborn, Russell Square

🚌 19, 38, 45, 171A

Limited ♿

Open: Monday–Saturday, 10.00 a.m.–5.00 p.m.

£

Dr Johnson's House

17 Gough Square, EC4 (0171 353 3745)

Famous for his comment, 'When a man is tired of London, he is tired of life', Dr Johnson (1709–84) was more than a clever wordsmith. He compiled the first comprehensive English dictionary while he was living at 17 Gough Square between 1748 and 1759. It was here too that he entertained David Garrick and Oliver Goldsmith.

The house has been restored to the condition it was in during Johnson's stay and contains a fascinating collection of items relating to Johnson, such as first editions of the dictionary, letters, prints, mezzotints and portraits, reflecting the famous occupant and his period.

Θ Blackfriars, Chancery Lane

🚌 11, 15, 26, 171A

No ♿

Open: May–September, Monday–Saturday, 11.00 a.m.–5.30 p.m.; October–April, 11.00 a.m.–5.00 p.m.

£

Keats House

Keats Grove, Hampstead, NW3
(0171 435 2062: recorded information)

Hampstead has been home to many important literary figures. The Romantic poet Leigh Hunt (1784–1859) moved here to a small cottage in a hamlet known as the Vale of Health in 1816 and often wrote about its beauty in his poems. When his friend John Keats came to visit him, he was so taken by the area that he too moved to Hampstead and lived there from 1818 to 1820.

Unfortunately Leigh Hunt's house has been pulled down, but Keats' house has been turned into a museum open to the public. The house contains relics, books, manuscripts and letters of Keats, his fiancée Fanny Brawne and his family and friends. Occasional poetry readings and musical evenings are held here too and it is also the headquarters of the Friends of Keats House.

⊖ Hampstead

🚌 24, 46, 268

Limited ♿

Open: April–October, Monday–Friday, 10.00 a.m.–1.00 p.m., 2.00 p.m.–6.00 p.m., Saturday, 10.00 a.m.–1.00 p.m., 2.00 p.m.–5.00 p.m., Sunday, 2.00 p.m.–5.00 p.m.; Easter, spring and late summer bank holidays, 2.00 p.m.–5.00 p.m.; November–March, Monday–Friday, 1.00 p.m.–5.00 p.m., Saturday, 10.00 a.m.–1.00 p.m., 2.00 p.m.– 5.00 p.m., Sunday, 2.00 p.m.–5.00 p.m. (closed Good Friday, Easter Sunday and May Day)

Free, but donations welcome

Sherlock Holmes Museum

221b Baker Street, NW1 (0171 935 8866)

Possibly the most famous address in London, 221b was the home of Sir Arthur Conan Doyle's fictional detective, Sherlock Holmes. Since 1990, this museum has brought to life the house that Holmes shared with his partner Dr Watson. It has been faithfully re-created according to the book and devotees have a chance to see the famous first-floor study where they worked, as well as Mrs Hudson's (the housekeeper) rooms and the bedrooms of Holmes and Watson. Memorabilia from the adventures and a selection of letters written to and from Mr Holmes are also on display, along with a magnificent bronze bust of the detective himself. The museum has a shop and period restaurant.

⊖ Baker Street

🚌 13, 27, 30, 82, 113, 274

No ♿

Open: daily, 9.30 a.m.–6.00 p.m. (last admission 5.30 p.m.)

£

Wesley's Chapel, Museum of Methodism and Wesley's House

49 City Road, EC1 (0171 253 2262: recorded information)

John Wesley (1703–91) was one of the most influential personalities of the eighteenth century. A fervent Christian, he began preaching in the open air at Bristol in 1739. Over the next fifty years his 'field preaching' gradually extended throughout the British Isles. Founder of the Methodist Movement, he built Wesley's Chapel as his London base. Known as the Cathedral of World Methodism, the chapel is the centrepoint of several historic buildings here and contains John Wesley's tomb. Today, the Chapel is still an active centre for Methodism and regular services are held each week on Thursdays and Sundays.

Nearby is Wesley's house, which he built in 1779. He lived here when not travelling and preaching elsewhere. It also provided a home for the preachers of the Chapel. It still retains its Georgian interior and provides a fascinating glimpse into domestic life at this time.

This site also contains the Museum of Methodism, which provides an excellent introduction to the movement from its beginnings to the present day, with the most comprehensive collection of Methodist ceramics and displays of chapel architecture, Methodism and the arts and the World Methodist scene.

⊖ Moorgate, Old Street

🚌 55, 141, 214, 271

Limited ♿ (ground floor only)

Open: Wesley's Chapel and John Wesley's tomb Monday–Saturday, 10.00 a.m.–6.00 p.m.; Museum of Methodism and John Wesley's House Monday–Saturday, 10.00 a.m.– 4.00 p.m.

Chapel and tomb free, £ for museum and house

PERFORMING ARTS

Fenton House

Windmill Hill, Hampstead, NW3 (0171 435 3471)
See also page 91

The William and Mary house provides an attractive setting for the collection of early keyboard instruments. Known as the Benton Fletcher Collection, the instruments date from 1540 to 1805 and include a seventeenth-century Flemish harpsichord.

⊖ Hampstead

🚌 46, 210, 268

Limited ♿ (ground floor)

Open: March, Saturday and Sundays 2.00 p.m.– 5.00 p.m.; April–end October, Wednesday–Friday, 2.00 p.m.–5.30 p.m., Saturday, Sunday and bank holiday Monday, 11.00 a.m.–5.30 p.m.

£ (free to National Trust members)

Museum of Instruments

Royal College of Music, Prince Consort Road, South Kensington, SW7 (0171 591 4346)

This internationally renowned collection of 600 instruments from *c*.1480 to the present day includes keyboard, stringed and wind instruments from Europe, Asia and Africa. Among the earliest instruments is possibly the oldest surviving stringed keyboard instrument, an anonymous clavicytherium probably made in southern Germany *c*.1480 and one of the earliest dated harpsichords, made by Alessandro Trasuntino in Venice in 1531.

⊖ South Kensington

🚌 9, 10, 52, 74

♿

Open: every Wednesday during termtime except January, 2.00 p.m.–4.30 p.m.

£

Museum of the Moving Image (MOMI)

South Bank, Waterloo, SE1 (0171 401 2636: recorded information)

Become the star of the latest blockbuster movie in an interview with film journalist Barry Norman, fly high over London like Superman or even read the 'News At Ten' during a visit to the Museum of the Moving Image. The museum utilizes many ingenious displays to illustrate the history and magic of cinema and television in a journey through time. From early Chinese shadow theatre, you pass to the birth of television and international cinema up to the latest in television technology. Look out for the actor-guides in costume bringing the exhibits to life and try out some basic animation techniques for yourself.

Nothing has been overlooked at the award-winning museum that is packed with original posters, film and television clips and costumes, notably Marilyn Monroe's 'Shimmy Dress' from *Some Like It Hot*. Allow an absolute minimum of two hours to visit this entertaining and educational museum that appeals to both adults and children. Facilities include a shop and a café.

⊖ Embankment, Waterloo

🚇 Waterloo

🚌 26, 68, 168, 171, 171A, 176

♿

Open: daily except 24–26 December, 10.00 a.m.–6.00 p.m. (last admission 5.00 p.m.)

£

Puppet Centre

Battersea Arts Centre, Lavender Hill, SW11 (0171 228 5335)

Formed in 1974 to promote the arts of puppetry and animation, the Puppet Centre has an excellent collection of puppet figures, rare photographs, slides, posters and memorabilia on display at the Battersea Arts Centre and in the Fantasy in Action touring exhibition.

Puppet performances are given regularly too (see page 135).

🚇 Clapham Junction

🚌 77, 77A, 345

♿

Open: Monday–Friday, 2.00 p.m.–6.00 p.m. 12 noon–10.00 p.m.

Free (£ for performances)

Rock Circus

London Pavilion, Piccadilly Circus, W1 (0171 734 8025: recorded information)

The history of rock 'n' roll through the ages is told through a series of tableaux featuring life-size wax models of all the major stars, from Elvis Presley to Madonna. The highlight of the exhibition is a rock show where the audio-animatronic waxwork stars appear to come alive and dance and play along to their greatest hits.

⊖ Leicester Square, Piccadilly Circus

🚌 3, 6, 9, 11, 12, 13, 14, 15, 19, 22, 23, 53

♿

Open: Sunday, Monday, Wednesday and Thursday, 11 a.m.–9.00 p.m.; Tuesday, 12 noon–9.00 p.m.; Friday and Saturday, 11 a.m.–10.00 p.m.

££

Royal Military School of Music

Kneller Hall, Kneller Road, Twickenham, Middlesex
(0181 898 5533)

Alongside the Royal Military School of Music is an important collection of musical instruments, the W.F. Blandford Collection. All the instruments have military connections.

🚇 Whitton
🚌 281
No &

Open: by appointment only, Monday–Friday
Free

Royal Opera House Archives

Royal Opera House, Covent Garden, WC2 (0171 240 1200)

Established in the 1960s, the Royal Opera House Archives were formed to record the history of the Royal Opera House and its companies since it opened in 1732. Materials contained in the archives range from eighteenth-century prints of performers to administrative and financial records, head-dresses and jewellery to costume and set designs.

Visual material includes eighteenth- and nineteenth-century prints and song-sheet covers. There are also photographs, which include pictures of the stage sets for the first Covent Garden performance of 'The Ring' in 1892 and of the first London season by Diaghilev's 'Ballets Russes' in 1911, as well as performance photographs of many contemporary performers.

Press cuttings range from announcements of eighteenth-century performances to detailed coverage of opera at Covent Garden and other London theatres since 1847. For costume and textile enthusiasts there are hundreds of original designs, including 1,100 costume designs by Attilio Comelli, house designer at the Royal Opera House from the 1890s to the 1920s.

The Archives are also home to several special collections, including the Dame Eva Turner Collection of costumes, head-dresses and jewellery, the Harold Rosenthal Collection of Press Notices with reviews of performances at the Royal Opera House from 1847 to 1937 and of opera performances at other major London theatres between 1865 and 1937, a photographic record of the Royal Opera House and the Royal Ballet Benevolent Fund Collection of material relating to the early history of the Vic Wells/ Sadler's Wells Ballet.

⊖ Covent Garden
🚌 4, 6, 9, 11, 13, 15, 23, 26, 76
Limited &

Open: by appointment only for research on Monday–Friday, 10.30 a.m.–1.00 p.m., 2.30 p.m.–5.30 p.m. (closed Wednesday)
Details of admission charges available on request

❖

Shakespeare's Globe Exhibition and Guided Tour

New Globe Walk, Bankside, SE1 (0171 928 6406)

Built in 1599 and destroyed by fire in 1613 when an ember from a stage cannon used in a performance of *Henry VIII* set light to the thatch, the original Globe Theatre was a famous Elizabethan theatre where many of Shakespeare's plays were performed. The theatre is now being rebuilt as an entertainment, education and cultural complex.

When completed, the Globe will be a celebration of Shakespeare's life and work – a living, working theatre, with his plays performed in the open air to audiences seated on wooden benches just as three centuries ago. In the special exhibition you can see craftsmen using seventeenth-century techniques to complete the timber-frame construction of the new Globe Theatre. The exhibition also tells the history of the old theatre and describes the research that has gone into the design for the new one.

Θ/▣ London Bridge

🚌 P11, 344

Limited ♿

Open: daily, 10.00 a.m.–5.00 p.m.

£ (including guided tour)

The Theatre Museum

Russell Street, Covent Garden, WC2
(0171 836 7891; 0171 836 2330: box office)

Situated in the heart of Theatreland, the Theatre Museum is a celebration of 400 years of Britain's theatrical heritage. The museum was created in 1974 out of three major collections to become a separate entity under the umbrella of the Victoria & Albert Museum. Although called the Theatre Museum, it encompasses all live performing arts, including circus, magic, opera and ballet.

The museum's excellent permanent collections include exhibitions that explore the British stage and its stars. The story is told using a wealth of costumes, props, drawings, photographs, posters and audio-visual displays. In your journey through the museum look out for the reconstructions of early theatres including the Globe, a display illustrating the restoration of the Savoy Theatre to its Art Deco form of 1929 and the memorabilia of Noel Coward and great actors such as Garrick, Kean and Irving.

Included in the price of the entry ticket is the daily tour guide service, costume workshops and make-up demonstrations. Children particularly enjoy these, especially when they see their friends transformed into animals!

It is a good idea to phone in advance to find out about temporary exhibitions, events and talks before your visit. The museum also has a souvenir shop and a box office should you wish to step straight out of the museum and into a West End production.

Θ Covent Garden

🚌 4, 6, 9, 11, 13, 15, 23, 26, 76

♿

Open: Tuesday–Sunday, 11.00 a.m.–7.00 p.m.

£

BT Museum

145 Queen Victoria Street, EC4 (0171 248 7444; 0800 289 689: recorded information)
BT's museum describes the history of telecommunications through a series of 'touch and try' displays, videos and exhibits. The display is constantly changing to adapt to the massive leaps in technology and communication that continue today.
⊖ Blackfriars, Mansion House
▣ Blackfriars
🚌 11, 15, 26, 45, 63
♿ (advance notice preferred)
Open: Monday–Friday, 10.00 a.m.–5.00 p.m.
Free

Brunel Exhibition Rotherhithe

Brunel's Engine House, Railway Avenue, Rotherhithe, SE16 (0181 318 2489)
One of the foremost engineers of the nineteenth century, Sir Marc Isambard Brunel built the engine house in Rotherhithe for the boilers which provided the power to drain the tunnel under the Thames. The tunnel was the first major underwater thoroughfare in the world. Its construction between 1825 and 1843 was a triumph of ingenuity and perseverance in the face of floods, financial losses and human disaster. It was opened to pedestrians in 1843 and sold to a railway company in 1865. It now carries the London underground trains between Rotherhithe and Wapping.

Sadly at one time the building was neglected and became increasingly derelict. After the East London line was electrified in 1913 the building was no longer required for railway purposes and gradually fell into disuse. Fortunately in 1975 the building, now scheduled as an Ancient Monument, was leased to the London Borough of Southwark and through them to the Brunel Exhibition Project for restoration and for use as a museum.

The museum opened in 1980 and contains a fascinating account of the building of the tunnel. It also houses the sole surviving example of a compound horizontal V-steam pumping engine built by J & G Rennie of Southwark in 1855. To enjoy the museum most and to get a better understanding of the technology involved here, it is a good idea to go on a guided tour and watch the video display.
⊖ Rotherhithe
▣ New Cross, New Cross Gate, then East London line
DLR: Shadwell, then East London line
🚌 P11, 47, 188
Limited ♿
Open: first Sunday each month, 12 noon–4.00 p.m.
£

Charles Darwin Memorial Museum

Downe House, Luxted Road, Downe, Orpington, Kent (01689 859119: recorded information)
Charles Darwin (1809–82) was one of the nineteenth century's most influential scientists, best known for his theory on the evolution of species. He lived at

Downe House from 1842 until his death and his large collection of books, notes and scientific evidence can be viewed by the public today.

🚊 Petts Wood, then bus

🚌 R2 (Monday–Friday and Saturday shopping hours only)

Limited ♿

Open: Wednesday–Sunday and bank holiday Monday, 1.00 p.m.–5.30 p.m.

£

Kew Bridge Steam Museum

Green Dragon Lane, Brentford, Middlesex (0181 568 4757)

The highlights of this museum are five Cornish beam engines, two of which can be seen working every weekend. Originally used to pump West London's water supply for more than a century, the five engines are led by Grand Junction 90, the world's largest working beam engine.

The museum also has other items to interest steam enthusiasts, including a Bagneel steam locomotive called Wendy and a presentation of London's water supply from its early beginnings in the eighteenth century to the present day. The forge and nineteenth-century machine shop are examples of the facilities essential to a steam-powered pumping station. The museum is 'in steam' only at weekends. Facilities include a café (weekends only) and a bookshop.

⊖ Gunnersbury, Kew Gardens

🚊 Kew Bridge

🚌 65, 237, 267, 391

Limited ♿

Open: daily, 11.00 a.m.–5.00 p.m.

£

London Gas Museum

British Gas, Twelvetrees Crescent, Bromley-by-Bow, E3 (0171 538 4982)

The museum traces the development of the gas industry from the foundation of the Gas-Light and Coke Company in 1812 to the present day. The enormous impact of gas lighting and heating is presented through period room sets. Look out for 'Sir Fred' taking a bath in a Victorian bathroom and the lady of the house sitting by the fire in an Edwardian drawing room. Appliances through the ages are shown beside the most modern gadgets, including gas ovens, waffle makers and even a gas-operated fan and a radio.

⊖ Bromley-by-Bow

DLR: Devons Road

🚌 52, 108

Limited ♿

Open: by appointment only

Free

London Planetarium

Marylebone Road, NW1 (0171) 935 6861: recorded information)

A journey through time and space with regular shows and lectures about the planets and stars in our solar system. There are plenty of special effects, enhanced by the installation of the most advanced star projector in the world – the Digistar Mark II. The shows last thirty minutes and start every forty minutes. No children under five. If you are also visiting Madame Tussaud's, the combined admission ticket saves money.

⊖ Baker Street

🚌 C2, 2, 13, 18, 27, 30, 74, 82, 113, 135, 139, 159, 274

♿

Open: Monday–Friday, 12.20 p.m.–5.00 p.m. (last show starts then); Saturday and Sunday, 10.20 a.m.–5.00 p.m.

£–££

The Natural History Museum
See page 47

Science Museum
See page 49

Tower Bridge Museum
Tower Bridge, SE1 (0171 403 3761)
There are splendid views from the enclosed high-level walkway across the top of the towers on the bridge – you can either climb the 200 steps or take the lift. There is also a museum with various interesting exhibits, plus Victorian engine rooms with the original steam engines used to open the bridge to let ships through. Today, the hydraulic lifting mechanisms are powered by electricity.

⊖ Tower Hill

DLR: Tower Gateway, Tower Hill

🚌 42, 78

♿

Open: April–October daily, 10.00 a.m.–6.30 p.m.; November–March, 9.30 a.m.–6.00 p.m.

££

Tower Hill

by District line

The Tower of London, HMS Belfast, St Katharine's Dock, River Trips to Greenwich and Westminster ... and a fabulous view from the top of Tower Bridge. All a few steps from Tower Hill Station.

Go Green, Go District

Wimbledon Windmill Museum

Windmill Road, Wimbledon Common, SW19 (0181 947 2825)

On the west side of Wimbledon Common, near the car park, there is a rare, hollow-post windmill which has been converted into a museum illustrating the story of windmills. There is a café.

⊖/🚆 Wimbledon

🚌 93

No ♿

Open: Easter to end October, Saturday, Sunday and public holiday, 2.00 p.m.–5.00 p.m.

£

VISUAL ARTS • 78

Bramah Tea and Coffee Museum

The Clove Building, Maguire Street, SE1 (0171 378 0222)

Tea is the nation's favourite drink. However, when tea was first introduced to this country, in the seventeenth century, it was an expensive commodity that could only be afforded by the very wealthy and was locked away in special tea caddies to stop the servants from stealing it!

This museum tells the story of tea and coffee through a glittering collection of pictures, silver and ceramics. It is also interesting to learn how the tea bag and instant coffee came about. Apparently, in the 1960s the coffee giants Nestlé and General Foods thought that if they introduced coffee as soluble powder like cocoa, the British might take to it more. The tea traders responded to this challenge to their traditional market by producing a tea that would infuse more quickly. These teas were marketed as quick brew, fast brew and super brew and were but one small step away from the tea bag which currently accounts for seventy per cent of British tea sales. After visiting the museum you can stop for tea or coffee in their café, or buy your own from the shop.

⊖ Tower Hill, London Bridge

DLR: Tower Gateway

🚌 P11, 47, 188

Limited ♿

Open: daily, except 25–26 December, 10.00 a.m.–6.00p.m.

£

London Dungeon

28–34 Tooley Street, London Bridge, SE1 (0171 403 0606: recorded information)

Not for the faint-hearted, the London Dungeon cleverly manages to create a gruesome atmosphere where you can frighten yourself out of your wits.

Passing through the cold, damp candlelit 'dungeons', you discover a history of blood-thirsty and barbaric methods of punishment used in Britain over the centuries re-created in tableaux. The story begins with a human sacrifice at Stonehenge by Druids and Boadicea spearing a Roman soldier to death. Punishments were still fairly barbaric in Tudor times and you can see Anne Boleyn, one of Henry VIII's less fortunate wives, being beheaded. You can also experience special effects originally conceived for major television and film productions. Although this museum is often fascinating, it can be a welcome relief once you reach the end and daylight outside.

⊖/🚃 London Bridge

🚌 17, 21, 35, 40, 47, 133

♿

Open: daily, April–September, 10.00 a.m.–5.30 p.m., October–May, 10.00 a.m.–4.30p.m.

££

Madame Tussaud's

Marylebone Road, NW1 (0171 935 6861: recorded information)

Without doubt one of the most popular museums in London. The constantly long queues to enter in the summer can be avoided by booking tickets in advance. Madame Tussaud herself was a Frenchwoman born in 1761. Her widowed mother was a housekeeper to a doctor who taught the girl wax modelling skills. When only seventeen she modelled Voltaire – the figure is on display in the museum. Her work at a Paris exhibition led to an invitation to the court of Louis XVI and Marie Antoinette, where she supervised the artistic education of the King's sister for nine years before the Revolution broke out. Her connection with the royal family made her 'guilty by association' and she was imprisoned, sharing a cell with the future Empress Josephine and only narrowly escaping the guillotine. On her release she was compelled to make death masks of executed nobles; some of these masks can still be seen in the museum.

Leaving her husband in France, she moved to Britain with her two children and for the next thirty-three years she travelled all over the country exhibiting her collection of models. In 1835 she established a permanent base in London, known as 'The Bazaar, Baker Street', visitors being charged sixpence for admission. In 1884 her grandsons moved the exhibition to its present site.

The museum aims to have some topical displays by including authentic waxworks of the latest celebrity, pop star or sportsman. In the Grand Hall you will find historical, political, military and royal figures, while in the refurbished Chamber of Horrors notorious criminals are re-created almost too realistically with spine-chilling sound effects.

If you are also visiting the London Planetarium, the combined admission ticket saves money.

⊖ Baker Street

🚌 C2, 2, 13, 18, 27, 30, 74, 82, 113, 135, 139, 159, 274

Limited ♿

Open: October–March: daily, 10.00 a.m.–5.30 p.m.; April–September, 9.00 a.m.–5.30 p.m.

££

National Postal Museum

King Edward Building, King Edward Street, EC1 (0171 239 5420)

For over 350 years the British Post Office has provided postal services to the public and today the Post Office and Royal Mail are part of our everyday lives. Their unique heritage and impact on society is explored in this museum, which has displays of stamps, from the Penny Black to the latest issues, early examples of letter boxes, post horns, medals and model mail coaches.

⊖ St Paul's

🚌 8, 22B, 25, 56

Limited ♿

Open: Monday–Friday, 9.30 a.m.–4.30 p.m. (closed bank holiday Monday)

Free

Ragged School Museum

46–50 Copperfield Road, E3 (0181 980 6405)

This is the East End's own history museum with a special interest in the work of Dr Barnardo and the development of education in London. It is based in a Victorian warehouse which from 1896 was part of the largest Ragged (free) School in London and known as the Copperfield Road Ragged School. From 1877 to 1908 thousands of poor local children received a free education with free meals in the winter and help towards finding their first job.

As well as displays on Dr Barnardo and the school, there is a re-created Victorian classroom used by school groups for re-enacted Victorian lessons. There is also a lively programme of varied events for children, families and adults, such as treasure hunts and Christmas traditions workshops, while the history club gives regular talks on the East End on the third Wednesday of each month during the winter.

⊖ Mile End

BR/DLR: Limehouse

🚌 D6, D7, 25, 277, 309

No ♿

Open: Wednesday and Thursday, 10.00 a.m.–5.00 p.m.; first Sunday of each month, 2.00 p.m.–5.00 p.m.

Free, but donations welcome

Salvation Army Heritage Centre

117–121 Judd Street, WC1 (0171 387 1656)

The Salvation Army was founded by General William Booth (1829–1912) and its aim is to spread the Gospel and improve social conditions throughout the world. This museum tells the story of the movement with exhibits such as photographs, documents and examples of the Salvation Army Uniform. There is a free audio guide and a bookshop.

⊖ King's Cross

🚌 10, 30, 73, 91

Limited ♿

Open: exhibition Monday–Friday, 9.30 a.m.–3.30 p.m.; Saturday, 9.30 a.m.–12.30 p.m.; archives by appointment only

Free, but donations welcome

Twinings in the Strand

216 Strand, WC2 (0171 353 3511)

Twinings have been importing tea into England since the seventeenth century. The company has a fine collection of items relating to the history of tea and the Twining family on display here.

⊖ Charing Cross, Embankment, Temple

🚆 Charing Cross

🚌 4, 6, 9, 11, 13, 15, 23, 26

Limited ♿

Open: Monday–Friday, 9.30 a.m.–4.00 p.m. (large groups not possible; occasionally closed at short notice)

Free

Arsenal Museum

Arsenal Stadium (North Stand), Avenell Road, N5 (0171 226 0304)
Arsenal Football Club was formed in 1886 by workers from
the Royal Munitions Factory in Woolwich. The club moved
to Highbury in 1913 and has been there ever since. This
museum is a nostalgic record of the club through the years
on its rise to the top of the Premier League in London.
Mementoes abound and include photographs, players' kit
and footballs. There is also a twenty-minute film high-
lighting all the great moments in Arsenal's history.

⊖ Arsenal

🚌 4, 19, 236

♿

Open: May–July, Friday and Saturday, 9.30 a.m.–4.00 p.m.;
August–April, Friday, 9.30 a.m.–4.00p.m.

£

MCC Museum

Lord's Cricket Ground, St John's Wood, NW8
(0171 289 1611: Curator; 0171 266 3825:
Tours Department)
Lord's was established in 1787 by Thomas Lord, a
keen cricketer and wealthy property developer. It
is the home of the Marylebone Cricket Club,
founded in 1787 when cricket was emerging
from its medieval village roots to become a
popular game with the aristocracy. The club's
leading position was at once recognized and in
1788 it laid down a code of laws. The MCC has been the
guardian of the laws of cricket ever since and today receives suggestions
from governing bodies worldwide.

The museum at Lord's is a treasure house of cricketing history. As befits the
gentlemanly atmosphere, visitors are encouraged to dress appropriately and
wear a shirt and jacket in the pavilion and indoor areas. The highlight of the
tour around Lord's is a visit to the Long Room, the inner sanctum where MCC
members can watch matches. It is also a cricketing art gallery and there are
portraits of the founder, Thomas Lord and C.B. Fry, the English all-rounder
who was offered, and refused, the crown of Albania. There are also paintings
of other famous cricketing stars, including Douglas Jardine, Sir Pelham 'Plum'
Warner, Sir Donald Bradman and W.G. Grace. You can also see a display of
bats used by such great stroke players as Trumper, Compton, Hutton and
Hobbs.

No visit to the museum would be complete without seeing the famous Ashes.
Whoever wins them every two years, England or Australia, they are kept here
permanently, safe in a terracotta urn.

Cricket is not the only sport played at Lord's; there has been a long tradition of real tennis too. Henry VIII's favourite game is still played here today and you can visit the unusual tennis courts.

The shop attract enthusiasts of all ages.

⊖ St John's Wood

🚌 13, 46, 82, 113, 139

Limited ♿

Open: guided tours (book in advance) at 12 noon and 2.00 p.m. daily. (subject to changes in times); no tours during Test and Cup matches

£

The Museum of Rugby

RFU Ground, Rugby Road, Twickenham, Middlesex, TW1 (0181 892 2000)

Twickenham, home of England rugby since 1909, welcomes visitors. The Museum of Rugby is designed to appeal to enthusiasts of all ages with interactive displays, rugby memorabilia and a continuous film show. 'The Twickenham Experience Tour' gives visitors a fascinating glimpse behind the scenes with a visit to the England dressing room and the players' tunnel.

🚉 Twickenham

🚌 281

♿

Open: Museum: non-match days, Tuesday–Saturday, 10.30 a.m.–5.00 p.m.; Sunday, 2.00 p.m.–5.00 p.m. (last admission 4.30 p.m.); match days, 11.00 a.m.–1 hour prior to kick-off (match ticket holders only). Tour: Tuesday–Saturday, 10.30 a.m., 12 noon, 1.30 p.m., 3.00 p.m.; Sunday, 2.30 p.m.

£

Wimbledon Lawn Tennis Museum

Church Road, Wimbledon, SW19 (0181 946 6131)

If you are one of those people who are glued to a television set for two weeks of the year when the Wimbledon Championships are on in the summer but lose interest during the rest of the year, then you should visit the Wimbledon Lawn Tennis Museum to rekindle your enthusiasm. Here, the story of lawn tennis from its origins in medieval real tennis is told through a collection of paintings, costume, ornaments and jewellery. You can also enjoy the highlight of the previous year's Championship in the video theatre, to remind yourself of the best moments. There are also an excellent tea room and shop.

⊖ Southfields

🚉 Wimbledon

🚌 93

♿

Open: Tuesday–Saturday, 10.30 a.m.–5.00 p.m.; Sunday 2.00 p.m.–5.00 p.m.

£

London Transport Museum

Covent Garden, WC2 (0171 836 8557: recorded information)

Located off the Piazza in the heart of Covent Garden, the London Transport Museum takes you on a journey through 200 years of transport history. This fascinating museum is dedicated to the world's largest urban passenger transport system and its impact on the growth of London and its suburbs.

The museum's chief exhibits are the buses, trams, and trains which are brought to life by actors playing a range of characters. The museum benefits from video displays, interactive exhibits and simulators where you can actually find yourself in the driving seat of a London bus or tube train. There are free guided tours at weekends and bank holidays and film showings related to different aspects of London Transport.

Strolling through the museum you begin to realise how much importance has always been attached to the design of London's transport, from the vehicles themselves to the station environment, from the world-famous Underground map to the outstanding posters. From 1908 the country's leading artists were commissioned to produce posters promoting travel to favourite destinations such as Kew Gardens or the Zoo. There are now around 5000 in the collection which can all be seen on the Resource Centre computers, and some of which will be featured in striking exhibitions.

The museum's shop is stacked full of gifts, souvenirs, books, posters and postcards, enabling you to buy a copy of your favourite poster reproduced from the museum's huge archive. The café is also recommended as you can sit overlooking the Piazza and enjoy the street musicians and entertainers.

⊖ Covent Garden

🚌 4, 6, 9, 11, 13, 15, 23, 26

♿

Open: daily except Friday, 10.00 a.m.–6.00 p.m. (last admission at 5.15 p.m.); Friday, 11.00 a.m.–6.00 p.m.

£

North Woolwich Old Station Museum

Pier Road, E16 (0171 474 7244)

Indoor and outdoor exhibits in and around a Victorian railway station tell the story of the railways.

🚆 North Woolwich

🚌 69, 101, 473

Limited ♿ (ground floor only)

Open: April–September, Saturday and Sunday, 10.00 a.m.–5.00 p.m. (school parties and groups by arrangement at other times)

Free

4
HISTORIC HOUSES
AND BUILDINGS

TOWN HOUSES, GRAND royal residences, country estates and even Roman ruins are all part of London's rich heritage of historic buildings. Such landmarks as the Tower of London and Buckingham Palace are famous the world over and should be top of any visitor's list of places to see. Just as interesting are less well-known buildings, including Sutton House (now owned by the National Trust in Hackney, Leighton House in Kensington with its uniquely designed exotic interior and Forty Hall in Enfield, a magnificent Jacobean manor house. For sheer opulence, Apsley House at Hyde Park Corner cannot be surpassed.

For easy reference, the entries have been grouped alphabetically within geographical areas.

CENTRAL

Apsley House
Hyde Park Corner, W1 (0171 499 5676)

'No 1, London'
was the popular name for Apsley House, the Duke of Wellington's Hyde Park Corner residence. Now it's the Wellington Museum, filled with the treasures which the Iron Duke acquired on his campaigns.

Read all about it in our *Visitor's London* guide-book, £1.20 at London Transport shops and Travel Information Centres, and at all the best book shops.

We'll bring London to your door.

Built by Robert Adam between 1771 and 1778, Apsley House acquired the popular name 'Number One, London', because of its position just past a toll gate into the capital from the west. The 1st Duke of Wellington made his London home here after a successful military career in India, Spain and Portugal, culminating in his defeat of Napoleon at Waterloo in 1815.

When the Duke bought Apsley House in 1817, he was the most powerful commander in Europe and his huge popular support gave him enormous political influence. Wellington enlarged the house to reflect his increased status and enriched it with his magnificent collection of paintings, silver, porcelain, sculpture and furniture from the Napoleonic age. His military success had brought him impressive gifts from all round the world.

Wellington never met his adversary, Napoleon Bonaparte, but the staircase hallway is dominated by a huge 3.45-metre (11 foot 4-inch) statue of the French Emperor by Canova. The house also contains 83 pictures seized in 1813 following the Battle of Vitoria from Joseph Bonaparte, who had stolen them from the Spanish royal collections. In addition to seventeenth-century Spanish pictures, there is a large group of Dutch and Flemish Old Masters and works by the nineteenth-century British school. The collection also contains important works by Goya, Rubens, Correggio, Velázquez, Breughel, de Hooch, Wilkie and Lawrence. Highlights include Velázquez' 'Waterseller of Seville' and 'Spanish Gentleman' and the Duke's favourite picture (so it is believed), 'The Agony in the Garden' by Correggio.

The house, once described as the 'most renowned mansion in the capital', was used for entertaining on a grand scale and oozes with opulence and splendour. The windows in the 27-metre (90-foot) long Waterloo Gallery are fitted with sliding mirrors, enhancing the chandeliers, and each room shimmers with gold decoration. Here too, Wellington's great dinner and dessert services are on display. The Sèvres Egyptian Dessert Service was commissioned by Napoleon for his Empress Josephine and represents the monuments of the Pharaohs of Ancient Egypt. Other highlights include the silver parcelgilt Portuguese Service, with an 8-metre (26-foot) long centrepiece, which was used at the annual Waterloo Banquet, a great event at which the Duke entertained the officers who had served under him at Waterloo and in the Peninsular War.

⊖ Hyde Park Corner

🚌 2, 8, 9, 10, 14, 16, 19, 22, 36, 38

Limited ♿

Open: Tuesday–Sunday and bank holiday Monday, 11.00 a.m.–4.50 p.m. (closed Good Friday, 24–26 December and New Year's Day)

£

Banqueting House

Whitehall, SW1 (0171 930 4179)

This impressive Stuart hall was built in 1619 for James I and it was from here that Charles I stepped on to the scaffold on 30 January 1649 to be executed. From an artistic point of view, it is worth visiting for the splendid ceiling paintings by Rubens that were commissioned by Charles I.

⊖ Charing Cross, Embankment, Westminster

🚇 Charing Cross

🚌 3, 11, 12, 24, 53, 77A, 211

No ♿

Open: Monday–Saturday, 10.00 a.m.–5.00 p.m. (closed at short notice for functions)

£

Buckingham Palace

SW1 (0171 839 1377: visitors' office)

In 1762 George III bought Buckingham House from the Duke of Buckingham. His son, George IV, had the building substantially redesigned by Nash and the work was completed during the reign of Queen Victoria. The palace is still used as the official London residence of the royal family, as well as the centre of operations for their administrative and domestic staff.

Since 1993, the palace has thrown open its doors every August and September to allow people into its State Rooms – the Grand Hall, Throne Room, Green Drawing Room, State Dining Room, Music Room and the Silk Tapestry Room

Buckingham Palace

– along with several galleries. It is a fascinating opportunity to see many items from the Royal Collection and the rooms where important Heads of States are entertained. (See also the Queen's Gallery, page 17.)

Just around the corner from Buckingham Palace are the royal mews. These house the Queen's horses and the elegant carriages used on state occasions.

⊖/🖳 Victoria

🚌 2, 8, 38, 52, 73, 82

Open: Palace August–September, daily, 9.30 a.m.–5.30 p.m.

&

££

Open: Mews late March–late September, Tuesday–Thursday, 12 noon–4.00 p.m.; early October–late March, Wednesday, 12 noon–4.00 p.m.

&

£

Houses of Parliament

Parliament Square, SW1 (0171 219 4272) Possibly the best-known building in London, the Houses of Parliament are the home of English democracy. Officially known as the Palace of Westminster, the building was rebuilt from 1834 onwards, after a fire destroyed most of the original buildings. The only important parts to have survived are the Great Hall, built by William II between 1097 and 1099, and the crypt and cloisters of St Stephen's Chapel.

The palace was a royal residence from the reign of Edward the Confessor to the reign of Henry VII and it is now the seat of government. The buildings are vast, covering 3.24 hectares (8 acres), with eleven courtyards, 3 kilometres (2 miles) of corridors and over 1,000 rooms. Big Ben, the most famous clock tower in Britain, was probably named after Sir Benjamin Hill, who commissioned the enormous bell and completed the work on the 97-metre (316-foot) tower in 1859.

Although the building is not open to the public, you can arrange to go on a tour. British citizens should write to their MP, while citizens from other countries have to apply in writing to the Public Information Office of the House of Commons. It is also possible to watch your MP at work in a Parliamentary debate. The galleries are open to the public and priority is given to those with tickets (obtainable from your MP or, for overseas citizens, from your embassy or High Commission).

⊖ Westminster

🚌 3, 11, 12, 24, 53, 77A, 211

&

Open: by arrangement only (see above)

Free

Roman Bath

5 Strand Lane, WC2 (0171 798 2064: answerphone)

The remains of a bath restored in the seventeenth century and believed to be Roman are visible all year round through a window from the pathway.

⊖ Temple

🚇 Blackfriars, Charing Cross

🚌 6, 9, 11, 13, 15, 23, 26, 171A

♿

Open: Through window from pathway all year. Also, May-end September, Wednesday, 1.00 a.m.–5.00 p.m. by appointment only

£ (free to National Trust members)

Sir John Soane's Museum

13 Lincoln's Inn Fields, WC2
(0171 405 2107; 0171 430 0175: recorded information)
See also page 104

Designed by the architect Sir John Soane, this house served as his private London residence and as home to his collection of antiquities and works of art between 1813 and 1837.

Soane was born in 1753, the son of a small country builder and died, after a long and distinguished career, in 1837. One of London's foremost architects, his work can be seen all across the capital from Chelsea to Ealing.

An exceptionally rich source of knowledge and inspiration from the past, the house and museum is almost full to the brim of Soane's extensive collection. Soane began collecting from all over Europe in 1790 and his works of art include Egyptian, Greek, Roman, Oriental and medieval objects, sculpture, architectural fragments, antique marbles, bronzes, paintings, watercolours, drawings, prints, stained glass and models. Every inch of space has been utilized and the attention to detail is quite staggering. Wandering through the house, one can imagine Soane constantly adding and rearranging items to his satisfaction.

⊖ Holborn

🚌 8, 22B, 25, 68, 91, 168

Limited ♿

Open: Tuesday–Saturday, 10.00 a.m.–5.00 p.m. (first Tuesday of each month, also 6.00 p.m.–9.00 p.m.); public lecture tour every Saturday, 2.30 p.m.

Free

EAST

HM Tower of London

Tower Hill, EC3 (0171 709 0765)

The Tower of London is one of the city's oldest landmarks. Built by William I as a fortress, it has also served as the Royal Mint, Royal Observatory and Armoury and as a prison.

❖

In the Medieval Palace above Traitor's Gate the rooms have been carefully re-created to suggest what life was like in the Tower in the 1280s during the reign of Edward I. Historians dressed in replica medieval costume are present in every room to explain the contents and to demonstrate thirteenth-century activities such as calligraphy and quill-making.

The crowning glories of the building are the Crown Jewels – the 106.5 carat Koh-i-noor dates back to the thirteenth century and is set in the Crown of Queen Elizabeth, the Queen Mother. However, the 'jewel in the crown' so to speak is the diamond in the Sceptre with Cross, symbolizing the monarch's power. It is surmounted by the First Star of Africa, the world's largest cut diamond at 530 carats.

Free guided tours of the Tower by Yeomen Warders (which take place at regular intervals during the day) include a visit to Traitor's Gate, St Thomas's Tower, the Middle Tower, Byward Tower, Bloody Tower (where, according to legend, the Little Princes were murdered in 1485) and the Bell Tower.

It is only possible to watch the nightly Ceremony of the Keys by making written application to the Clerk of Ceremony of the Keys, Queen's House, HM Tower of London, EC3N 4AB.

Θ Tower Hill

DLR: Tower Gateway

🚌 15, 42, 78, 100

Limited ♿

Open: March–October, Monday–Saturday, 9.00 a.m.–6.00 p.m.; Sunday, 10.00 a.m.–6.00p.m.; November–February, Monday–Saturday, 9.00 a.m.–5.00 p.m.; Sundays 10.00 a.m.–5.00 p.m.

££

Beefeaters

The Tower of London is guarded by the Yeomen Warders, or the 'Beefeaters', a company founded by Henry VII in 1485, who still wear Tudor costume, with blue tunics carrying the sovereign's monogram on the chest. The origin of the name 'Beefeater' is not clear. One possible reason is that the Yeomen Warders wear the same uniform as the yeomen who once served the buffet at St James's Palace and became known as Buffetiers.

Sutton House

2 & 4 Homerton High Street, Hackney, E9 (0181 986 2264)

The oldest and one of the grandest houses in London's East End, Sutton House is now a multi-arts centre as well as a museum. One of its most pleasing features is its relaxed atmosphere. It is less expensive to visit than many historic houses and once inside you are left to wander through the house as you please. In each room there is a folder of information to read through, packed with useful notes.

Dating back to Tudor times, Sutton House has had a varied history and the displays successfully convey a sense of how the house has changed personality over the centuries. Built in 1535, Sutton House was home to Ralph Sadleir, a Privy Councillor and diplomat who survived imprisonment in the Tower of London under Henry VIII and lived on to be Mary, Queen of Scots' jailer. Rooms from this period include the panelled Linenfold Room and the Great Chamber.

In later centuries the house became a rich merchant's house, a girls' school, a home for Huguenot silk merchants and an Edwardian church institute. More recently, the house was occupied by squatters in the mid-1980s. As with the other inhabitants, they too left their mark and pieces of their graffiti are on display too.

Sutton House is now an important social and arts centre in Hackney. Varied events and exhibitions take place here regularly and it is home to the Early Music Centre and the Young National Trust Theatre. Concerts are performed regularly in the 'Barn' and there is an excellent café for refreshments after your visit and a shop.

⊖ Bethnal Green, Manor House, Whitechapel

▣ Hackney Central, Hackney Downs, Homerton

🚌 W15, 52, 236, 276

Limited ♿

Open: Wednesday, Sunday and bank holiday, 11.30 a.m.–5.30 p.m.

£ (free to National Trust members)

William Morris Gallery

Lloyd Park, Forest Road, Walthamstow, E17 (0181 527 3782)

William Morris, designer, craftsman, poet and socialist, was born in Walthamstow in north-east London in 1834 and died in Hammersmith, west London, in 1896. From 1848 to 1856, the Morris family home was The Water House, an elegant mid-eighteenth-century building set in its own grounds. Since 1950, it has housed the William Morris gallery, a permanent collection of works illustrating the achievements and influence of William Morris.

Morris's work both as a designer and writer on the applied arts revolutionized the taste of the late nineteenth century, in Britain and abroad. The gallery's permanent displays show the development of his career, from the medievalism of his early designs in the 1860s to the virtuoso patterns of the 1880s and 1890s. Wallpapers, printed and woven textiles, embroideries, rugs and carpets, furniture, stained glass and ceramics are all represented in the collection, designed by

'Forget six counties overhung with smoke, Forget the snorting steam and piston stroke, Forget the spreading of the hideous town.'

WILLIAM MORRIS

Morris and his contemporaries (Burne-Jones, Rossetti and Philip Webb) who formed the firm of Morris & Co.

The gallery also displays decorative arts by followers of Morris in the Arts and Crafts movement, which flourished from the mid-1800s to the 1920s. Included are works by Arthur Mackmurdo's Century Guild and furniture by Sidney Barnsley.

The collection of decorative and applied arts is complemented by the Brangwyn Gift of paintings and drawings by the Pre-Raphaelites and their contemporaries and work by Sir Frank Brangwyn himself.

The gallery also has a library containing manuscript material and original photographs relating to Morris and his circle, as well as books and articles. These may be consulted by appointment.

⊖ Walthamstow Central

🚌 34, 97, 97A, 123, 215, 275

Limited &

Open: Tuesday–Saturday, first Sunday of each month, 10.00 a.m.–1.00 p.m., 2.00 p.m.–5.00 p.m.

Free

The Woodpecker Tapestry, William Morris Gallery

NORTH

Burgh House

New End Square, Hampstead, NW3 (0171 431 0144)
See Hampstead Museum, page 52.

Fenton House

Windmill Hill, Hampstead, NW3 (0171 435 3471)
Fenton House, one of the best William and Mary houses to survive intact in London, has an excellent collection of early keyboard instruments (see also page 70). There is also an important collection of English porcelain (including Bow, Chelsea and Worcester) and German figures, as well as a room devoted to Oriental ware.

There is an attractive walled garden in which you can sit.

⊖ Hampstead

🚌 46, 210, 268

Limited &

Open: March, Saturday and Sunday 2.00 p.m.–6.00 p.m.; April to end October, Wednesday–Friday, 2.00 p.m.–5.30 p.m.; Saturday, Sunday and bank holiday Monday, 11.00 a.m.–5.30 p.m.

£ (free to National Trust members)

Forty Hall

Forty Hall, Enfield, Middlesex (0181 363 8196)

A beautiful Jacobean house built between 1629 and 1636 for a wealthy haber-dasher and later Lord Mayor of London, today the house is owned by the Enfield Council and is open to the public.

The interior bears the mark of two principal periods: the original work and some late eighteenth-century decoration and the rooms on view include the dining room, drawing room and five first-floor rooms. The other ground-floor rooms have been altered over the centuries and feature two galleries. The Raynton Room holds exhibitions of paintings by local artists and the Exhibition Gallery houses various interesting community displays.

Outside, the buildings flanking the former stable courtyard have been converted into a reception area comprising a banqueting suite, a small lecture hall and café. The gardens are worth visiting too and much of the estate is open to the public for walks. The park rangers hold regular guided walks and also run a wildlife club (for eight to twelve year olds). Other outdoor events include painting exhibitions, an annual Shakespearean play, equestrian events and Fun Days.

🚃 Enfield Town, then bus

🚌 191, 231

Limited ♿

Open: Thursday–Sunday, 11.00 a.m.–5.00 p.m.

Free

Kenwood House

Hampstead Lane, NW3 (0181 348 1286)

A beautiful eighteenth-century house, now managed by English Heritage, Kenwood was once the home of the 1st Earl of Iveagh. He left the house and its collection of paintings and furniture to the nation in 1927. Known as the Iveagh Bequest, the pictures include 'The Guitar Player' by Vermeer, a late self-portrait by Rembrandt and 'Mary, Countess of Howe' by Gainsborough. Turner's 'The Iveagh Seapiece' hangs in the Breakfast room. English School portraits are found elsewhere, including 'Lady Hamilton' by Romney and 'Mrs Musters as Hebe' by Reynolds.

There are also impressive gardens and a lake which is the centrepiece of regular outdoor classical concerts (see page 187) in the summer. Amenities include the Brewhouse restaurant.

⊖ Archway, Golders Green, then bus

🚌 21

♿

Open: 1 April–30 September, daily, 10.00 a.m.–6.00 p.m., 1–31 October, 10.00 a.m.–6.00 p.m. (or dusk if earlier); 1 November–31 March, daily, 10.00 a.m.–4.00 p.m. (closed 24 and 25 December)

Free

Croydon Palace

Old Palace Road, Croydon, Surrey (0181 668 3349)

Now part of a girls' school (the Old Palace School of John Whitgift), and run by the Whitgift Foundation, the Old Palace comprises a fifteenth-century Great Hall and Guard Room, a Tudor Long Gallery and domestic Chapel.

The foundation of the palace dates back over 1,000 years. In Saxon times it was called a manor and its lord was the Archbishop of Canterbury. Over the centuries, the Archbishops used the Palace as a country residence and as their headquarters when engaged on diocesan business.

🚆 East Croydon, West Croydon, then 10-minute walk

🚌 264

P

No ♿

Open: accompanied 2-hour tours, school holidays, 2.00 p.m. (phone to check days)

£ (tea included)

Lambeth Palace and Library

Lambeth Palace Road, SE1 (0171 928 8282: Palace; 0171 928 6222: Library)

Home of the Archbishops of Canterbury, the most prestigious position in the Church of England, a palace has stood on this site for nearly 800 years. As well as being a private residence, it is a busy office and visitors are only allowed in after making an appointment with the Hospitality Secretary on 0171 928 8282. There is usually a long waiting list.

Once inside, you will find a collection of portraits of former archbishops. In the Guard Room hang pictures of seventeenth- and eighteenth-century archbishops, including Sir Joshua Reynolds' portrait of Secker and George Romney's Moore. Other portraits are in the great corridor and picture gallery.

The library has an excellent collection of books and manuscripts. It was started by a bequest from Archbishop Bancroft who died in 1610. Today, it comprises over 3,500 volumes of manuscripts and 150,000 printed books. Works include an important collection of records of the Church of England, early versions of the English Bible and Henry VIII's treatise against Martin Luther which earned him the title of 'Defender of the Faith'.

⊖ Lambeth North

🚌 3, C10, 77, 344

♿ (by prior arrangement)

Open: by appointment only, Palace Wednesday or Thursday afternoon by arrangement with the Hospitality Secretary; Library Monday–Friday, 10.00 a.m.–5.00 p.m. (phone first)

Free, but donations welcome

Ranger's House

Chesterfield Walk, Blackheath, SE10 (0181 853 0035)

Ranger's House was probably first built *c*.1700 for Captain, later Admiral, Hosier, on wasteland adjacent to Greenwich Park. At that time, the house had a superb view and Greenwich, easily accessible from London by road and river, was already beginning to attract wealthy residents. By the early nineteenth century, the house had been passed to the Crown and it became the official residence of the Ranger of Greenwich Park, which is how it acquired its name.

In 1974, it became the home of the Suffolk Collection of paintings, including a series of full-length Jacobean portraits by William Larkin, which show in great detail some of the most elaborate costumes of the time. On the first floor of the house is the bulk of the Dolmetsch Collection of early musical instruments, on loan from the Horniman Museum (see page 64).

In the Architectural Study Centre housed in the coach house, visitors are able to see at close quarters a selection of architectural artefacts (including balustrades, plaster and wooden cornices, iron railings, glass, bricks and tiles) from London houses of many periods.

⊖ New Cross, then bus 53

🚆 Blackheath, Maze Hill, Greenwich (then 15 minutes' walk)

🚌 53

Limited ♿

Open: daily, 1 April–31 October, 10.00 a.m.–1.00 p.m., 2.00 p.m.–6.00 p.m.; 1 November–31 March, Wednesday–Sunday, 10.00 a.m.–1.00 p.m.; 2.00 p.m.–4.00 p.m..

£ (free to English Heritage members)

The Royal Hospital Chapel
The Royal Naval Museum
The Painted Hall
Greenwich Hospital

NEW CROSS GATE or
NEW CROSS STATION
thence bus 53, 153, tram 36, 38, 40

Royal Naval College

King William Walk, Greenwich, SE10 (0181 858 2154)

See also National Maritime Museum, page 62

Designed by Sir Christopher Wren in 1695, the Royal Naval College was originally built as a hospital for naval pensioners. The painted hall and chapel are open to visitors. Both are stunning: the painted hall is the dining hall of the college and is covered with magnificent paintings including an allegorical painting of William III and Mary II handing liberty and peace to Europe. The chapel is almost as lavishly decorated and was designed by James Stewart after the original was destroyed by fire in 1779.

🚆 Greenwich

🚌 188, 199

No ♿

Open: daily, 2.30 p.m.–4.45 p.m. (last admission 4.30 p.m.)

Free

WEST

Boston Manor

Boston Manor Road, Brentford, Middlesex (0181 570 0622)

Although the house is open only on Sundays in the summer months, it is worth visiting, as it is a charming example of a Jacobean building. Built in 1623, it was bought by the Clitherow family in 1670 and remained their home until 1924.

❖

The highlights of the house include the drawing room, with its magnificent ceiling designed in 1623 that is divided into panels representing the senses, the elements, Peace, Plenty, War and Peace and Faith, Hope and Charity. Also on view are the main bedroom and another smaller room.

⊖ Boston Manor

🚌 E8

No ♿

Open: last Saturday and Sunday in May to last Saturday and Sunday in September, 2.30 p.m.–5.00 p.m.

Free

Carlyle's House

24 Cheyne Row, Chelsea, SW3 (0171 352 7087)
Only minutes away from the hustle and bustle of the King's Road and located in the heart of residential Chelsea is the eighteenth-century town house of the great Victorian writer Thomas Carlyle (1795–1881), who was best known for his historical works.

Carlyle lived and worked in this house for fifty years, entertaining among others Charles Dickens and Alfred Tennyson. At the time, his house was considered modest and not in a fashionable part of London. The house contains much of the Carlyles' original furniture, books, prints and personal relics.

⊖ Sloane Square

🚌 11, 19, 22, 49, 211

No ♿

Open: April to end October, Wednesday, Sunday and bank holiday, 11.00 a.m.–5.00 p.m.

£ (free to National Trust members)

Chiswick House

Burlington Lane, Chiswick, W4 (0181 995 0508)
Built for Lord Burlington (1695–1753), Chiswick House is one of the finest Palladian houses in Britain. Lord Burlington was a great admirer of the architecture of ancient Rome and of sixteenth-century Italy and he chose to make Chiswick House a setting worthy of his excellent art collection and library.

A good way to start your visit is to watch the special video on the house, which explains the background to the collection in detail. Then wander through the elegant and highly ornamented, gilded rooms, which give the building the feeling of a gallery rather than a home. The most elaborate room is the central saloon, or Tribunal, which has a carved frieze and an impressive domed ceiling.

The whole house is a remarkable example of the precision and symmetry typical of the eighteenth century and contrasts strongly with the garden. The grounds of Chiswick House are, historically, among the most important in England, for it was here that Lord Burlington and William Kent (1684–1748) experimented with the natural style of gardening. There is also a café and a book-shop.

🚇 Chiswick
🚌 E3, 190
Limited ♿

Open: 1 April–30 September, daily, 10.00 a.m.–1.00 p.m., 2.00 p.m.–6.00 p.m.;
1 October–31 March, Wednesday–Sunday, 10.00 a.m.–1.00 p.m., 2.00 p.m.–4.00 p.m.
(Closed 24–26 December and 1 January)
£ (free to English Heritage members)

Ham House

Ham, Richmond, Surrey (0181 940 1950)
This beautiful Stuart house set in a wonderful position overlooking the Thames just west of Richmond was one of grandest buildings of its age. Home to the Lauderdale family, it was first built in *c.*1610, and then enlarged, redecorated and furnished in the 1670s.

It has been restored to its original glory by the National Trust, which aims for the house to be an almost intact presentation of seventeenth-century life. As with any restoration work, modern replica materials have had to be used, which has led

The Queen's Bed Chamber, Ham House

to criticism in certain quarters. But the National Trust knows that it cannot please everyone all the time and most visitors appear delighted with the results.

The furniture, fireplaces and ceilings all display the craftsmanship of the early seventeenth century, while the ceilings show the progress from geometric-type plasterwork to garlands and spandrels. Other works of art include tapestries, paintings, antique carpets and porcelain.

⊖ Richmond, then bus

🚉 Kingston, Richmond, then bus

🚌 65, 371

Limited ♿

Open: April–October, Monday–Wednesday, 1.00 p.m.–5.00 p.m.; Saturday and Sunday, 12 noon–5.30 p.m.; November–Christmas, Saturday and Sunday, 1.00 p.m.–4.00 p.m.

£ (free to National Trust members)

Hampton Court Palace

Hampton Court Road, Middlesex (0181 781 9500)

In 1514 Cardinal Wolsey ordered building to begin on Hampton Court Palace and in 1525 gave it to Henry VIII in a vain attempt to retain his favour. The palace today bears the distinct and varied mark of almost five centuries of royal history.

Hampton Court has been divided into six different routes, which make it far easier for visitors to enjoy and appreciate. Don't be surprised if you bump into some unusual-looking characters – the guides here dress up in period costume which helps to give an atmosphere of life in the palace and adds some colour to a visit. It is well worth joining the guided tours around each part as the guides are full of fascinating information about the palace. Tours usually start in the Clock Court and run every couple of hours (check the timetable when you arrive).

In Henry VIII's State Apartments you will see the grand rooms for dining and waiting upon the king. Most visitors to the palace in Tudor times would never have gone past the Great Hall as only a few of the king's most trusted men would be allowed close contact with him.

The Queen's State Apartments were intended for Mary II who sadly died before the palace was completed. They were decorated and furnished in later reigns. The smaller Georgian Rooms provide an insight into the lives and pastimes of the Georgian court. William III's Cartoon Gallery displays eighteenth-century copies of Raphael's cartoons.

Following the fire in 1986, the rooms in the King's Apartments, built and decorated

Overleaf: Hampton Court Palace

for William III, have now been restored to their original appearance and give an insight into both his public and private life. The Wolsey Rooms and the Renaissance Picture Gallery, built for Cardinal Wolsey, Henry VIII's chief minister, now display important Renaissance paintings from Her Majesty the Queen's collection.

The reconstruction of the huge Tudor kitchens is unrivalled anywhere in Britain. A range of activity was undertaken here, with businesslike precision, and to get a good overview of it, examine the detailed model first. Inside the complex of rooms, you will find a herb room, cooking areas, with massive fires which are lit every day and a remarkable *pâtisserie* area where the King's favourite cakes were made.

The palace gardens are well worth visiting too. As well as the Maze and the Great Vine, there is a wonderful reconstruction of King William's Knot Garden and the recently restored Privy Garden. Amenities include cafés and a shop.

🚇 Hampton Court

🚌 R68, 111, 216, 411, 461

〰 from Charing Cross, Kingston, Richmond or Westminster

Limited ♿

Open: mid-March–mid-October, Tuesday–Sunday, 9.30 a.m.–6.00 p.m.; Monday, 10.15 a.m.–6.00 p.m.; mid-October–mid March, Tuesday–Sunday, 9.30 a.m.–4.30 p.m., Monday, 10.15 a.m.–4.30 p.m.

££

Hogarth's House

Great West Road, Chiswick, W4 (0181 994 6757)

Just 45 metres (50 yards) from the busy Hogarth roundabout on the Great West Road lies this charming early eighteenth-century house which was once the country home of William Hogarth, the painter and engraver. It is now a gallery where most of his best-known engravings are on display, including 'Harlot's Progress', 'Rake's Progress', 'Marriage à la Mode' and 'Gin Lane'.

In nearby Chiswick Mall there are houses of a similar period and Hogarth's tomb is in the grave-yard outside St Nicholas's Church.

⊖ Gunnersbury

🚌 E3, 190

Limited ♿

Open: phone for details

Free

Kensington Palace State Apartments and Royal Ceremonial Dress Collection

W8 (0171 937 9561)

William III and Mary II purchased what was then called Nottingham House from the Earl of Nottingham for £14,000 and, while alterations begun by Sir Christopher Wren were still under way, they moved the Court there in 1689.

It continued to be a principal residence of successive monarchs until George III moved the court to Buckingham Palace. Indeed, it was not until the nineteenth century that the apartments were again needed for members of the Royal family. In 1798 the Duke of Kent, father of Queen Victoria, was allocated rooms at the Palace. His daughter was born there in 1819 and was also at the Palace in 1837 when she learned that she had become Queen.

It is possible to visit several State Apartments and to see the popular Court Dress Collection which contains examples of the special clothes associated with royal ceremonial. Many examples date back to the eighteenth century. More modern additions have been made to the collection by the present Queen and her family, and plans for the State Apartments include projects to display these important items of current royal fashion.

⊖ High Street Kensington, Notting Hill Gate, Queensway

🚌 9, 10, 12, 27, 28, 31, 49, 52

Limited ♿

Open: May to September, daily, 9.45 a.m.–5.00 p.m. (tours only)

Kew Palace

Royal Botanic Gardens, Kew, Surrey (0181 940 1171)

Also known as the 'Dutch House', Kew Palace was built by Samuel Fotrey, a London merchant of Dutch parentage. The house is built in the Dutch gabled style and Fortrey commemorated its completion with a monogram and the year, 1631, over the front door. George III lived here, the smallest of the royal palaces, with his wife Queen Charlotte and their fifteen children for some years.

Downstairs the rooms are all panelled: the dining room in white eighteenth-century style, the breakfast room in early seventeenth-century style and the library ante-room in reset sixteenth-century linenfold. In the pages' waiting room also downstairs there is an exhibition of royal possessions including snuff boxes, alphabet counters and babies' rattles. Upstairs, the rooms have all been re-papered from the original wallpaper blocks.

⊖/🚇 Kew Gardens

🚌 65, 391

Limited ♿

Open: Monday–Saturday, 9.30 a.m.–4.30 p.m.; Sunday, 9.30 a.m.–5.30 p.m.

£

Leighton House

12 Holland Park Road, Kensington, W14 (0171 602 3316)

From the exterior, Leighton House looks just like all the other smart red-brick houses in this Kensington road, but once inside the exotic Arab Hall you are

Leighton House

immediately transported to a Moorish palace. This magnificent house was home to Lord Leighton (1803–96), a major Victorian artist. He gave vent to his taste for the exotic when he commissioned the architect George Aitchison (1825–1910) to build the house. The Arab Hall is the centrepiece of Leighton House and the dazzling gilt mosaic frieze, depicting birds and mythological scenes and a fountain in the centre, and the intricate design of the Isnik tiles, all contribute to an extraordinary impression of the Orient.

Leighton House also has a fascinating collection of Pre-Raphaelite and High Victorian paintings, including works by Burne-Jones, Millais and Leighton. Do not forget to visit Leighton's studio, the heart and purpose of the house, with its great windows and gilded dome. You can also visit the garden which is open from April to September.

⊖ High Street Kensington

🚌 9, 10, 27, 28, 31, 49

No ♿

Open: Monday–Saturday, 11.00 a.m.–5.30 p.m.; tours by prior arrangement

Free

Linley Sambourne House

18 Stafford Terrace, Kensington, W8 (0181 742 3438: recorded information)

One of the purposes of renovating a property and its interior to its original period is to be able to imagine what it was like to have lived there at that time. However, even the best restoration work cannot match the real thing and Linley Sambourne House is a rare and fascinating survivor. A large late-Victorian house in a smart

Kensington road, it was home to Linley Sambourne, a leading cartoonist for the satirical magazine *Punch* in the late Victorian and Edwardian periods. Since his death, his family have kept the magnificent interior largely unchanged, together with many of Sambourne's own pictures and those of his friends.

Administered by the Victorian Society, whose aim is to preserve important Victorian buildings and other architecture, the house offers the chance to see how this successful artist lived and worked.

⊖ High Street Kensington

🚌 9, 10, 27, 28, 31, 49

No ♿

Open: 1 March–1 October, Wednesday, 10.00 a.m.–5.00 p.m.; Sunday, 2.00 p.m.– 5.00 p.m.; guided tours available at 3.00 p.m.

£

Marble Hill House

Twickenham, Middlesex (0181 892 5115)

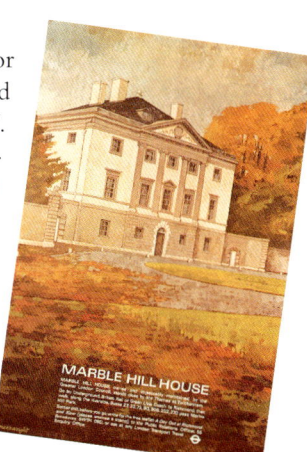

MARBLE HILL HOUSE

Marble Hill House is a beautiful Palladian house built for George II's mistress, the Countess of Suffolk, in 1724–9, and later occupied by Mrs Fitzherbert, the mistress of George IV. The building has been restored and contains a good collection of early eighteenth-century English paintings and furniture, as well as an overmantel and overdoor painted by G.B. Panini in 1738.

After looking around Marble Hill House, you can take a small ferry boat and hop over to the Surrey side of the Thames and visit Ham House (see page 96).

⊖ Richmond, then bus

🚉 St Margaret's, Twickenham

🚌 H22, 30, R68, R70, 90, 290

Limited ♿ (ground floor only)

Open: 1 April–30 September, daily, 10.00 a.m.–1.00 p.m.; 2.00 p.m.–6.00 p.m.; 1 October–31 March, Wednesday–Sunday, 10.00 a.m.–1.00 p.m.; 2.00 p.m.–4.00 p.m.

Free

Livery Companies' Halls

The only way to visit the halls of the ancient livery companies of the City is to apply to the City Information Office (0171 606 3030/332 1456) early in the year for tickets from the small allocation which it receives each February. The livery companies participating in the scheme include the Goldsmiths, the Tallow Chandlers, the Skinners, the Fishmongers and the Haberdashers.

It is also possible to visit the impressive Fishmongers' Hall at other times by contacting their archivist on 0171 626 3531. Public companies often hold their Annual General Meetings in City livery halls, giving shareholders an opportunity of seeing them.

Osterley Park

Jersey Road, Osterley, Isleworth, Middlesex (0181 560 3918)

Osterley is one of the best places to see the work of the eighteenth-century interior designer, Robert Adam. The original house at Osterley was built in Tudor times for Sir Thomas Gresham and was totally transformed in the eighteenth century for its owner, Sir Francis Child, by Sir William Chambers and Robert Adam.

Child was a highly successful financier, a one-time Lord Mayor and banker to Charles II. His enormous wealth allowed Chambers and Adam a free reign at Osterley and they produced stunning results. The exterior was redesigned by Chambers into a neo-classical mansion. The neo-classical theme was continued inside by Adam, the finest executioner of this style in the eighteenth century. What is remarkable at Osterley is Adam's attention to detail. You can see his work everywhere, from ceilings and walls to door handles and carpets.

The main rooms to visit are the hall, library, eating room and the state bedchamber. The tapestry room contains the French Gobelins – beautiful tapestries that were made specially for the room in the eighteenth century and among the few items in the house to outshine any of Adam's work.

⊖ Osterley

🚌 111, 120

Limited ♿

Open: April–October, Wednesday–Sunday, 1.00 p.m.–5.00 p.m.; bank holiday Monday, 11.a.m.–5.00 p.m.

£ (free to National Trust members)

Pitshanger Manor Museum

Mattock Lane, Ealing, W5 (0181 567 1227)

This Grade I listed building was owned by Sir John Soane as his country house from 1800 to 1810 (his London house is described on page 88). He extensively rebuilt the house and used it as a showplace for his collections.

Among the main features of the house are the palatial dimensions, the ornate plaster ceilings and life-sized classical statues. The house also reflects Soane's passion for light and space: mirrors above fireplaces and in door panels reflect light from the large windows, while a skylight in the vestibule offers maximum daylight for the stairs.

⊖ Ealing Broadway

🚌 E2, E8, 207

Limited ♿

Open: Tuesday–Saturday, 10.00 a.m.–5.00 p.m.

Free

Royal Hospital, Chelsea

Royal Hospital Road, Chelsea, SW3 (0171 730 0161)

The Royal Hospital, Chelsea was founded by Charles II in 1682 as a retreat for veterans of the regular army who had become unfit for duty, either after long service or because of wounds. The provision of a hostel rather than some system of pension was probably inspired by the Hôtel des Invalides in Paris founded by Louis XIV.

Designed by Sir Christopher Wren for Charles II, this impressive building was intended to house all army pensioners. Some of the interiors were designed by Robert Adam, while Sir John Soane designed many of the buildings on the outer sides of the East and West Roads and an infirmary in the north-west corner of the grounds (destroyed by bombing during the Second World War).

Today, the Royal Hospital is home for about 400 veteran soldiers aged sixty-five and over. The public are allowed to wander round the grounds, as well as visit the Chapel and the Great Hall inside the Hospital. There is also a small museum devoted to the history of the Royal Hospital.

⊖ Sloane Square

🚌 11, 211

Limited ♿

Open: Monday–Saturday, 10.00 a.m.–12 noon, 2.00 p.m.–4.00 p.m.; Sunday, 2.00 p.m.–4.00 p.m. (museum closed October–March).

Free

Syon House

Syon Park, London Road, Brentford, Middlesex (0181 560 0881)

Facing Kew Gardens from across the River Thames is Syon House and Park. The house was built on the site of a Brigittine convent soon after Henry VIII's Dissolution of the Monasteries and it has belonged to the Dukes and Earls of Northumberland since the Reformation – the Northumberland lion can be clearly seen on the roofline.

The splendid interior was designed by Robert Adam in the eighteenth century. Every room is stunning, from the Ante Room with its vivid colouring and solid gilding to the magnificent Red Drawing Room where even the carpet was designed by Adam. The house is full of wonderful furniture and paintings too (mostly family portraits) by such artists as Van Dyck and Rubens.

It is worth visiting the gardens at the same time as the house. Designed by Capability Brown between 1767 and 1773, the centrepiece is the Great Conservatory, designed by Charles Fowler between 1820 and 1827. Inside the conservatory are cacti, ferns and other plants.

🚉 Kew Bridge

🚌 116, 117, 237, 267

Limited ♿ (house)

Open: House April–end September, Wednesday–Sunday; Sunday only October–mid-December, 11.00 a.m.–5.00 p.m.; Gardens daily, 10.00 a.m.–6.00 p.m. or dusk (closed 25–26 December)

£ (for house)

Overleaf: *Aldwych Theatre*

PERFORMING
ARTS

5
THEATRE

L ONDON'S THEATRE SCENE spreads across the heart of the West End out into the suburbs. Many of the best-known theatres are in what is called 'Theatreland', stretching from Shaftesbury Avenue to Covent Garden. These theatres stage both new productions and old favourites, from musicals to thrillers, and usually have some stars topping the bill. Perhaps ironically, neither of London's theatrical flagships – the Royal National Theatre and The Barbican, home of the Royal Shakespeare Company – are in 'Theatreland'.

Britain's National Theatre, the culmination of sixty years of campaigning for and planning a state-subsidized theatre, was founded in 1963, when Sir Laurence Olivier established the Company in its temporary home at the Old Vic (see page 129).

In 1969, work began on a new building on the South Bank of the Thames which opened in 1976. Although the architecture of the South Bank complex of arts venues may have its critics, the artistic importance of these centres cannot be denied.

The Royal National Theatre is a multi-arts centre. Its spacious foyers and river terraces are open to everyone all day every day. There is also a research and development wing called the National Studio that encourages and pursues theatrical experimentation. There are free exhibitions and live music, theatre tours, bars, buffets, a restaurant and bookshop. Regular talks, known as Platforms, are held in one of the three theatres – prestigious writers and directors from across the arts talk about their latest projects. Guests have included Dirk Bogarde, Stephen Sondheim and Alan Bennett. Keep an eye out in the listings magazines for forthcoming events.

The National Theatre

The National operates on the repertory system, offering at any one time an average of nine different productions. Since its inception, the National has staged over 400 plays, covering the work of 250 writers and spanning 2,500 years from Aeschylus through Shakespeare and other classic dramatists to modern playwrights. Among the numerous successes here in recent years are Alan Bennett's *The Madness of George III* and *Mother Courage and her Children* by Bertolt Brecht.

Tickets for the National are usually cheaper than those in many other London theatres, and in the Olivier and Lyttelton all prices are reduced for previews and Saturday matinées. Any unsold tickets will be reduced two hours before all performances.

Opened in March 1982, the Barbican Centre is Europe's largest multi arts and conference venue. It was built as 'the City's gift to the nation' by the Corporation of London (the local authority for the City) and the range and quality of activity taking place under one roof are unrivalled.

The Barbican is home to the Royal Shakespeare Company and the London Symphony Orchestra (see pages 141). The Barbican Art Gallery (see page 27) mounts major exhibitions and there are free exhibitions throughout the Centre's foyers. Visitors can also enjoy a wide range of free foyer music and performance art with regular lunchtime and early evening concerts from classical, jazz, world and roots artists.

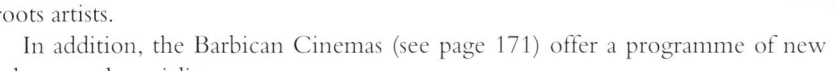

In addition, the Barbican Cinemas (see page 171) offer a programme of new releases and specialist seasons.

The Centre also hosts special children's events and popular bank holiday festivals, as well as mounting an annual multi-media festival based on a central theme.

The Barbican has excellent places to eat and drink, open all day. There is a Brasserie (level 2), the Waterside Restaurant (on the ground floor) and a Balcony Café (level 1), as well as bars and buffets in the foyer. There is also a tropical rooftop Conservatory open to the public at weekends.

Barbican Theatre and The Pit

Barbican Centre, Silk Street, EC2 (0171 638 8891: box office)
The 1,166-seat Barbican Theatre and 200-seat studio theatre, The Pit, are the London homes of the Royal Shakespeare Company. The RSC's work at the Barbican Centre is an integral part of the company's programme, and it gives around 600 performances of some 16 different productions a year, ranging from classical to new work. The RSC regularly performs to over a million people a year in London, Stratford-upon-Avon, a five-week season in Newcastle-upon-Tyne and on tour.

The RSC places emphasis on ensemble work. A core of actors is formed each year to perform in a range of productions over a two-year cycle, first in Stratford and then in London, and the RSC aims to be the leading classical theatre company in the English-speaking world.

Artistic directors of the RSC have included Trevor Nunn, Terry Hands and Adrian Noble, whose recent major productions include *King Lear*, with the late Sir Robert Stephens, and the ground-breaking production of *A Midsummer Night's Dream*.

⊖ Barbican and Moorgate

🚌 4, 56

♿

££

Royal National Theatre

South Bank, SE1 (0171 928 2252)

Within the Royal National Theatre (the 'Royal' was granted in 1988) are three auditoriums, each with its own style and characteristics. The largest and most radical of the three is, the open-stage theatre named after Lord Olivier, the National's first artistic director, from 1962 to 1983. It is designed to be flexible enough to serve dramatists of every period. No seat is far from the actor and the proximity of the seats adds a new relationship between actor and audience.

The proscenium-arched Lyttelton is named after the National's first chairman (1962–71), Oliver Lyttelton. As in the other two theatres, the walls are made of roughly finished concrete to promote efficient acoustics.

The Cottesloe is the smallest of the three theatres and the most flexible. On three sides of the auditorium there are two tiers of pillared galleries, which correspond to the inn yards used for theatre in medieval times. The theatre was named after Lord Cottesloe, the first chairman (1962–77) of the South Bank Theatre

---

Booking tickets

You can book tickets directly with a theatre, but here are some alternatives:

First Call: Credit card booking for all prices of tickets at most West End theatres on 0171 420 0000 (24-hour service). Depending on the individual show, there is up to a 15 per cent surcharge on each ticket, which is sent to you by first class mail or held for collection at the relevant theatre.

Half-price tickets: The Society of London Theatres has a booth in Leicester Square, WC2, which sells half-price tickets for the same day for major West End productions. Open Monday–Saturday, from 12 noon to 30 minutes before curtain up for matinées, from 2.30 p.m. to 6.30 p.m. for evening performances. A small surcharge is made.

Theatre/Travel tickets: Combined West End theatre and rail tickets are available at reduced prices from British Rail Ticket Theatre and Concert Rail Club, PO Box 1, St Albans, Herts (01727 841115).

Ticketmaster: Credit card booking for theatre (and sporting events) on 0171 344 4444 (24-hour service). Also available through all travel branches of W.H. Smith, American Express, Co-op Travelcare and the London Tourist Board Information Centre at Victoria Station.

Board responsible for building the National Theatre and, on completion, handing it over to the National Theatre Board.

Refreshments are available at the Mezzanine and Terrace Café and there are bars and buffets open throughout the day.

θ Embankment, Waterloo

🚇 Waterloo

🚌 26, 68, 171, 171A, 188, 211

♿

££

For more diverse theatre, look away from the West End to alternative, local and pub theatres. Tickets are generally cheaper than in the West End. Many of these venues have an excellent reputation for high-quality drama, often featuring the work of new writers and exploring new themes, and offering a great opportunity to support the lifeblood of London's thriving arts scene.

Children too have an excellent choice of theatrical entertainment. London is probably the world centre for pantomime and throughout the Christmas season television and film's biggest stars appear in shows both in the West End and locally. Puppet theatre is usually popular with children and there are several good puppet theatres in London. Many theatres put on Saturday shows and workshops for children and the Polka Theatre and Unicorn Children's Theatre (see pages 136 and 137) stage high-quality productions especially for children.

Don't underestimate the ability of children to enjoy 'grown-up' drama though. Musicals are always popular but it is worth trying something a little more demanding such as Shakespeare if children are interested – by taking plays out of the classroom context, they are far more likely to enjoy drama. There are also about sixty touring children's theatre companies that perform in venues throughout London.

WEST END THEATRES

This section features all the main theatres in London with box office telephone numbers. All the theatres included have at least one bar and facilities to buy snacks, such as ice creams, chocolate and crisps. The quality and variety of refreshments does not vary greatly from one theatre to another, but there are some exceptions and I have picked out theatres with particularly noteworthy cafés or restaurants. To avoid the inevitable crush at the bar in the interval, it is wise to order drinks beforehand.

Adelphi Theatre

Strand, WC2 (0171 379 8884)

Although the current theatre was designed in the 1930s, a theatre has stood here since 1806. Hits include a revival of *My Fair Lady* in the late 1970s, *Me and My*

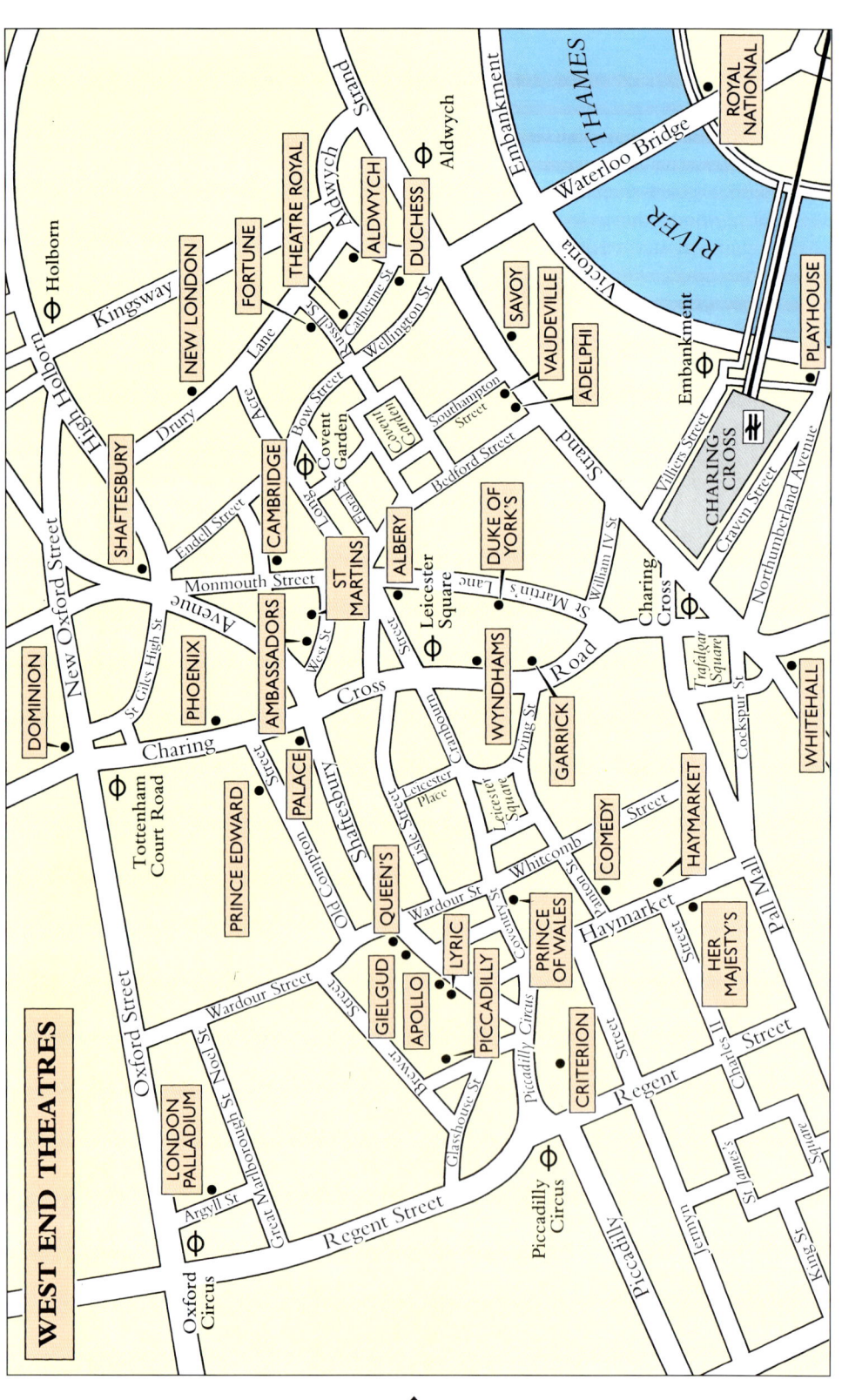

Girl in the mid-1980s and Andrew Lloyd Webber's *Sunset Boulevard*. There are four bars and hot and cold refreshments are available.

⊖ Charing Cross, Embankment

🚌 6, 9, 11, 13, 15, 23

♿

££

Aldwych Theatre

Aldwych, WC2 (0171 416 6003)

Built in 1905 as a pair to the Waldorf (now the Strand) Theatre, the Aldwych was named after the road that was also built at this time between Drury Lane and the Law Courts. From 1960 to 1982 the theatre was home to the Royal Shakespeare Company before it moved to the Barbican. Previous productions include Arthur Miller's *A View from the Bridge* and Tom Stoppard's *Hapgood*. There are three bars.

⊖ Holborn, Temple

🚌 6, 9, 11, 15, 23, 26, 68, 76, 91, 171A

♿

££

Albery Theatre

St Martin's Lane, WC2 (0171 369 1730)

An elegant Edwardian theatre, it was built on behalf of the actor-manager Charles Wyndham in 1903. Originally known as the New Theatre, its name was changed to the Albery in 1973.

The theatre boasts the first appearance of Sir John Gielgud in the West End, in a 1925 production of Margaret Kennedy's *The Constant Nymph*. It was also the venue for the first run of Lionel Bart's *Oliver!* in the 1960s and Schaffer's *Equus* in the 1970s. The main hit of the early 1990s was *Five Guys Named Moe*. The theatre has three bars.

⊖ Leicester Square

🚌 6, 13, 15, 24, 29, 176

♿

££

Ambassadors Theatre

West Street, WC2 (0171 836 6111)

A small, appealing theatre, the Ambassadors was built in 1913. Whereas most theatres change their productions after a few weeks or possibly a few months, remarkably the Ambassador Theatre staged the same play from 1952 to 1974! The play was Agatha Christie's *The Mousetrap* which then moved next door to St Martin's Theatre. Later successes have included *Les Liaisons Dangereuses* which ran from 1986 to 1990. There are two bars.

⊖ Leicester Square

🚌 14, 19, 24, 29, 38, 176

♿

££

Apollo Theatre

Shaftesbury Avenue, W1 (0171 494 5070)

Designed in the French Renaissance style, the Apollo was one of the first theatres to be built in Shaftesbury Avenue, in 1905. Next to the entrance is the theatre's lucky mascot – a silver buckle and chain with a flying lizard supported by rampant lions. This motif comes from the badge of a German tribe of gypsies associated with the Lowenfield family who built the theatre.

Hits include Alan Bennett's *40 Years On* in 1968, starring Sir John Gielgud, who also appeared in David Storey's *Home* in the 1970s and Hugh Whitemore's *The Best of Friends* in 1988. The theatre continues to stage new plays and attracts established stars. There are two bars.

θ Piccadilly Circus

🚌 14, 19, 38

Limited ♿

££

Apollo Theatre

Apollo Victoria
17 Wilton Road, SW1 (0171 416 6070)

Andrew Lloyd Webber's highly successful and fast-moving show on roller skates, *Starlight Express*, opened here in the mid-1980s. The futuristic show contrasted with the splendid interior of the listed building with its elaborate decoration and plasterwork. It was built in 1930 as a cinema and originally known as the New Victoria. There are three bars.

⊖/🖳 Victoria
🚌 11, 24, 211
♿
££

Cambridge Theatre
Earlham Street, WC2 (0171 494 5080)

A wonderful Art Deco theatre built in 1930, the Cambridge Theatre is a popular venue for musicals such as *Fame – The Musical*; previous hits include *Return to the Forbidden Planet*. There are three bars.

⊖ Covent Garden, Leicester Square
🚌 14, 19, 24, 29, 38, 176
♿
££

Comedy Theatre
Panton Street, SW1 (0171 369 1731)

Although originally constructed specifically for comedy productions, all types of plays and shows are performed here today, ranging from *The Rocky Horror Show* to serious drama by Arthur Miller and Tennessee Williams.

A Grade II listed building, it was built in 1881 by the Victorian architect Thomas Verity. There are three bars.

⊖ Piccadilly Circus
🚌 3, 12, 53, 88
♿
££

Criterion Theatre
Piccadilly Circus, W1 (0171 369 1747)

The most unusual feature of the Criterion is that the auditorium is underground! Built by Thomas Verity, the theatre is a wonderful piece of elaborate Victorian design.

Both serious drama and light comedy are staged here, with hits including Ray Cooney's *Run For Your Wife*. There are three bars.

⊖ Piccadilly Circus
🚌 3, 6, 9, 12, 14, 15, 19, 22, 23, 38, 53
♿
££

Dominion Theatre

Tottenham Court Road, WC2 (0171 416 6060)

Built to function either as a cinema or a theatre, the Dominion dominates the eastern end of Tottenham Court Road. With its large auditorium and wide stage, it is mostly used for musicals such as *Grease* and big band concerts. There are four bars.

⊖ Tottenham Court Road

🚌 10, 24, 29, 38, 73, 134

♿

££

Duchess Theatre

Catherine Street, WC2 (0171 494 5075)

An underground theatre, like the Criterion (see page 115), the Duchess was built in 1929 by Ewan Barr and mainly stages popular British comedy. It is one of the smallest West End theatres, but has two bars.

⊖ Covent Garden

🚌 6, 9, 11, 13, 23, 77A

Limited ♿

££

Duke of York's Theatre

St Martin's Lane, WC2 (0171 836 5122)

Originally called the Trafalgar Square Theatre when it opened in 1892, it changed its name to the Duke of York's in 1895 in honour of Queen Victoria's grandson, later George V. Its most famous production was *Peter Pan* by J.M. Barrie which opened in 1904 and was revived there every Christmas until 1915.

More recently, the theatre has staged new drama by such writers as Alan Ayckbourn and Arthur Miller with actors including Glenda Jackson and Paul Scofield in leading roles. There are two bars.

⊖ Charing Cross, Leicester Square

🚆 Charing Cross

🚌 6, 11, 15, 24, 29, 176

Limited ♿ (to Royal Circle only)

££

Fortune Theatre

Russell Street, Covent Garden, WC2 (0171 836 2238)

An elegant Art Deco theatre built in 1924, visually it is quite a contrast to the majestic Theatre Royal opposite. It was named after the original Fortune Theatre in the Barbican where Shakespeare performed in the sixteenth century but mostly modern plays are staged now. There are two bars.

⊖ Covent Garden

🚌 6, 9, 11, 13, 15, 23

Limited ♿

££

Garrick Theatre

Charing Cross Road, WC2 (0171 494 5085)

While this theatre was being built in the late 1880s, work had to be halted when an underground river flooded the building's foundations! Luckily, the builders managed to overcome this problem and the Garrick Theatre, which was named after the famous eighteenth-century actor David Garrick (1717–79), opened in 1889.

Popular comedies such as *No Sex Please – We're British* are among recent, long-running hits, as well as serious drama. There are three bars. Incidentally, keep an eye out for the ghost of Arthur Bourchier, a one-time theatre manager here.

⊖ Charing Cross, Leicester Square
🚇 Charing Cross
🚌 24, 29, 176
♿

££

Gielgud Theatre

Shaftesbury Avenue, W1 (0171 494 5065)

When the theatre opened in 1906, it was called the Hicks after the actor-manager Sir Seymour Hicks (1871–1949) but its name was changed to the Globe in 1909 and renamed in 1994 in honour of the actor Sir John Gielgud (1904–). The theatre has a splendid Louis XVI-style interior and contains three bars. Comedy and straight drama are staged here.

⊖ Piccadilly Circus
🚌 14, 19, 38
♿

££

Haymarket Theatre Royal

Haymarket, SW1 (0171 930 8800)

Now one of the smartest theatres in London, the Theatre Royal did not start out so well. Opened in 1720, the 'Little Theatre in the Hay', as it was known, did not have the royal patent needed for it to be able to present plays for its first forty years and so had to open illegally. A patent was finally granted in 1766, although performances at the new Theatre Royal were limited to the summer months when the other royal theatres, Drury Lane and Covent Garden, were closed.

The Haymarket's first play was Richard Sheridan's *The Rivals*. More recent hits include revivals and new plays, such as David Mamet's *A Life in the Theatre* in the late 1980s.

The theatre was redesigned by John Nash in the 1820s and throughout the nineteenth century various alterations were made to its elegant interiors. There are four bars.

⊖ Piccadilly Circus
🚌 6, 13, 14, 15, 19, 22, 38
♿

££

Her Majesty's Theatre

Haymarket, SW1 (0171 494 5400)

The first theatre on this site was built by the architect and playwright, Sir John Vanburgh (1664–1726) in 1705 and originally named after Queen Anne. It soon became a popular venue for opera and was known as the Italian Opera House. By the late nineteenth century, the name of the theatre had been changed to Her Majesty's in honour of Queen Victoria and a new theatre was built in 1897 for the actor-manager Sir Beerbohm Tree (1853–1917).

In the early 1980s Peter Schaffer's *Amadeus* had a long run here. It was replaced by Andrew Lloyd Webber's even longer running *Phantom of the Opera*. There are three bars.

⊖ Piccadilly Circus

🚌 3, 6, 12, 14, 19, 38, 53

&

££

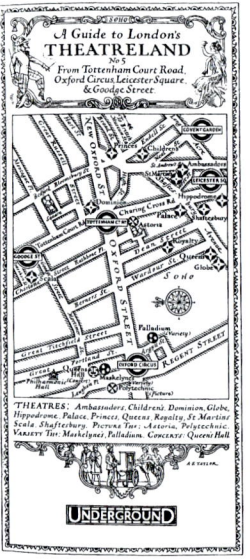

London Palladium

Argyll Street, Oxford Circus, W1 (0171 494 5020)

Home of variety and musicals, the theatre was built in 1868 and was redesigned in 1910 by Frank Matcham. This theatre is often used for Royal Variety Shows. At other times it mainly stages musicals, such as *Oliver!* Other hits include a revival of *Joseph* and *Singin' in the Rain*. There are three bars.

⊖ Oxford Circus

🚌 7, 8, 10, 25, 55, 73

&

££

Lyric Theatre

Shaftesbury Avenue, W1 (0171 494 5045)

A nineteenth-century theatre with a 1930s Art Deco interior, the Lyric is one of the oldest theatres in Shaftesbury Avenue. Excellent new drama is performed here, such as *Burn This* by Lanford Wilson in 1990 and plays by Alan Ayckbourn and Alan Bennett. There are four bars.

⊖ Piccadilly Circus

🚌 14, 19, 38

&

££

New London Theatre

Drury Lane, WC2 (0171 405 0072)

The musical *Cats* opened here in 1981 and became the longest-running musical in British theatre. There are two bars and a coffee bar in the main foyer.

⊖ Covent Garden, Holborn

🚌 11, 15, 26, 68, 91, 171A

Limited &

££

The Palace Theatre

Shaftesbury Avenue, W1 (0171 434 0909)

It was built as an opera house in 1891, but insufficient interest in opera was shown by British audiences and it changed its name and purpose in 1892. The new name was the Palace of Varieties and since then the theatre has staged a range of variety shows and musicals, including Cameron Mackintosh's *Les Miserables*. There are four bars. The Palace Brasserie, next to the Stalls Bar, is open one hour before a performance.

⊖ Leicester Square

🚌 14, 19, 24, 29, 38, 176

♿

££

Phoenix Theatre

Charing Cross Road, WC2 (0171 369 1733)

The Phoenix is closely associated with the playwright Noel Coward (1899–1973) who performed here with actress Gertrude Lawrence (1898–1952) in several of his plays, including *Private Lives*, the production which opened the theatre in 1930. There is even a bar named after him in the foyer. There are four other bars too.

Successful productions include Willy Russell's *Blood Brothers*, *The Merchant of Venice* with Dustin Hoffman, and Derek Jacobi as *Richard II* and *Richard III*.

⊖ Leicester Square, Tottenham Court Road

🚌 14, 19, 24, 29, 38, 176

♿

££

Phoenix Theatre

Piccadilly Theatre

Denman Street, W1 (0171 369 1734)

Built of white Portland stone in 1928, the Piccadilly is in a short street a few yards from the bustle of Piccadilly Circus.

Musical hits have included *Mack and Mabel*, *Mutiny* and *A Little Night Music*. Willy Russell's highly successful play *Educating Rita* was staged here in the early 1980s. There are four bars.

⊖ Piccadilly Circus

🚌 3, 6, 9, 14, 19, 38

♿

££

Playhouse Theatre

Northumberland Avenue, WC2 (0171 839 4401)

Originally opened in 1882, the Playhouse Theatre has seen such stars as Laurence Olivier (1907–89), Noel Coward (1899–1973) and Alec Guinness (1914–) perform here. The memory of some other famous names associated with the theatre lives on, as three of the four boxes are named after George Bernard Shaw (1856–1950), Marie Tempest (1864–1942) and Gladys Cooper (1888–1971).

The theatre closed in the early 1980s, but fortunately not for long. Sir Peter Hall's attempts to make it the base for his theatre company failed, but the theatre itself survived and subsequently many good plays and some lively shows – the Chippendales performed here – have been produced at the Playhouse. There are three bars. There is also a café bar which serves light snacks, coffee and tea from 6.00 p.m. to 9.00 p.m.

⊖ Embankment

🚌 6, 9, 11, 13, 15, 23

♿

££

Prince Edward Theatre

Old Compton Street, W1 (0171 734 8951)

The first of several new theatres to be built in the 1930s, the Prince Edward was at one time a casino. It became a theatre once again in the 1940s and in the 1970s it was turned into a dual-purpose theatre and film venue.

Concentrating mainly on musicals, productions include revivals of George and Ira Gershwin's *Crazy For You*, and Cole Porter's *Anything Goes*, as well as Andrew Lloyd Webber and Tim Rice's *Chess*. There are four bars.

⊖ Leicester Square, Tottenham Court Road,

🚌 14, 19, 24, 29, 35, 176

♿

££

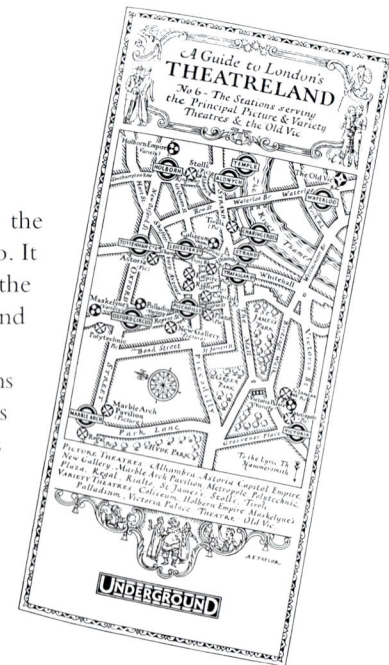

Prince of Wales Theatre

Coventry Street, W1 (0171 839 5987)

The Prince of Wales first opened in 1884 and was redesigned in 1937 in typical 1930s style. There are two bars (the one in the stalls includes a champagne bar).

⊖ Piccadilly Circus

🚌 3, 6, 9, 14, 19, 38

♿

££

Queen's Theatre

Shaftesbury Avenue, W1 (0171 494 5040)

Named after Queen Alexandra, this theatre was built in 1907. Its exterior suffered major war damage during the Second World War and was not rebuilt until 1959. Inside, the Edwardian interior survived and the theatre has three bars.

This theatre has a reputation for top dramas, with such stars as Vanessa Redgrave, as well as popular musicals, including *Prisoner Cell Block H.*

⊖ Piccadilly Circus

🚌 14, 19, 38

♿

££

Savoy Theatre

Strand, WC2 (0171 836 8888)

This attractive theatre has been wonderfully restored after a fire all but destroyed it in 1990. Next door to the Savoy Hotel, it was built in 1881 as a lyric playhouse. Revivals of Noel Coward and plays by other twentieth-century playwrights are popular here, as well as new British comedy and occasional musicals.

There are four bars in the theatre, but it is more fun (even though more expensive) to have a drink before a show in the American Bar at the Savoy.

⊖ Charing Cross, Covent Garden, Embankment

🚆 Charing Cross

🚌 6, 9, 11, 13, 15, 23

♿

££

Shaftesbury Theatre

Shaftesbury Avenue, WC2 (0171 379 5399)

An attractive Edwardian theatre, it almost had to close down in 1973 when part of the roof collapsed just before the start of a performance of *Hair*. It was rescued through the fund-raising efforts of the Save London's Theatres Campaign.

In recent years, hits have included *M. Butterfly* with Antony Hopkins and musicals such as *Return to the Forbidden Planet*. There are five bars and cold food is available in the Foyer Bar.

⊖ Covent Garden, Holborn, Tottenham Court Road

🚌 14, 19, 24, 29, 38, 176

♿

££

St Martin's Theatre

West Street, Cambridge Circus, WC2 (0171 836 1443)
St Martin's took over performances of Agatha Christie's *The Mousetrap* in 1974 from the Ambassadors Theatre. It has become the world's longest-running play. There are three bars.

⊖ Leicester Square
🚌 14, 19, 24, 29, 38, 176
Limited ♿ (please phone in advance)
££

Strand Theatre

Aldwych, WC2 (0171 930 8800)
Opened in 1905 as the Waldorf Theatre, it was renamed the Strand in 1909. It is a major venue for musicals such as *Buddy*. There are four bars.

⊖ Charing Cross, Embankment, Temple
🚋 Charing Cross
🚌 11, 15, 26, 68, 91, 171A
♿
££

Theatre Royal

Drury Lane, WC2 (0171 494 5000)
The oldest site in London to have been continually used as a theatre, the Theatre Royal is riddled with legends and old theatre lore. The current building is the fourth to stand here (it was built in 1812); two of the previous ones were destroyed by fire and the third was demolished.

Among the more fantastic tales about the theatre is that it has its own ghost, the 'Man in Grey' who is said to haunt the upper circle, especially during matinées. He is thought to be the ghost of a man whose bones were found behind a wall in 1840. The theatre has also carried on various traditions passed down through generations of actors. One of these is the Twelfth Night Cake. The actor Robert Baddeley who died in 1794 left money to provide a cake and wine for the green room every year on Twelfth Night.

This splendid old theatre has been home to a long line of top musicals including *Miss Saigon*. Refreshment for the audience is possible every night (Monday – Saturday) at the Café Theatre Royal, with a themed Oriental and European cuisine. There are also six bars.

⊖ Covent Garden
🚌 11, 15, 26, 68, 91, 171A
♿
££

Vaudeville Theatre

Strand, WC2 (0171 836 9987)

A venue for light drama, revues and comedies, the Vaudeville originally dates from the late seventeenth century, but was rebuilt in 1891. There are three bars.

⊖ Charing Cross, Embankment

▣ Charing Cross

🚌 6, 9, 11, 13, 15, 23

♿ , but users are not allowed to remain in wheelchairs

££

Victoria Palace Theatre

Victoria Street, SW1 (0171 834 1317)

Originally a Victorian music hall and then a variety hall, the Victoria Palace Theatre became a traditional theatre in the 1930s. *Buddy* played here in the late 1980s, before transferring to the West End. Since then, there has been a regular turnover of successful musicals. The theatre has five bars.

⊖/▣ Victoria

🚌 C1, 8, C10, 11, 24, 211

♿

££

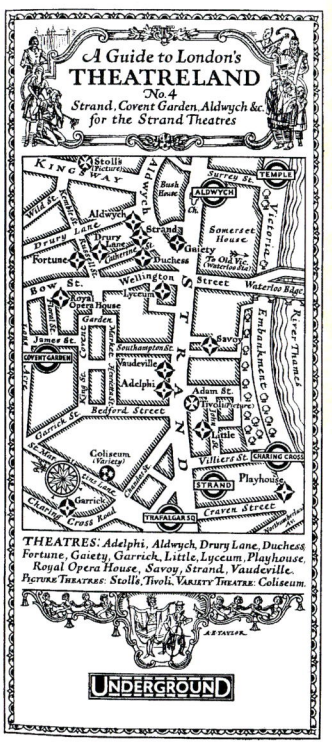

Westminster Theatre

Palace Street, Buckingham Palace Road, SW1 (0171 828 9361)

Although there have been no major hits produced here, the Westminster Theatre enjoys regular success with drama revivals.

The theatre was converted from a 1920s cinema in 1931. It had originally been built as a chapel in 1776. There is a pub next to the theatre and inside the theatre there is a café that opens one hour before a performance.

⊖/▣ Victoria

🚌 C1, C10, 11, 211

♿

££

Whitehall Theatre

Whitehall, SW1 (0171 369 1735)

A grand Art Deco theatre, the Whitehall stages revivals, musicals and comedy. It has two bars.

⊖ Charing Cross, Embankment

▣ Charing Cross

🚌 3, 11, 12, 24, 53, 77A

♿

££

Wyndham's Theatre

Charing Cross Road, WC2 (0171 369 1736)

An attractive, small theatre, built in 1899, the Wyndham is named after the Victorian actor-manager, Charles Wyndham. The theatre took over the major 1980s hit, *Serious Money* by Caryl Churchill from the Royal Court Theatre and since then has staged more new drama, as well as musicals and revivals. It has three bars and tea and coffee are available during Saturday matinées.

⊖ Leicester Square

🚌 14, 19, 24, 29, 38, 176

♿

££

ALTERNATIVE AND LOCAL THEATRES

These have been grouped together alphabetically within geographical areas.

CENTRAL

Donmar Warehouse

41 Earlham Street, WC2 (0171 369 1732)

Best known for its excellent work by director and producer Sam Mendes (with such stars as Judi Dench), the Donmar Warehouse has earned an excellent reputation for both its own new productions and those of touring companies.

Originally the site was a rehearsal studio built for the ballerina Margot Fonteyn. As the Warehouse, it became the Royal Shakespeare's studio theatre in London, opening in 1977 to show plays that had proved successful at Stratford's The Other Place as well as the works of young British playwrights. When the RSC moved to the Barbican in 1982, the theatre became the Donmar Warehouse. Recent hits include Terry Johnson's *Insignificance* and *Company* by George Firth.

⊖ Covent Garden

🚌 14, 19, 24, 29, 38, 176

♿

£–££

Drill Hall Theatre

16 Chenies Street, WC1 (0171 637 8270)

The Drill Hall stages a wide range of innovative productions, particularly reflecting gay and lesbian culture. There are performances, workshops, international collaborations, exhibitions and an excellent vegetarian restaurant downstairs.

⊖ Goodge Street

🚆 Euston

🚌 10, 24, 29, 73, 134

♿

£–££

ICA

Nash House, The Mall, SW1 (0171 930 3647;
0171 930 0493: membership enquiries)
See also pages 25, 147 and 154

A programme of various types of avant-garde performances, termed 'Live Art' by the ICA, is held here, ranging from dance and talks, to improvised movement and video. Two recent productions, *True Stories*, an experimental solo character show by Penny Arcade, an American, who was raised by a band of drag queens and was a teenage superstar for Andy Warhol, and *Fade*, an exploration about how we prepare for and finally overcome loss, are typical of the exciting, and challenging, work performed here.

⊖ Charing Cross, Piccadilly Circus
▣ Charing Cross
🚌 9, 14, 19, 22, 29, 38
♿
£–££

Players' Theatre

The Arches, Villiers Street, WC2 (0171 839 1134)

Hugely popular with overseas visitors, the Players' offers a wonderfully nostalgic evening of Victorian music hall entertainment, performed by the Players' Theatre Company. In addition the theatre stages classic Victorian musicals, melodramas and pantomimes, such as *Babes in the Wood* and *The Sleeping Beauty*, using the original scripts.

⊖ Charing Cross, Embankment
▣ Charing Cross
🚌 6, 9, 11, 13, 15, 23
♿
££

Hackney Empire

291 Mare Street, Hackney, E8 (0181 985 2424)

See also pages 160 and 164

Designed by the theatre architect Frank Matcham in 1901, this theatre provides a venue for traditional variety, new variety, comedy, music, dance, theatre shows, musicals and shows for children.

⊖ Bethnal Green, then bus

🚆 Hackney Central

🚌 D6, 48, 55, 106, 253

♿

£–££

Mermaid Theatre

Puddle Dock, Blackfriars, EC4 (0171 236 2211)

The dream of actor and director Lord (Bernard) Miles (1907–91) and his wife who had always wanted to build an Elizabethan-style theatre, the Mermaid is a performance space for plays as well as offering facilities for rehearsals, lectures and presentations. A broad spectrum of plays are performed, and the theatre often presents a themed season of productions.

Overlooking the Thames, the Mermaid has a self-service restaurant, a River Room and two bars.

⊖/🚆 Blackfriars

🚌 11, 15, 26, 45, 63

♿

£–££

NORTH

Almeida

Almeida Street, Islington, N1 (0171 359 4404)

An important London theatre, in the heart of Islington, the Almeida stages contemporary and classical drama, opera (see page 164) and dance throughout the year. Recent hits include *The Silver Tassie* by Sean O'Casey and *Venice Preserved* by Thomas Otway. The theatre has an excellent restaurant which is open even when a production is not on.

⊖ Angel, Highbury & Islington

🚆 Highbury & Islington

🚌 4, 19, 30, 43

Limited ♿

££

Hampstead Theatre

Swiss Cottage Centre, NW3 (0171 722 9301)

A well-respected theatre, the Hampstead opened in 1962. Since then it has staged a host of brilliant performances from visiting companies as well as its own productions.

The first plays staged here were Harold Pinter's *The Room* and *The Dumb Waiter*, while more recent productions have included Arthur Miller's double bill, *Danger: Memory!* and *Sweet Panic*.

Membership is required to attend a play here, but ticket prices are reasonably low to make up for this.

⊖ Swiss Cottage
🚌 C11, 13, 31, 46, 82, 113
Limited ♿
£–££

New End Theatre

27 New End, Hampstead, NW3 (0171 794 0022)
A range of works, from Shakespearean plays to new works by women ex-offenders, are performed here. One of the annual highlights is a festival of Restoration comedy held every summer.

⊖ Hampstead
🚌 46, 210, 268
Limited ♿
£–££

Old Bull Arts Centre

68 High Street, Barnet, Herts (0181 449 0048)
The Old Bull Arts Centre offers a full programme of top-quality touring theatre, dance (see page 160), music, cabaret, comedy and children's shows as well as a picture gallery. A generous innovation is the regular Tuesday 'pay what you can' idea, an excellent way to encourage people to go to the theatre.

⊖ High Barnet
🚆 New Barnet
🚌 34, 84, 107, 234, 263
♿
£–££

Theatro Technis

26 Crowndale Road, Camden Town, NW1 (0171 387 6617)
An unusual theatre company, Theatro Technis is Greek Cypriot in origin but international in vision. Set up in the 1950s to answer the cultural needs of the recently immigrated community of Greek Cypriots, the company expanded to encompass the theatrical works of other European countries. Today, a whole spectrum of plays is performed in various languages, ranging from Ancient Greek tragedies to modern Spanish writing.

⊖ Camden Town
🚌 24, 27, 29, 214, 253
Limited ♿
£–££

Tricycle Theatre
269 Kilburn High Road, NW6 (0171 328 1000)
The Tricycle Theatre has become an invaluable community resource in a multi-racial neighbourhood and has received much critical acclaim for its productions of black and Irish drama. Many of the plays premiered at the Tricycle have been seen subsequently in the West End or on television. *Half the Picture*, a dramatization of the Scott 'Arms to Iraq' Inquiry, was the first play ever to be performed in the Houses of Parliament and, on a more frivolous level, the Tricycle's first musical, *Ain't Misbehavin'*, went on to enchant West End audiences.
⊖ Kilburn
▣ Brondesbury
🚌 16, 16A, 28, 31, 32
♿
£–££

SOUTH

Ashcroft Theatre
Fairfield Hall, Park Lane, Croydon, Surrey (0181 688 9291)
Calling itself 'South London's Premier Art and Entertainment Centre', the Fairfield Hall is truly a multi-arts centre. The Ashcroft Theatre stages ballet (see page 160), opera, pantomime, drama, children's shows and even wrestling. The centre also has a concert hall, a gallery, restaurant (the Green Room) and coffee shop.
▣ East Croydon
🚌 50, 60, 197, 204, 250, 392
♿
£–££

Battersea Arts Centre
176 Lavender Hill, Battersea, SW11 (0171 223 2223)
See also pages 30, 128 and 135
Battersea Arts Centre (or BAC as it is more commonly known) opened in 1974 in what was previously Battersea's town hall. The striking Victorian listed building contains three theatre spaces, a gallery, bookshop, bar and restaurant. It is one of the busiest independent theatres in the country, staging plays from established writers such as Jean Anouilh to young new writers. Each autumn BAC holds 'Short BAC & Sides', the best Edinburgh preview season (recent productions include a one-woman show by the television presenter Annabel Giles).
▣ Clapham Junction
🚌 77, 77A, 135
♿
£-££

The Brixton Shaw Theatre
Brixton Hill, SW2 (0171 733 4443)
The resident company, Counterpoint Theatre, produces four plays a year and the theatre is also used by touring companies. An eclectic range of plays are

performed, with the aim of encouraging audiences in an area of London that does not have a strong theatrical tradition.

⊖/🚉 Brixton
🚌 45, 109, 118, 133
Limited ♿
£–££

Greenwich Theatre

Crooms Hill, Greenwich, SE10 (0181 858 7755)
A venue for all types of plays and shows from mainstream stand-up comics to revivals of plays by Ibsen and Chekhov, the Greenwich Theatre has an eclectic programme to suit all tastes.
🚉 Greenwich
🚌 53, 180, 188, 199, 286
♿
£–££

The London Bubble Theatre

5 Elephant Lane, Rotherhithe, SE16 (0171 237 4434)
See also page 189
The acclaimed London Bubble Theatre is a leading exponent of 'forum theatre', a technique that encourages audience participation. Works range from Shakespeare to music theatre and have a strong multi-cultural context.
⊖ Rotherhithe
🚌 P11, 47, 188
No ♿
£–££

The Old Vic

Waterloo Road, SE1 (0171 928 7616)
Originally a centre for music hall and variety in the mid-nineteenth century, the Old Vic became a temperance hall in the late nineteenth century under the management of social reformer Emma Cons. She was succeeded by her niece Lillian Baylis who was determined to bring good-quality drama to even the poorest people. The Old Vic presented all thirty-seven of Shakespeare's plays between 1915 and 1923.

In the 1960s the Old Vic became the home of the National Theatre Company under Laurence Olivier until it moved to the Royal National Theatre in 1976. Today, a wide variety of plays and musicals are performed, ranging from *Carmen Jones* to *The Wind in the Willows*. There are three bars.
⊖/🚉 Waterloo
🚌 68, 168, 171, 176, 188
♿
£–££

Overleaf: *The Old Vic*

Southwark Playhouse

62 Southwark Bridge Road, SE1 (0171 620 3494)
Set up in the early 1990s, the Southwark Playhouse produces and performs a range of diverse, script-based plays. Winner of the 1995 *Time Out* drama award for Jack Shepherd's *Choosing the Moment*, the Southwark Playhouse continues to build on its excellent reputation.

⊖ Borough
🚌 P3, 21, 35, 40, 133, 344
No ♿
£–££

Young Vic Theatre

66 The Cut, Waterloo, SE1 (0171 928 6363)
Located on the south bank of the Thames, the Young Vic Theatre is a highly acclaimed venue, attracting such top stars as Helen Mirren and Siân Phillips and inspiring excellent performances. Recent revivals such as *Peer Gynt* have been as popular as new plays, such as *Zenobia* by Nick Dear. Plays are performed by an in-house theatre company or guest companies and artists.

⊖/🚆 Waterloo
🚌 45, 63, 68, 168, 171, 176, 188
♿
£–££

The Gate

11 Pembridge Road, W11 (0171 229 5387)

An award-winning theatre, the Gate performs an international selection of plays. A recent German season was particularly successful, as was a sell-out trilogy of Greek stories, *Agamemnon's Children*.

⊖ Notting Hill Gate

🚌 27, 28, 31, 52, 302

No ♿

£–££

Labatt's Apollo

Queen Caroline Street, Hammersmith, W6 (0171 416 6080)

A major venue in west London, Labatt's Apollo presents a range of popular musicals and shows. Recent triumphs have been *Riverdance* and *Joseph* (see also page 152).

⊖ Hammersmith

🚌 9, 10, 33, 72, 211, 266

♿

££

Lyric Hammersmith

King Street, W6 (0181 741 2311)

An elegant Victorian theatre, built in 1895, shrouded in a modern frontage, the Lyric is a major theatre venue in west London and stages plays for adults and children. The theatre often invites companies from regional theatres to stage plays, such as a recent co-production of *The Cabinet of Doctor Caligari* with the Nottingham Playhouse.

⊖ Hammersmith

🚌 9, 10, 27, 72, 190, 220, 267, 283, 295, 391

No ♿

£–££

Riverside Studios

Crisp Road, Hammersmith, W6 (0181 741 2251)

Considered 'one of the country's most adventurous venues', according to the actress Vanessa Redgrave, the Riverside has an excellent international reputation for introducing British audiences to new and established actors, writers, directors and musicians from all over the world.

The Riverside is equally popular with film buffs (see page 175), and regularly shows new and classic art films, as well as excellent films for children.

There is also a great newly refurbished café and bar open every day from 11.00 a.m. to 11.00 p.m.

⊖ Hammersmith

🚌 33, 72, 190, 211, 220, 295

♿

£–££

Royal Court

Sloane Square, SW1 (0171 730 1745; 0171 730 2554: box office Theatre Upstairs)
Many of the twentieth century's leading playwrights first had their work performed in this theatre, home of new writing and exciting plays. Among its most famous successes are John Osborne's *Look Back in Anger* with Alan Bates, Martin Sherman's *Bent* with Ian McKellen and work by Caryl Churchill, including *Top Girls* and *Serious Money*, which transferred to the West End.

A theatre has stood on this site since 1870 and it provides two performance areas: the main theatre and the Theatre Upstairs, where repertory works are staged (by such dramatists as Sam Shepherd). The theatre also runs a Young People's Theatre School for young playwrights, who it is hoped will contribute to the theatre's reputation as the 'National Theatre of New Writing'. There are two bars.

⊖ Sloane Square
🚌 C1, 11, 19, 22, 137, 137A, 211
Limited ♿
£–££

Royal Court Theatre

The Royal Court Theatre will be closed for two years from the beginning of September 1996 because of a major rebuilding project. During this time the Company will move its productions to two theatres in the West End – the Duke of York's and the Ambassadors.

Waterman's Arts Centre

40 High Street, Brentford, Middlesex (0181 568 1176)
Overlooking the River Thames, Waterman's Arts Centre is a lively arts and entertainment venue. It has an excellent reputation for exciting theatre and for its live music. There is also late-night cabaret, events for children and a cinema.

⊖ Gunnersbury, South Ealing, then bus
🚊 Brentford, Gunnersbury
🚌 116, 117, 237, 267
♿
£–££

PUB THEATRES

Bush Theatre

Shepherd's Bush Green, W12 (0181 743 3388)
Well known for producing innovative plays by new writers, the Bush Theatre has a long history of encouraging and developing new talent. Over 1,000 scripts are received each year and of these only the very best are produced. Recent hits include *Trainspotting* by Harry Gibson, adapted from the novel by Irvine Welsh, which transferred to the West End along with *Killer Joy* by Tracey Letts.

Some of the most innovative directors and designers work in this theatre and the quality of its work attracts actors of the highest calibre.

⊖ Shepherd's Bush

🚌 49, 95, 207, 237, 260, 283

No ♿

£–££

King's Head Theatre Club

115 Upper Street, Islington, N1 (0171 226 1916)

Top-quality theatre has been performed upstairs at this pub since 1970. It is an important venue for new plays and works by established writers, and alumni include Kenneth Branagh, Ben Kingsley and Maureen Lipman. Plays staged here in recent years range from *Burning Blue* by David Greer to *Kvetch* by Stephen Berkoff and *Stairway to Heaven* by Kevin Metchear and Tom Morgan.

⊖ Angel, Highbury & Islington

🚌 4, 19, 30, 43

♿

£–££

The Man in the Moon

392 King's Road, Chelsea, SW3 (0171 351 2876, 0171 351 5701)

Comedy, plays and one-man shows are performed upstairs at the Man in the Moon pub. Late-night performances are a regular feature.

⊖ Sloane Square, then bus

🚌 11, 19, 22, 211

No ♿

£–££

Old Red Lion Theatre

418 St John Street, Islington, EC1 (0171 837 7816)

Once the drinking haunt of Lenin when he was in London, or so the legend goes, the Old Red Lion pub has been home to a small but innovative theatre since the late 1970s. Plays generally comprise either new works or revivals of old plays produced in a new way.

⊖ Angel

🚌 19, 38, 171A

No ♿

£–££

Orange Tree Theatre

1 Clarence Street, Richmond, Surrey (0181 940 3633)

A unique theatre-in-the-round with an intimate atmosphere producing an exciting mix of rare and contemporary classics, new plays, musicals and plays for young people.

⊖/🚆 Richmond

🚌 H22, 65, 190, 290, 337, 391

♿

£–££

CHILDREN'S THEATRE

Battersea Arts Centre

Old Town Hall, Lavender Hill, SW11 (0171 223 2223)
See also page 128
Special events are held for children at weekends and holidays, including puppet performances – the BAC is home of the Puppet Centre Trust. The Puppet Centre is in charge of puppet theatre in venues across London; phone them on 0171 228 5335 to find out about performances.
🚇 Clapham Junction
🚌 35, 77, 77A, 156, 170, 295, 345
♿
£

Little Marionette Theatre

14 Dagmar Passage, Cross Street, Islington, N1 (0171 226 1787)
Children from five to thirteen are catered for at the Little Marionette Theatre. On Saturday mornings there are short shows aimed at under-fives, while in the afternoon older children can enjoy a full-length play, which could be anything from a

---

Pantomime

Pantomime dates back to Roman times, although it has changed considerably since then. It was originally considered extremely scandalous and dangerously subversive. In the fifth century anyone associated with pantomime was thrown out of every city in the Roman Empire apart from Alexandria, which is said to be its birthplace. It was so popular there that it was feared that any expulsion might cause a riot.

Originally, pantomime was based on dance to the accompaniment of music and song. Modern pantomime developed from the popular Italian Night Scenes performed in London by the *commedia dell'arte* from the sixteenth to the eighteenth centuries. An unnamed dancing master from Shrewsbury is credited with writing the first British pantomime. In 1702 his first production *The Tavern Bilkers* was performed at Drury Lane, now regarded as the home of British pantomime.

At that time the main feature of pantomime was the Harlequinade, where the character of the Harlequin could turn himself into someone else in a short operetta which slowly merged into a well-known fairy story such as *Cinderella*. In the nineteenth century actresses were cast as young heroes, while the comic elderly characters were performed by men, dressed as women and known as Dames.

Children's shows are also held at the Riverside Studios, Royal National Theatre, Sadler's Wells, and the Lyric Hammersmith. The Barbican Centre holds regular weekend festivals and fun days for all the family too.

❖

traditional folk story to a Christmas pantomime. The theatre also puts on extra shows during half-terms and holidays.

⊖ Highbury & Islington
🚇 Essex Road
🚌 4, 19, 30, 43
♿
£

Movingstage Marionette Company

Puppet Theatre Barge, Blomfield Road, Little Venice, W9 (0171 249 6876)

Water and marionettes work in harmony together at the Movingstage Marionette Company. Based in an old working barge on the pretty backwater of the Regent's Canal at Little Venice, the Puppet Theatre Barge is an unusual and fascinating theatre for children and adults. Plays are selected from existing works and poems and occasionally new work is commissioned from contemporary poets. During the winter the company develops ideas for its plays and carves the hand-puppets. The shows are toured up and down the Thames during the summer. You can catch the shows in London from November to June.

⊖ Warwick Avenue
🚌 6, 46
No ♿
£

London Transport offers this poster as a diversion and a greeting. Its three figures, cut out and made up, will provide puppets or hanging decorations. Copies cost 10/- each from the Poster Shop, 280 Marylebone Road, NW1 (near Edgware Road Circle Line station), including a leaflet giving simple instructions. Call between 10 and 4 on Mondays to Fridays or send 11/6 to include postage and packing.

Polka Theatre for Children

240 The Broadway, Wimbledon, SW19 (0181 543 4888)

The Polka Theatre is the only theatre in London entirely devoted to children and has two shows daily for families and schools. Shows vary from plays, mime, magic and music and are suitable for children of all ages. As well as theatre, there is a museum of puppets and toys, an adventure room, a workshop and a café. In the summer holidays there is a summer school, while in the shop there is a special selection of souvenirs affordable with pocket money.

⊖ South Wimbledon, Wimbledon
🚇 Wimbledon
🚌 57, 93, 155
♿
£

Tricycle Theatre

269 Kilburn High Road, NW6 (0171 328 1000)
See also page 128
The imaginative and varied programme of
Saturday shows and drama workshops has earned
a deservedly loyal following among local children
and young people.
⊖ Kilburn
▣ Brondesbury
🚌 16, 16A, 28, 31, 32
♿
£

Unicorn Theatre

Great Newport Street, WC2 (0171 836 3334)
Founded in 1947, the Unicorn is the oldest professional children's theatre in
London and aims to introduce live theatre to all children and promote their
enjoyment of it. Two productions are always on, one for fours to sevens and the
other for eights to twelves. From Tuesday to Friday, the company performs for
school groups, but at weekends the theatre is open to the general public.
Performances take place on Saturday at 11.00 a.m. and 2.30 p.m. and on Sundays
at 2.30 p.m.

   The theatre also holds open days, where visitors can take part in an afternoon
of free workshops, chats with actors and face-painting.
⊖ Leicester Square
🚌 24, 29, 176
♿
Free (£ for performances)

Waterman's Arts Centre

40 High Street, Brentford, Middlesex (0181 568 1176)
A regular Saturday afternoon theatre performance for over-threes is held. Shows
vary from magic and music to puppet shows. Performances start at 2.30 p.m.
⊖ Gunnersbury, South Ealing, then bus
▣ Brentford, Gunnersbury
🚌 116, 117, 237, 267
♿
£

MIME THEATRE

Forget Marcel Marceau, today mime theatre is an umbrella term for a host of
exciting performance art, from Indian classical dance drama to mask theatre and
often these performances include speech. The venues are equally varied:
   Battersea Arts Centre (see page 135)
   The Circus Space (see page 178)

Cochrane Theatre, Southampton Row, WC1 (0171 242 7040)
Drill Hall Theatre (see page 124)
ICA (see page 125)
Jackson's Lane, 269a Archway Road, N6 (0181 341 4421)
Lilian Baylis Theatre (see page 160)
Lyric Hammersmith (see page 132)
Old Bull Arts Centre (see page 127)
The Place Theatre (see page 155)
Riverside Studios (see page 132)
Royal Festival Hall (see page 155)
Sadler's Wells Theatre (see page 159)
Turtle Key Arts Centre, 74 Farm Lane, SW6 (0171 385 4905)
Waterman's Arts Centre (see page 137)
Young Vic (see page 131)

BACKSTAGE TOURS

Find out what goes on behind the scenes by taking a backstage tour. The Royal National Theatre has tours daily at 10.15 a.m., 12.30 p.m., 2.45 p.m., 5.30 p.m. and 6.00 p.m., except on Olivier matinée days when the times are different. For more details phone 0171 633 0880 (between 10.00 a.m. and 11.00 p.m.).

Other theatres hold similar tours. Listed below are useful numbers to find out where and when these take place:

Act 1 Theatre Travel Club, Theatreland Tours (0171 494 2304);

Tour Guides Ltd (0171 495 5504);

Stage by Stage Tours (0171 328 7558).

6
MUSIC

CLASSICAL MUSIC

FROM LUNCH-TIME concerts in City churches and symphony concerts and recitals in the major venues throughout the year to those held in the grounds of historic houses on summer weekend evenings and the pomp and ceremony of the last night of the Proms at the Royal Albert Hall, lovers of classical music are almost spoilt for choice. Every Christmas there are dozens of carol concerts (see page 199, The Entertainment Year) – check your local newspapers in December – and you can listen to superb singing in choral services in Westminster Abbey and Westminster Cathedral on most days.

Several orchestras are based in the capital, including the London Symphony (at the Barbican) and the Philharmonic (at the Royal Festival Hall and the Royal Albert Hall). The city also plays host to many overseas and touring orchestras, choirs and soloists. Unlike theatres which are frequently booked up weeks in advance, it is often possible to buy tickets for a classical concert just before it begins, and they will generally be much less expensive than for a play or a top rock band. For a really good deal, book tickets for a series of concerts.

To attend a concert being performed for a radio recording, apply to the Ticket Unit, BBC, Broadcasting House, Portland Place, W1 (0171 580 4468).

London and composers

London has always been hospitable to foreign musicians. Handel first visited London in 1710 and returned two years later to dominate London's artistic life for nearly half a century. While he was here, he composed the famous 'Water Music' for George I and the 'Firework Music' for George II.

Mozart stayed in Frith Street, Soho in 1764, when touring as an infant prodigy, and there composed his first, or 'London' Symphony at the age of eight. Haydn came to London in 1791 and stayed for eighteen months. While he was here, he wrote six of the 'Salomon' symphonies. He returned to London in 1794 and wrote the last five of the 'Salomon' symphonies.

❖

Barbican Centre

Silk Street, EC2 (0171 638 8891: box office)
See also pages 27, 109 and 171
The 2,000-seat Barbican Hall offers a breadth
and depth of programming unsurpassed in
London. Presentations range from symphony
orchestras and chamber ensembles to solo
artists from both the national and international scene. The Hall also plays host to
some of the leading names from the fields
of jazz, folk and world music.

The Centre's resident London
Symphony Orchestra promotes around
eighty-five concerts at the Barbican
each year. Founded in 1904, the self-
governing LSO is London's oldest
orchestra, and became the first
orchestra to have a home when it
moved to the Barbican Centre in
1982.

This residency has enabled the
orchestra to develop an identity and artistic profile
unique for a London orchestra, establishing a reputation for excel-
lence with its award-winning programming and pioneering ventures including
themed music festivals. The Centre also mounts themed music series, together
with annual multi-media festivals. Keep an eye out in the listings magazines for
details of these important events in London's music calendar.

⊖ Barbican, Moorgate
🚌 4, 11, 56, 100, 133, 141, 214, 271
&
££

Royal Albert Hall

Kensington Gore, SW7 (0171 589 8212)
Prince Albert suggested that the profits from the Great Exhibition in 1851 should
be used to make South Kensington a centre for the arts and education. The Natural
History, Science and V & A museums (see pages 47, 49 and 37) were subsequently
built but the plans drawn up for a hall containing libraries, a lecture theatre and
exhibition rooms were abandoned for some reason. After Prince Albert's death in
1861 a public fund was opened to finance both the Albert Memorial and the hall.
Again the plans had to be shelved, this time for lack of funds. Then in 1863 Henry
Cole, chairman of the Society of Arts, proposed that the building should be
financed by selling 999-year leaseholds of seats. This proved successful and the hall
was opened in 1871 and named the Royal Albert Hall of Arts and Sciences.

The Royal Albert Hall is one of the most important concert halls in London.
The whole building is a huge oval rising to an impressive glass dome in the centre.
Around the outside is a huge frieze illustrating 'The Triumph of Arts and

Royal Albert Hall

Sciences'. It is now best known for holding the Sir Henry Wood Promenade Concerts here every summer but, interestingly, these concerts only moved here in 1941 for the 47th season after their original venue at the Queen's Hall was destroyed by a bomb (see also page 195).

The Royal Albert Hall is a busy venue for the rest of the year too, with both pop and classical concerts, sometimes with multi-coloured laser displays.

⊖ High Street Kensington, Knightsbridge.

🚌 9, 10, 52

♿

££

Royal Festival Hall, Queen Elizabeth Hall and Purcell Room

South Bank Centre, SE1 (0171 960 4242: box office 10.00 a.m.–9.00 p.m.)

Classical music is performed almost every night in at least one of the South Bank's cluster of concert halls. The main venue, and the largest, is the Royal Festival Hall where such orchestras as the London Philharmonic and the Philharmonia perform. Top international conductors are regularly invited to appear in a series of works.

The two smaller halls are equally busy with performances of a wide variety of classical music, including choral work. Tickets are usually less expensive for these concerts.

⊖ Embankment, Waterloo
🚆 Waterloo
🚌 26, 68, 171, 171A, 188, 211
♿ to all three halls
£–££

FRESH THINGS NOT CANNED
NOURISH BEST THE SPIRITS
ON PLEASURE BENT

St James's

Piccadilly, W1 (0171 734 4511; 0171 437 5053: box office)

Lunch-time recitals take place regularly in this Wren church. Concerts are also held on some Thursday, Friday and Saturday evenings. Beethoven, baroque and piano sonatas are popular here. Phone for details.

⊖ Piccadilly Circus
🚌 8, 9, 14, 19, 22, 38
♿
£–££ for evening concerts

St John's

Smith Square, SW1
(0171 222 1061: 10.00 a.m.–5.0 0 p.m.)

This former church is one of the foremost venues for classical music in London. It hosts both lunch-time and evening concerts regularly. Lunch-time concerts are held every Monday and on alternate Thursdays. Unlike most other lunch-time concert venues, there is a small charge but you can become a 'Friend' which entitles you to two free tickets for the Thursday concerts and reduced prices for the evening concerts. The music performed ranges from series of early music and chamber ensembles to soprano soloists and organ recitcals.

⊖ Westminster
🚌 3, C10, 77A, 159, 507
♿ (phone first)
£–££

St Martin-in-the-Fields

Trafalgar Square, WC2 (0171 930 0089: box office)
Concerts of baroque music are held here every
Thursday, Friday and Saturday at 7.30 p.m. by
candlelight which creates a wonderful atmosphere.
There are also regular (free) lunch-time concerts
on Monday, Tuesday, Wednesday and Friday
where young musicians perform a broad repertoire of classical music. There is also a bookshop
and a café in the crypt.
⊖/🚇 Charing Cross
🚌 6, 9, 11, 13, 15, 23
♿

££ (lunch-time free, but donations welcome)

Wigmore Hall

36 Wigmore Street, W1 (0171 935 2141)
Classical music is performed at the Wigmore
Hall virtually seven days a week (every month
except August). A particular pleasure is to go
to one of the Sunday morning concerts, an
excellent way to unwind at the weekend;
coffee, sherry or fruit juice is included in the
price of the tickets, together with a compli-
mentary programme.
⊖ Bond Street
🚌 7, 10, 12, 25, 73, 94
♿
£–££

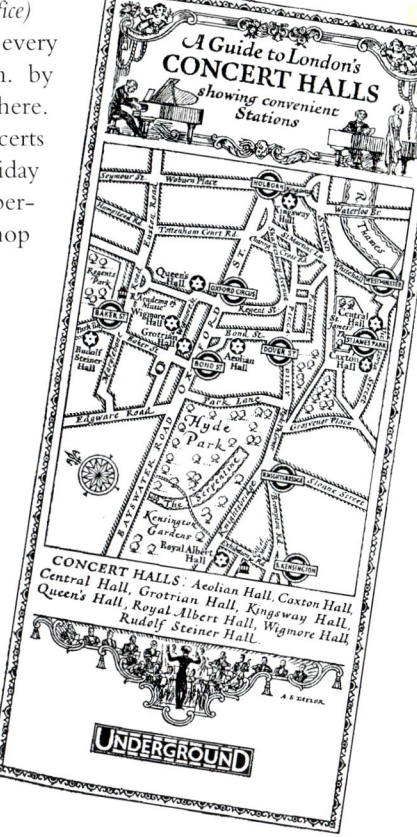

CITY CHURCHES

St Anne and St Agnes

Gresham Street, EC2 (0171 606 4986)
Concerts take place every Monday and some Friday lunch-times at 1.10 p.m. The
repertoire here includes chamber music, trios and duos and string quartets.
⊖ St Paul's
🚌 4, 8, 22B, 25, 26, 56
♿

Free, but donations welcome

St Bride's

Fleet Street, EC4 (0171 353 1301)

Lunch-time recitals of classical music are given every Tuesday, Wednesday and Friday at 1.15 p.m.

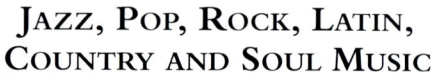

θ/🚇 Blackfriars

🚌 11, 15, 26, 171A

No ♿

Free, but donations welcome

St Mary-le-Bow

Cheapside, EC2 (0171 248 5139)

Come to the lunch-time concerts in this City church every Thursday at 1.05 p.m. and listen to a selection of baroque, instrumental and piano music.

θ St Paul's

🚌 8, 22B, 25, 56

♿

Free, but donations welcome

JAZZ, POP, ROCK, LATIN, COUNTRY AND SOUL MUSIC

Live music can be found every night of the week all across London. The biggest bands play at the huge venues, such as Wembley Stadium. The shows there are always spectacular, but tickets can be expensive. Smaller venues, with an established name, such as the Borderline near Tottenham Court Road or the Mean Fiddler in Harlesden, can attract some top bands too. Dozens of pubs also have regular live music nights; they have a more intimate atmosphere than an arena or stadium and often serve food too.

The following is a selection of the best places to see live music.

JAZZ VENUES

CENTRAL

Pizza Express

10 Dean Street, Soho, W1 (0171 439 8722)

There's jazz on the lower ground floor at this Pizza Express, the first of the chain to be opened back in the 1960s. Modern and mainstream jazz feature and the pizzas are good too.

θ Tottenham Court Road

🚌 7, 8, 10, 25, 55, 73

No ♿

££

Pizza on the Park

11 Knightsbridge, Hyde Park Corner, SW1
(0171 235 5273)
Regular jazz is performed in this spacious restaurant facing Hyde Park.
⊖ Hyde Park Corner
🚌 9, 10, 14, 19, 22, 52
♿
££

Polar Bear

30 Lisle Street, Leicester Square, WC2 (0171 437 3048)
Free modern jazz is played most nights of the week in this pub in the heart of Chinatown.
⊖ Leicester Square
🚌 14, 19, 24, 29, 38, 176
No ♿
££

Ronnie Scott's Club

47 Frith Street, Soho, W1 (0171 439 0747)
One of the most famous jazz venues in London, Ronnie's attracts international artists alongside British jazz performers. The main act each evening plays two sets, around 10.30 p.m. and 1.00 a.m. Food is served and it is a good idea to book a table.
⊖ Leicester Square, Tottenham Court Road
🚌 14, 19, 24, 29, 38, 176
No ♿
££

Blue Note

1 Hoxton Square, Islington, N1 (0171 729 8440)
This is a small venue that features acid jazz, hip hop and jungle with plenty of room to dance.
⊖ Old Street
🚌 55, 141, 271
No ♿
££

Jazz Café

5 Parkway, Camden Town, NW1 (0171 916 6060)
Part of the Mean Fiddler chain of clubs, this is a large modern venue with jazz played in the evening and at lunch-time on Sunday. Food is served upstairs and it is mostly standing downstairs. It is wise to book in advance.
⊖ Camden Town
🚌 C2, 24, 27, 29, 124, 135, 168, 274
Limited ♿ (ground floor only)
££

The Rhythmic

89–91 Chapel Market, Islington, N1 (0171 713 5859)
A large jazz venue. A broad range of music is performed with the emphasis on international funk and R&B.
⊖ Angel
🚌 4, 19, 30, 38, 43, 56
♿
££

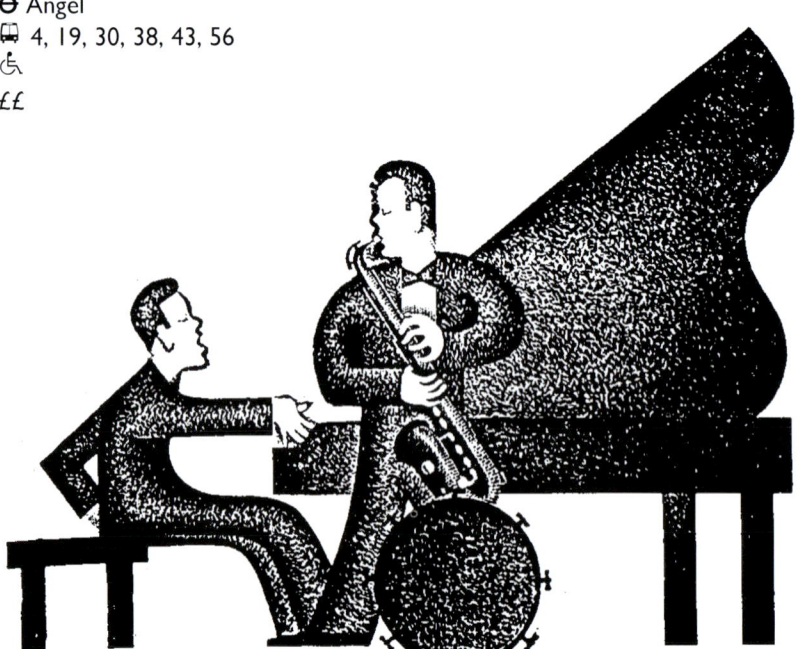

The Vortex

139–141 Stoke Newington Church Street, N16 (0171 254 6516)

Based above a second-hand bookshop, this is the place to see the leading contemporary British players in jazz and free improvisation. Food is available and jazz is played every evening and at lunch-time on Sunday.

🚊 Stoke Newington

🚌 67, 73, 106, 149, 276

No ♿

££

WEST

606 Club

90 Lots Road, Chelsea, SW10 (0171 352 5953)

Tucked away near Chelsea Harbour, this is a popular jazz venue. Enter by a discreet door and go down into the basement where you can eat and drink while listening to a wide range of jazz every night. If you visit here regularly, you will save money on your bills if you become a member. There is no entrance charge to non-members but a cover charge is added to the bill.

⊖ Sloane Square, then bus

🚌 C3, 11, 22

No ♿

££

Bulls Head

373 Longsdale Road, Barnes, SW13 (0181 876 5241)

A centre for be-bop and mainstream jazz, the Bulls Head is the oldest pub in Barnes, dating back to 1684. International jazz performers play here alongside home-grown talent. There is an informal and friendly environment, pub prices and good food in the adjoining Stable restaurant. Jazz is performed every evening and also at lunch-time on Sunday.

🚊 Barnes Bridge

🚌 9, 9A

♿

£

Other Venues

See also the following venues, which host jazz as part of their mixed programmes:

100 Club (page 148);

Barbican Centre (Page 140);

Battersea Arts Centre (page 128);

ICA (page 147);

The Mean Fiddler (page 151);

The Old Bull Arts Centre (page 127);

Royal Festival Hall, Queen Elizabeth Hall and Purcell Room (page 142)

Waterman's Arts Centre (page 133)

CENTRAL

100 Club

100 Oxford Street, W1 (0171 636 0933)
Jazz and R&B are the mainstay of this venue. There is a fast-food menu and music is played every night from 7.30 p.m. onwards.
⊖ Tottenham Court Road
🚌 7, 8, 10, 25, 55, 73
No ♿
££

Astoria

157 Charing Cross Road, WC2
(0171 434 0403)
Along with its sister venue, the LA2 (see page 149), the Astoria is a major club and music venue. Concerts take place at 8.00 p.m.
⊖ Tottenham Court Road
🚌 14, 19, 24, 29, 38, 176
No ♿
££

Black Horse

6 Rathbone Place, W1 (0171 580 0666)
Modern jazz, R&B and soul are performed in this intimate pub venue every night from 8.30 p.m. onwards.
⊖ Tottenham Court Road
🚌 7, 8, 10, 25, 55, 73
Limited ♿
££

Borderline

Orange Yard, off Manette Street, W1 (0171 734 2095)
It is advisable to book tickets to see Indie and British pop bands here seven nights a week. The bands play from 8.30 p.m. to 11.00 p.m. and the disco takes over from 11.30 p.m. until 3.00 a.m.
⊖ Tottenham Court Road
🚌 14, 19, 24, 29, 38, 176
♿
££

Break for the Border

Goslett Yard, 127 Charing Cross Road, WC2 (0171 437 8595)
A range of pop music, including classic covers from the 1960s to the 1990s, is

played here from Thursday to Saturday, 8.30 p.m.–3.00 a.m. Food is available.

⊖ Tottenham Court Road

🚌 14, 19, 24, 29, 38, 176

♿

£

Dover Street Wine Bar

8–9 Dover Street, W1 (0171 629 9813)

A popular drinking hole and restaurant, the Dover Street Wine Bar offers a mix of jazz, soul and rhythm every night from 8.00 p.m. onwards.

⊖ Green Park

🚌 8, 9, 14, 19, 22, 38

No ♿

££

LA2 (London Astoria Two)

161 Charing Cross Road, WC2 (0171 434 0403)

A major live music venue and club in the West End and sister to the Astoria (see page 148). Bands play from 11.00 p.m.

⊖ Tottenham Court Road

🚌 14, 19, 24, 29, 38, 176

Limited ♿ (phone in advance)

££

Marquee

105 Charing Cross Road, WC2 (0171 437 6603)

The original Marquee was in Wardour Street (on the site where the restaurant Mezzo now stands). Today's Marquee is still a prime venue, attracting many top bands. Doors open at 8.00 p.m.

⊖ Leicester Square, Tottenham Court Road

🚌 14, 19, 24, 29, 38, 176

Limited ♿ (phone in advance)

££

Rock Garden

The Piazza, Covent Garden, WC2 (0171 240 3961)

In the centre of Covent Garden, the Rock Garden plays Indie on Wednesdays, rock and blues on Thursdays and presents a band showcase on Mondays. Bands usually start playing at 9.00 p.m.

⊖ Covent Garden

🚌 14, 19, 24, 29, 38, 176

♿

£

Twelve Bar Club

22 Denmark Place, Denmark Street, WC2 (0171 916 6989)

A popular folk venue, the Twelve Bar Club plays live music seven nights a week. The shows start at 8.30 p.m. Fast food is available.

⊖ Tottenham Court Road

🚌 14, 19, 24, 29, 38, 176

No &

£

EAST

Filthy MacNasty's & the Whiskey Café

68 Amwell Street, EC1 (0171 837 6067)

A great Irish pub, here you will find a lively mix of traditional and new Irish music, as well as regular jamming sessions (from 8.30 p.m. onwards).

⊖ Angel, King's Cross

🚌 19, 30, 38, 73, 171A, 214

No &

£

NORTH

Bull & Gate

389 Kentish Town Road, NW5 (0171 485 5358)

Indie rock and alternative jazz funk are on the menu at this pub seven nights a week from 9.00 p.m. to midnight. Food is not available.

⊖/🚆 Kentish Town

🚌 C2, 134, 135, 214

No &

£

Camden Palace

1a Camden High Street, NW1 (0171 387 0428)

This attractive old theatre makes a good venue for live rock and Indie music several nights a week (from 8.30 p.m. onwards). Fast food is available.

⊖ Camden Town

🚌 24, 27, 29, 134, 135, 168

&

££

Dublin Castle

94 Parkway, Camden Town, NW1 (0171 485 1773)

Indie and alternative pop music are played here live every Monday, while, on Friday, there is Rockabilly and Ska from 9.00 p.m. to midnight.

⊖ Camden Town

🚌 C2, 24, 27, 29, 134, 135, 168, 274

No &

£

Mean Fiddler

28a High Street, Harlesden, NW10 (0181 961 5490; 0171 344 0044: credit card booking)
Rock, Indie, blues and solo acts all play at this established club. The Mean Fiddler is the flagship club of the Mean Fiddler group, the largest group in London (see also The Grand, below, and the Shepherd's Bush Empire, page 153). Doors open at 8.00 p.m.
⊖/🚇 Willesden Junction
🚌 PR1, 18, 220, 226, 260
♿
££

Wembley Arena

Empire Way, Wembley, Middlesex (0181 900 1234)
A famous venue, with excellent acoustics, this is one of the best places in town to see the top national and international bands. Doors usually open at 7.30 p.m.
⊖ Wembley Central, Wembley Park
🚇 Wembley Central
🚌 PR2, 18, 83, 92, 182, 204, 297
♿
££

Wembley Stadium

Empire Way, Wembley, Middlesex (0181 902 8833; 0181 900 1234: box office)
This massive outdoor venue is a great place to see bands – so long as it's not raining! Some historic concerts have taken place here, perhaps the best known being the Live Aid Concert in 1985. Doors usually open at 7.30 p.m.
⊖ Wembley Central, Wembley Park
🚇 Wembley Central
🚌 PR2, 18, 83, 92, 182, 204, 297
♿
££

SOUTH

Brixton Academy

211 Stockwell Road, Brixton, SW9 (0171 924 9999)
A popular venue in south London, the Brixton Academy attracts many major bands. It is advisable to book and food is available (mainly sandwiches and pizzas). Concerts usually begin at 8.00 p.m.
⊖/🚇 Brixton
🚌 2, 3, 109, 133, 322, 345
Limited ♿ (phone in advance)
££

The Grand

1 St John's Hill, Battersea, SW11 (0171 738 9000)
Part of the Mean Fiddler group of clubs (see also The Mean Fiddler, Harlesden, above, and the Shepherd's Bush Empire, page 153), the Grand is a popular spot

with a good selection of live bands each week and a night club afterwards. The bands usually start at 8.30 p.m.

🚇 Clapham Junction

🚌 37, 39, 77A, 156, 170, 219

No ♿

££

Half Moon, Putney

93 Lower Richmond Road, Putney, SW15 (0181 780 9383)

An established venue with many popular bands, there are regular performances of blues, rock and country music here. Doors open at 7.30 p.m.

⊖ Putney Bridge

🚇 Putney

🚌 14, 22, 39, 74, 85, 93, 265, 270

♿

££

<hr/>

WEST

Bottom Line

Shepherd's Bush Green, W12 (0181 740 1304)

Blues, rock and Indie bands play here seven nights a week (from 8.30 p.m. onwards), also lunch-times on Sunday. It is best to book when a big name is playing. Food is available.

⊖ Shepherd's Bush

🚌 49, 95, 207, 237, 260, 283

♿

££

Labatt's Apollo

Queen Caroline Street, Hammersmith, W6 (0171 416 6080)

A venue for top artists; ticket prices vary depending on the act. Always book in advance. Concerts generally start at 8.00 p.m. (See also page 132)

⊖ Hammersmith

🚌 9, 10, 33, 211, 266, 267

♿

£–££

King's Head

4 Fulham High Street, SW6 (0171 736 1413)

Indie, rock and blues are all played live here in this dark, moody pub. Three bands play each night, apart from Sunday, when there are only two. Doors open at 8.30 p.m.

⊖ Putney Bridge

🚌 22, 39, 85, 93, 265, 270

♿

£

Orange

3 North End Crescent, North End Road, West Kensington, W14 (0171 371 4317)
On some nights up to four bands play in this converted snooker hall. From
Tuesday to Thursday, there is Indie, rock and pop, while on Friday and Saturday,
you will find jazz funk. There is a songwriters' night each Monday evening too.
Doors open at 7.30 p.m.
⊖ West Kensington
🚌 28, 391
No ♿
££

Shepherd's Bush Empire

Shepherd's Bush Green, W12, (0181 740 7474)
Another in the Mean Fiddler chain (see The Grand and The Mean Fiddler, page
151), the Empire is a venue for rock, Indie and some established artists. Doors
open at 7.30 p.m.
⊖ Shepherd's Bush
🚌 49, 95, 207, 237, 260, 283
Limited ♿ (phone in advance)
££

Tiffin

541a King's Road, Chelsea, SW6 (0171 610 6117)
This is one of the few places where you can hear Indian jazz. Massala Jazz, the in-
house band, plays each Sunday from 9.00 p.m. to 11.00 p.m. Tiffin also serves
excellent Anglo-Indian food.
⊖ Fulham Broadway
🚌 11, 22
♿
££

❖

7
BALLET, DANCE
AND OPERA

BALLET AND DANCE

LONDON HAS A lively tradition of ballet and dance ranging from performances of such favourite traditional ballets as 'Swan Lake' and 'Sleeping Beauty' to contemporary, Asian and African dance. The Royal Ballet Company is based at the Royal Opera House and performs all year round. As well as their dazzling home-grown dancers, guest artists from overseas also perform with the company.

Another popular ballet company is the English National Ballet which is based at the London Coliseum during the summer months and also has a Christmas season at the Royal Festival Hall, performing popular family ballets, including 'The Nutcracker' and 'Giselle'. The English National Ballet developed from the gala performances of ballet in London in 1949. The Polish-born impresario Julian Braunsweg recognized the appeal of these performances and proposed that the London season should be followed with regional tours.

Contemporary and world dance can be seen in dozens of venues across London. Among the best-known new dance companies that perform here and elsewhere is Dance Umbrella. Its programmes are always filled with premieres of the work by the best young British choreographers as well as productions by companies from around the world. In association with *Time Out* magazine, Dance Umbrella also sponsor the annual London Dance and Performance Awards for the best in new dance and performance.

The best venues to see ballet and dance in the capital are featured below, with information on the major ballet and dance companies that perform there.

MAJOR DANCE VENUES

ICA
Nash House, The Mall, SW1 (0171 930 3647;
0171 930 0493: membership enquiries)
See also pages 25, 125 and 147
A wide range of contemporary dance and performance art (a mix of movement, music, text and design) is performed here, as well as theatre, talks and exhibitions.
⊖ Charing Cross, Piccadilly Circus
🚇 Charing Cross
🚌 11, 12, 15, 22, 109, 176
♿
£–££

For London Spectacle
⊖ London Transport

London Coliseum

St Martin's Lane, WC2 (0171 632 8300: box office;
0171 240 5258: credit card booking)

Home to the English National Opera (see page 162) and the English National Ballet during the summer, the theatre is used by overseas touring companies too.

⊖ Charing Cross, Embankment
▣ Charing Cross
🚌 24, 29, 68, 91, 168, 176
♿
££

The Place

17 Duke's Road, WC1 (0171 387 0031)

The Place is a busy multi-arts centre with the emphasis on dance. Independent companies are based here and is also the home of the London Contemporary Dance School and the Academy of Indian Dance. The theatre presents work by independent companies.

⊖/▣ Euston
🚌 10, 30, 73, 91
No ♿
£–££

Queen Elizabeth Hall

South Bank Centre, SE1 (0171 960 4242)
See also page 155

About 800 events are held at the Queen Elizabeth Hall each year, including dance, mime, small orchestral and chamber music recitals, music, theatrical and film performances.

⊖/▣ Waterloo
🚌 26, 68, 168, 171, 171A, 188
♿
££

Royal Festival Hall

South Bank Centre, SE1 (0171 960 4242)
See also page 142

Dance performances are held here throughout the year. Highlights include such Christmas favourites as 'The Sleeping Beauty' and 'The Nutcracker'. Leading overseas ballet companies can be seen here.

⊖/▣ Waterloo
🚌 26, 68, 168, 171, 171A, 188
♿
££

Overleaf: *Royal Festival Hall*

❖

Royal Opera House

Bow Street, WC2 (0171 304 4000)
See also page 163

The company was created by Dame Ninette de Valois, dancer, choreographer and entrepreneur, who assembled a small company and school, the Vic-Wells Ballet, and in 1931 persuaded Lilian Baylis to provide it with a home at the Sadler's Wells theatre in Islington. After the Second World War, the company, by then called the Sadler's Wells Ballet, with its new star Margot Fonteyn, had moved to the Royal Opera House. In 1956, to mark its twenty-fifth anniversary, the name 'The Royal Ballet' was granted to the company by royal charter.

The Royal Ballet is Britain's largest and most prestigious ballet company. Led by its Director, Anthony Dowell, its principals include Darcey Bussell. The wide-ranging repertory embraces all the great three-act classical ballets, including 'Swan Lake', 'The Sleeping Beauty' and 'The Nutcracker', for example, together with works by the company's founder choreographer, Sir Frederick Ashton, principal choreographer Kenneth MacMillan, choreographers from the company and guest choreographers from abroad. Ballet is performed throughout the year, alternating with opera.

⊖ Covent Garden
🚌 4, 6, 9, 11, 13, 15, 23, 26, 76
♿
££

Royal Opera House

Sadler's Wells Theatre

Rosebery Avenue, EC1 (0171 713 6000 and 0171 278 8916)

A diverse variety of dance is performed at this theatre, which has an international reputation for presenting some of the finest dance from around the world.

⊖ Angel

🚌 19, 38, 171A

♿

££

Sadler's Wells

There has been a theatre at Sadler's Wells since the 1680s when a Mr Sadler built a 'Musick-House' to provide entertainment for the crowds that came to bathe in the healing waters of the well in his house. By 1744, the theatre offered pantomime and harlequinade. In the early nineteenth century huge water tanks were installed above and under the stage and Sadler's Wells became the home of 'nautical drama' and spectacular aqua theatre. The theatre blossomed under the manager Samuel Phelps during the mid-nineteenth century and after his departure it suffered a steady decline. The building was made into a skating rink, then a prize-fight arena before being restored to a theatre in 1878. In 1883 Sadler's Wells became a music-hall arena and later a cinema. In 1927 the old building was demolished and a new theatre built on the site, which still stands today.

LOCAL VENUES

EAST

Broadgate Arena

Corner of Liverpool Street and Eldon Street, EC2 (0171 588 6565: recorded information)

See page 184

⊖/🚆 Liverpool Street

🚌 11, 42, 100, 133, 214

♿

Free

Chisenhale Dance Space

64–84 Chisenhale Road, Hackney, E3 (0181 981 6617)

Chisenhale Dance Space has supported new and experimental dance work for over a decade. Its programme includes performances, workshops, classes for children and adults, residencies and commissions.

⊖ Mile End, then bus

🚌 277

No ♿

£–££

Hackney Empire

291 Mare Street, E8 (0181 985 2424)

See also pages 126 and 164

This theatre provides a venue for traditional variety, new variety, comedy, music, dance, theatre shows, musicals and shows for children.

⊖ Bethnal Green, then bus

▣ Hackney Central, London Fields

🚌 48, 55, 106

♿

£–££

Lilian Baylis Theatre

Arlington Way, Rosebery Avenue, EC1 (0171 713 6000)

A small studio dance theatre attached to Sadler's Wells Theatre (see page 159). South Asian dance, ballet and contemporary dance are performed here.

⊖ Angel

🚌 38, 56, 73, 171A

♿

£–££

<u>NORTH</u>

Old Bull Arts Centre

68 High Street, Barnet, Herts (0181 449 0048)

See also page 127

The Old Bull Arts Centre offers a packed programme of top-quality touring theatre, dance, cabaret and music, including premiers of new work.

⊖ High Barnet

▣ New Barnet

🚌 34, 84, 84A, 107, 234, 263

♿

£–££

<u>SOUTH</u>

Ashcroft Theatre

Fairfield Hall, Park Lane, Croydon, Surrey (0181 688 9291)

See also page 128

Touring dance companies perform in this theatre as well as other performing arts companies.

▣ East Croydon

🚌 50, 60, 197, 204, 250, 392

♿

££

Club Azul

Cage Theatre, The Landor, Landor Road, Clapham, SW4
(0171 358 1140: information)
A weekly club featuring the finest in flamenco, dance, music and song.
⊖ Clapham North
🚌 P5, 88, 155, 345
Limited ♿
£–££

Lewisham Studio Theatre

Rushey Green, SE6 (0181 690 0002)
A variety of dance, from ballet to Irish jigs, is performed here.
🚉 Catford Bridge
🚌 47, 54, 75, 136, 185, 199
Limited ♿
£–££

WEST

Riverside Studios

Crisp Road, Hammersmith, W6
(0181 741 2255)
The Riverside has an established reputation for introducing British audiences to new and established dancers, actors, writers, directors and musicians from all over the world.
⊖ Hammersmith
🚌 33, 72, 190, 211, 220, 295
♿
£–££

OPERA

The Royal Opera House is the focus of operatic activity in London. Home to the Royal Opera Company, it stages several productions each year, often featuring such celebrity guest stars as Luciano Pavarotti and Placido Domingo. The London Coliseum performs top-quality opera too, with the English National Opera, while smaller theatres across London stage occasional operas.

Opera is perhaps best suited to large-scale spectaculars and among the most popular recent events have been occasional open-air performances by leading singers. On a smaller scale, but just as enjoyable, are the regular annual outdoor opera performances held at Kenwood, Marble Hill and Holland Park (see pages 186, 187 and 188).

London Coliseum

St Martin's Lane, WC2 (0171 632 8300: box office; 0171 240 5258: credit card booking; 0171 836 7666: recorded information)

See also page 155

The London Coliseum is home to the English National Opera. This opera company began as a semi-professional team of singers who performed at the Old Vic Theatre in the late nineteenth century under the direction of social reformer Lilian Baylis. By the 1920s, Lilian Baylis's Old Vic theatre had moved to Sadler's Wells Theatre in Islington and in the mid-1930s an opera company was established that remained here until 1968.

At Sadler's Wells, the musical standards improved enormously with a professional chorus and eventually a permanent orchestra. The company moved to the Coliseum in 1968, prompted by the long-delayed and last-minute rejection of a proposal to build a National Opera House on the South Bank, next to the National Theatre.

The opera season runs through the winter months. A broad programme of opera is performed and always sung in English. Although this upsets some purist opera enthusiasts, it is very popular with most people.

⊖ Charing Cross, Embankment

▣ Charing Cross

🚌 24, 29, 68, 91, 168, 176

♿

London Coliseum

Royal Opera House

Bow Street, WC2 (0171 304 4000)

See also page 158

The company known today as the Royal Opera was created after the Second World War. Previous to it lies a tradition of operatic performance dating back more than 260 years at its home in Covent Garden. In each of the three theatres on this site since 1732, opera has played an important role.

The present theatre was built in 1858. During the Second World War it was used as a dance hall, but after the war the idea of public subsidy of the arts was accepted and the decision was made to establish the Royal Opera House as the permanent year-round home of the opera and ballet companies now known as the Royal Opera and the Royal Ballet.

The opera season runs from August to May, with performances alternated with ballets (see page 158). The price of tickets can be exorbitant, which often leads to critics claiming the ROH is an elitist establishment. However, it has to be remembered that the ROH is able to attract all the world's leading opera singers and stages some of the most stunning and memorable productions in the world. A less expensive way of enjoying opera here is to come to the prom season, held annually, when seats are removed from the stalls and places sold cheaply.

During the summer the Royal Opera House, in association with Midland Bank, occasionally relays performances direct from the stage of the Royal Opera House to an outdoor audience via a big screen in Covent Garden Piazza.

⊖ Covent Garden

🚌 4, 6, 9, 11, 13, 15, 23, 26, 76

♿

Temporary Closure of the Royal Opera House

The Royal Opera and the Royal Ballet are to move temporarily to the new, purpose-built Tower Bridge Theatre in Southwark for two years from autumn 1997, while the Royal Opera House is restored and renovated.

EAST

Hackney Empire
291 Mare Street, Hackney, E8 (0181 985 2424)
See also page 160
Opera is occasionally performed here.
⊖ Bethnal Green, then bus
🚆 Hackney Central
🚌 D6, 48, 55, 106, 253
♿

NORTH

Almeida Theatre
Almeida Street, Islington, N1 (0171 359 4404)
See also page 126
The Almeida holds a popular opera season each summer that often includes premieres of new operas.
⊖ Angel, Highbury & Islington
🚆 Highbury & Islington
🚌 4, 19, 30, 43
Limited ♿

SOUTH

Young Vic Theatre
66 The Cut, Waterloo, SE1 (0171 928 6363)
See also page 131
Some opera is performed here, alongside drama.
⊖/🚆 Waterloo
🚌 45, 63, 68, 168, 171, 176, 188
♿

8
CINEMA

MOST OF THE cinemas in the West End are owned by a handful of international companies and generally show the latest blockbusters. Leicester Square lies at the heart of London's movie kingdom, with five top cinemas: the MGM, the Empire, two Odeons and the Warner West End. These cinemas are often the venues for celebrity and royal premieres, where the stars of the latest film come to rub shoulders with their famous friends.

Alternatively, if you are interested in art-house, off-beat or foreign-language movies, there are plenty of places to see them in London too, from the ICA in the Mall to the Ritzy Cinema in Brixton. Serious movie buffs will enjoy the regular seasons of films at the National Film Theatre and the Barbican, and the highlight of the year is the London Film Festival in November.

Although the price of cinema tickets has soared in recent years, it is still possible to find bargains. Many cinemas have special discounts on Monday evenings and for films shown before 6.00 p.m., and most cinemas have two levels of tickets.

Cinema programmes generally change every one to three weeks – keep an eye out in the *Evening Standard* or *Time Out* and other listings magazines for new openings.

Popcorn, Coke and ice-cream are essential parts of the movie-going experience. All cinemas have a selection of refreshments, but at some repertory cinemas you are more likely to find a wider selection of more substantial snacks, like coffee and carrot cake.

Film Classifications

18: Films for adults only (no one under eighteen admitted)

15: Films for anyone aged fifteen or over

12: Films for anyone aged twelve or over

PG (parental guidance): Films for general exhibition, but parents are advised that the film may include material not suitable for young children

U: Films for general exhibition

CURRENT RELEASES

Empire

Leicester Square, WC1 (0171 437 1234)

A great place to see the latest blockbuster, even if it will cost you more than at most cinemas. Three screens.

⊖ Leicester Square

🚌 24, 29, 176

♿

£–££

MGM Cinemas

As well as being a mega movie maker, MGM owns a large chain of cinemas in the United Kingdom. With one exception they all show a selection of the latest releases – the largest of the London group is in the Trocadero, which has seven screens. The exception is the MGM Swiss Centre (see page 170), which shows 'art' and foreign films.

The telephone numbers given for the following MGM cinemas are all recorded information lines.

Baker Street Station, NW1 (0171 935 9772);
two screens; ⊖ Baker Street; 🚌 2, 13, 30, 74, 82, 113; no ♿; *£–££*

142 Fulham Road, SW10 (0171 370 0265);
five screens; ⊖ South Kensington; 🚌 14, 345; no ♿; *£–££*

63 Haymarket, SW1 (0171 839 1527);
three screens; ⊖ Charing Cross; 🚌 3, 12, 14, 19, 53, 88; no ♿; *£–££*

279 King's Road, SW3 (0171 352 5096);
four screens; ⊖ Sloane Square; 🚌 11, 19, 22, 211; no ♿; *£–££*

Panton Street SW1, (0171 930 0631);
two screens; ⊖ Piccadilly Circus; 🚌 3, 12, 14, 19, 53, 88; ♿; *£–££*

Piccadilly Circus, W1 (0171 437 3561);
two screens; ⊖ Piccadilly Circus; 🚌 3, 12, 14, 19, 53, 88; no ♿; *£–££*

135 Shaftesbury Avenue, WC2 (0171 836 6279);
two screens; ⊖ Leicester Square, Tottenham Court Road;
🚌 14, 19, 24, 29, 38, 176; no ♿; *£–££*

30 Tottenham Court Road, W1 (0171 636 6148);
three screens; ⊖ Goodge Street, Tottenham Court Road;
🚌 10, 24, 29, 73, 134; no ♿; *£–££*

Trocadero, Coventry Street, W1 (0171 434 0031);
seven screens; ⊖ Piccadilly Circus; 🚌 3, 12, 14, 19, 53, 88; ♿; *£–££*

Odeon Cinemas

The flagship Odeon in London is the Leicester Square and Mezzanine. The other Odeon in Leicester Square is called the Odeon West End. All five Odeons show the latest blockbusters.

The telephone numbers given for the following Odeon cinemas are all recorded information lines.

48 Haymarket, SW1 (01426 915353);
>one screen; ⊖ Piccadilly Circus; ⊞ 3, 12, 14, 19, 53, 88; ♿; £–££

Kensington High Street, W8 (01426 914666);
>six screens; ⊖ High Street Kensington; ⊞ 9, 10, 27, 28, 49; no ♿; £–££

Leicester Square, WC2 (01426 915683);
>main screen plus five screens in the adjacent Mezzanine;
>⊖ Leicester Square; ⊞ 24, 29, 176; no ♿; £–££

Marble Arch, W2 (01426 914501);
>one screen; ⊖ Marble Arch; ⊞ 2, 7, 10, 15, 16, 36; no ♿; £–££

West End, Leicester Square, WC2 (01426 915574);
>two screens; ⊖ Leicester Square; ⊞ 24, 29, 176; no ♿; £–££

Plaza

Lower Regent Street, SW1 (0171 437 1234)

This is the cinema where you will get to see blockbusters after they have stopped being new releases, so if you missed something good when it first came out, check to see if it is on here. Four screens.

⊖ Piccadilly Circus
⊞ 3, 12, 14, 19, 53, 88
No ♿
£–££

UCI Whiteleys

Queensway, W2 (0171 792 3332: information)

Among the many attractions of UCI Whiteleys is that its popcorn was voted the best in London, according to a survey carried out by *Time Out* magazine. On top of that, the seats are comfortable and with eight screens, you are sure of finding a film you want to see. The cinema complex is situated in a shopping centre which has numerous snack bars serving all types of food.

⊖ Bayswater, Queensway, Royal Oak
▣ Royal Oak
⊞ 7, 23, 27
No ♿
£–££

Whiteleys Shopping Centre
Over 60 shops, 13 restaurants and 8 cinemas
Open every day 'til midnight, shops open until 8 pm (except Sundays)
Nearest stations: Bayswater and Queensway

Warner West End

Leicester Square, WC2 (0171 437 4347)

The largest cinema in London with nine screens, Warner's is one of the giants in Leicester Square. Always busy, it screens the latest hits – tickets are expensive but worth the money for the experience.

⊖ Leicester Square
⊞ 24, 29, 176
No ♿
£–££

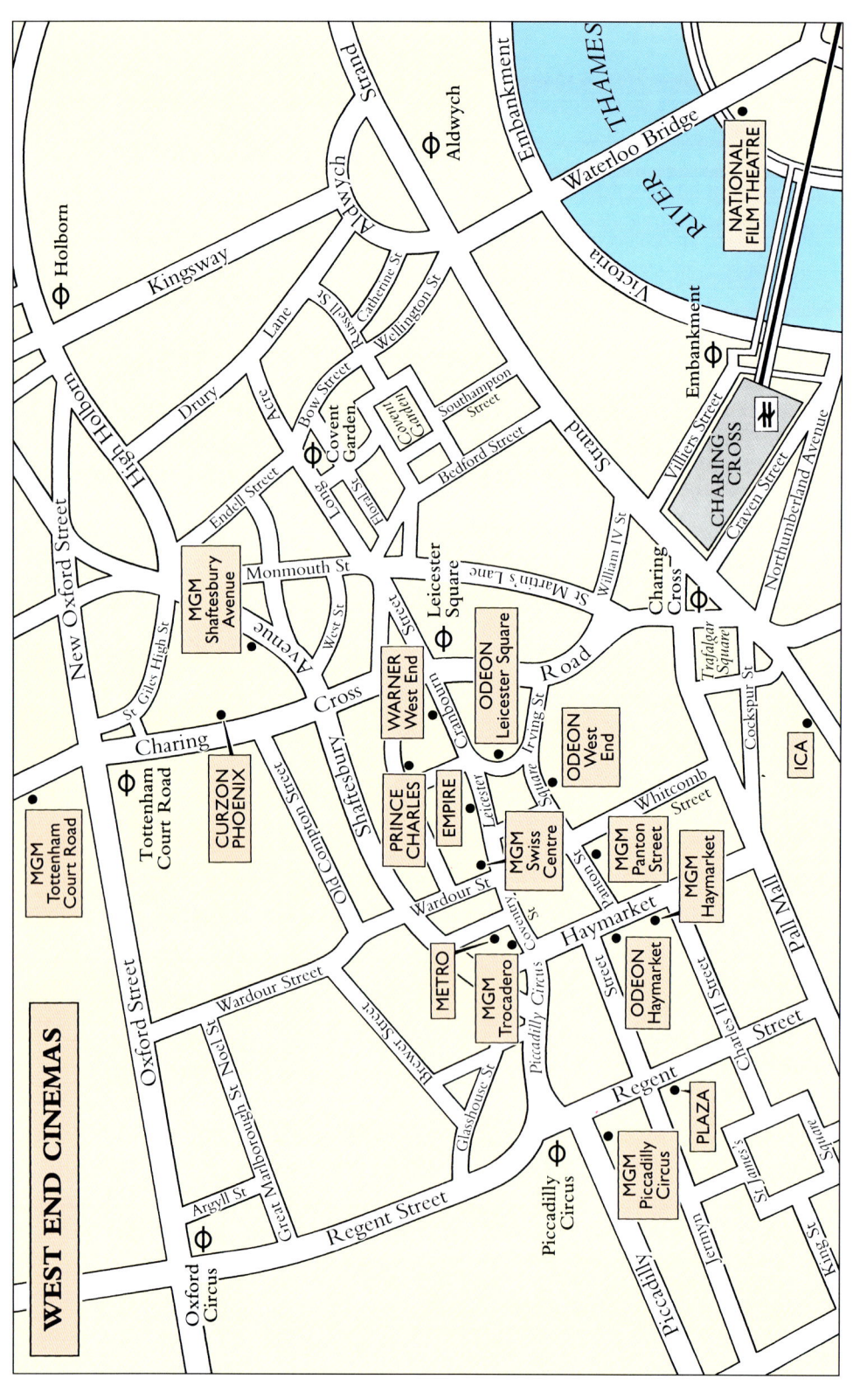

REPERTORY CINEMAS

Many of these cinemas show first-run films, as well as 'art' or foreign movies. They have been grouped alphabetically within geographical areas.

CENTRAL

Curzon Cinemas

Smart (and generally quite expensive), the three Curzon cinemas show the most popular 'art' films – from the latest Merchant Ivory offering to more obscure foreign movies. The same film is often featured over a long period (up to six weeks).

You will find Curzon cinemas at:

Curzon Mayfair, Curzon Street, W1 (0171 465 8865);
one screen; ✪ Green Park; 🚌 2, 10, 16, 36, 73, 74; no ♿; £–££
Curzon Phoenix, 110 Charing Cross Road, WC2 (0171 240 9661);
one screen; ✪ Leicester Square; 🚌 14, 19, 24, 29, 38, 176; no ♿; £–££
93 Shaftesbury Avenue, W1 (0171 369 1722);
one screen; ✪ Piccadilly Circus; 🚌 24, 29, 176; no ♿; £–££

ICA Cinema

Nash House, The Mall, SW1 (0171 930 3647; 0171 930 0493: membership enquiries)
See also pages 25, 125, 147 and 154

In common with its live art performances and visual art, it has to be said that the films shown at the ICA are rather eclectic. Foreign films feature strongly and there are often short seasons celebrating the work of a particular director. The cinematheque shows experimental films and classics. There is a restaurant/café serving tasty food (including vegetarian) for pre- or post-cinema snacks. One screen. Day and annual membership available.

✪ Charing Cross, Piccadilly Circus
🚇 Charing Cross
🚌 9, 14, 19, 22, 29
£–££ (concessions for members)

Lumiere

St Martin's Lane, WC2 (0171 836 0691)
One of the most centrally located cinemas where you can see 'art' films, the Lumiere always shows the latest releases of this genre. One screen.
✪ Leicester Square
🚌 24, 29, 176
No ♿
£–££

Metro

Rupert Street, W1 (0171 437 0757)

Since its refurbishment, the Metro has a smart exterior to tempt you in. The two screens are in the basement and show current 'art' films.

⊖ Piccadilly Circus

🚌 3, 6, 12, 14, 19, 38

No ♿

£–££

MGM Swiss Centre

Leicester Square, WC2 (0171 439 4470)

The entrance to the cinema is a little hard to find – you need to go round the side of the building in Wardour Street and then take a lift to the top floor. The cinema specializes in foreign films old and new. If you don't want to roam far afterwards for something to eat, you could do worse than go to the Swiss Centre's Marché Mövenpick, a rather good, Swiss-style self-service restaurant.

⊖ Leicester Square, Piccadilly Circus

🚌 24, 29, 176

No ♿

£–££

Minema

45 Knightsbridge, SW1 (0171 369 1723)

The problem with the Minema is that the seats are so comfortable there is a danger of falling asleep while watching a film! A small, expensive cinema in the heart of Knightsbridge, the Minema also has an excellent café selling delicious snacks and drinks, including wine. A particularly good deal is a meal and ticket for a film at a special price. One screen.

⊖ Hyde Park Corner

🚌 9, 10, 14, 19, 22, 52

No ♿

£–££

Prince Charles

Leicester Place, WC2 (0171 437 8181)

You do not have to be a member but by joining and paying a small annual fee, you will receive regular monthly programmes of forthcoming screenings, so you can plan what to see in advance. Perfect for the really serious movie-goer (ideally with plenty of free time), each week the Prince Charles shows between four and five movies in various slots from matinées to late evening, all at very reasonable prices. Two screens.

⊖ Leicester Square

🚌 24, 29, 176

No ♿

£ (with concessions for members)

Renoir Cinema

Renoir

Brunswick Square, WC1 (0171 837 8402)

Located close to London University, this cinema is particularly popular with students living nearby. It is part of a rather unattractive modern housing complex and shopping centre, but do not be put off; you will find some good vintage and modern foreign and 'art' films here. Two screens.

⊖ Russell Square

🚌 68, 91, 168, 188

No ♿

£–££

EAST

Barbican Cinemas

Barbican Centre, Silk Street, EC2 (0171 638 8891: box office)

Barbican Cinemas 1 and 2 present a diverse programme that successfully combines mainstream quality general releases with imaginative and varied specialist seasons devoted either to a particular theme, or to the work of a director, actor or country. The cinemas also present occasional talks, interviews and discussions with film and video clips, as well as silent films with live musical accompaniment.

⊖ Barbican, Moorgate

🚌 4, 56

♿

£–££

Museum of London

London Wall, EC2 (0171 600 3699; 0171 600 0807: recorded information)
See also page 65

Shown under the title 'Made in London' are documentaries about London and films made in London. Many of the films are connected with current exhibitions on view in the museum itself. Films are shown regularly, sometimes with two screenings a day.

⊖ Bank, Barbican, St Paul's

🚊 City Thameslink, Liverpool Street, Moorgate

🚌 56

♿

£ (in addition to admission charge)

Rio Dalston

107 Kingsland High Street, Dalston, E8 (0171 254 6677)

A popular community cinema, the Rio features a mix of blockbusters and 'art' films. There is a double bill late on Saturday afternoons, Saturday nights, and Sunday evenings of work by independent film makers (some of whom live locally). Once a month there is a classic midweek matinée.

🚊 Dalston Kingsland

🚌 67, 149

No ♿

£

NORTH

Everyman Cinema

Holly Bush Vale, Hampstead, NW3 (0171 435 1525)

A longtime favourite repertory cinema, this cinema shows a range of new and classic 'art' and foreign films. There is a cofee bar which serves homemade cakes, including carrot and banana, and a variety of ice-creams and soft drinks. One screen. Season tickets available.

⊖ Hampstead

🚌 46, 268

No ♿

£–££

MGM Hampstead

Pond Street, NW3 (0171 794 6603)

This cinema is popular with off-duty staff from the nearby Royal Free Hospital. Three screens.

⊖ Belsize Park

🚊 Hampstead Heath

🚌 C11, 24, 46, 168

♿

£–££

Phoenix Cinema

High Road, Finchley, N2 (0181 883 2233)
A good range of classic 'art' and foreign films are screened here, as well as selected current releases.
θ East Finchley
🚌 263
No ♿
£

SOUTH

Clapham Picture House

76 Venn Street, Clapham, SW4 (0171 498 2242)
A small, intimate cinema, the Clapham Picture House shows classic and contemporary 'art' films, changing the programme on a weekly basis. One screen.
θ Clapham Common
🚌 3, 4, 5, 35, 37, 137A
No ♿
£–££

Imperial War Museum

Lambeth Road, SE1 (0171 416 5000)
See also page 61
The museum has been collecting and preserving films for the past seventy-five years. A selection of film from the archive is regularly presented and ranges from documentaries to feature films. Often the films will be linked by a theme relating to a current exhibition.
θ Elephant & Castle, Lambeth North
🚌 12, 45, 53, 63, 68, 168
♿ (please phone to give 48 hours' notice)
£ (films included in admission charge)

National Film Theatre

South Bank, SE1 (0171 928 3232: box office; 0171 633 0274: recorded information)
The National Film Theatre is part of the South Bank arts complex. A mecca for film buffs, this is the place to see new releases, classics, foreign and 'art' films. If you want to go regularly, it is a good idea to take out membership as this will give you a discount on ticket prices. Tickets cost much less than in the West End anyway.

Films are screened almost every day in the two cinemas, with a rolling programme that changes regularly. There is a good self-service restaurant in the same building, as well as a coffee bar and a popular late-licensed bar. Don't forget to visit the Museum of the Moving Image if you come here to see a film. It is just next door and is full of fascinating movie memorabilia (see page 71).
θ/🚇 Waterloo
🚌 26, 68, 168, 171, 171A, 176
♿
£–££

Ritzy

Brixton Road, SW2 (0171 737 2121)
Newly released blockbusters are featured alongside classic and new 'art' and foreign films.
⊖/▣ Brixton
🚌 3, 109, 33
No ♿
£–££

WEST

Chelsea Cinema

206 King's Road, SW3 (0171 351 3742)
The latest foreign and artistic films are on offer here, and refreshments include homemade cake. The cinema also sells a selection of videos of films it has shown. Treat yourself to a pullman seat for more space and a guaranteed good view at a couple of pounds extra. One screen.
⊖ Sloane Square
🚌 11, 19, 22, 211
No ♿
£–££

Coronet

Notting Hill Gate, W11 (0171 727 6705)
One of only two cinemas in London where you can smoke (in the back few rows of the grand circle only), the Coronet has an attractive Edwardian interior. The cinema shows the most popular current releases, but the downside if you are tall is that the seats do not provide much leg room. Also the sound quality is not very good. However, the interior is worth seeing in itself. One screen.
⊖ Notting Hill Gate
🚌 27, 28, 31, 52, 94, 302
No ♿
£–££

The Film-lover travels UNDERGROUND

Piccadilly, Oxford Circus, Leicester Square, Strand Stations

Gate Cinema

87 Notting Hill Gate, W11 (0171 727 4043)
Traditionally an 'art' house, the Gate Cinema is gradually becoming more mainstream. Inside, the cinema is a long, low-ceilinged room gaily decorated with swags and bunches of fruit. The drawback though is that as the seats are not raked, you do not see well from the back. One screen.
⊖ Notting Hill Gate
🚌 27, 28, 31, 52, 94, 302
No ♿
£–££

Institut Français

17 Queensbury Place, South Kensington, SW7 (0171 589 6211)

A selection of new and classic French films is shown here. Sometimes there are themed seasons and there may be a short talk before the film starts. There is an attractive bright and airy café selling food and drinks before the performances, which are usually in early evening. One screen, *petit salle*, videothique.

⊖ South Kensington

🚌 C1, 14, 49, 74, 345

No ♿

£–££

Richmond Filmhouse

3 Water Lane, Richmond, Surrey (0181 332 0030)

Tucked away down a narrow alley that leads to the river's edge, the only sign the Filmhouse exists is a small noticeboard listing current and forthcoming films. The cinema shows a programme of two or three films on alternate days, with a change around every couple of weeks. One screen.

⊖/🚆 Richmond

🚌 33, H22, H37, R68, 90, 290

No ♿

£–££

Riverside Studios

Crisp Road, Hammersmith, W6 (0181 741 2255)

Part of a theatre complex, repertory, recent releases and regular festivals all feature in the programme at the Riverside. Sometimes the films shown have a connection with the play currently being performed.

⊖ Hammersmith

🚌 33, 72, 190, 211, 220, 295

♿

£

Late-Night Cinema

If you are naturally nocturnal, then you may want to go to the cinema late at night. There is a good choice in London, particularly at weekends. Most chain cinemas will have a late-night viewing of the latest release, while repertory cinemas usually offer classic and cult films, sometimes as double bills.

The following cinemas have regular late shows:

Empire, Leicester Square; Gate Cinema, Notting Hill; MGM Piccadilly; MGM Trocadero; Notting Hill Coronet; Odeon Kensington High Street; Odeon Leicester Square; Odeon Marble Arch; Odeon Swiss Cottage; Odeon West End; Rio Cinema, Dalston; Screen on the Green, Islington; and Warner West End.

Screen on the . . . chain

These cinemas are all excellent repertory venues, showing a broad sweep of 'art' and foreign films with a smattering of new releases as well. They are also situated in areas not only well served by public transport but with a wide range of pubs and restaurants nearby.

Screen on Baker Street
96 Baker Street, W1 (0171 935 2772);
two screens; ⊖ Baker Street; 🚌 13, 82, 113, 274; no ♿ ; £–££

Screen on the Green
Upper Street, Islington, N1 (0171 226 3520);
one screen; ⊖ Angel; 🚌 4, 19, 30, 43, 73, 171A; ♿ ; £–££

Screen on the Hill
199 Haverstock Hill, NW3 (0171 435 3366);
one screen; ⊖ Belsize Park; 🚌 C11, 168; no ♿ ; £–££

CHILDREN'S CINEMA

New films for children are always released to coincide with half-terms and holidays, but many cinemas in London also screen both new and classic children's films at other times. Some cinemas have children's film clubs, which also hold competitions and events. Tickets for these films are usually reasonably inexpensive. Remember too that many West End cinemas have half-price tickets for under-fourteens.

Below is a selection of cinemas with the most to offer children.

Barbican Splodge Club
Barbican Centre, Silk Street, EC2 (0171 638 8891)
The Splodge is a multi-activity scheme for children to join in – events range from music and drama to Christmas concerts and shows. The Children's Cinema Club shows films on Saturday afternoon.
⊖ Barbican
🚌 4, 56
♿
£

Clapham Picture House
Venn Street, SW4 (0171 498 2242)
Children's films are shown at lunch-time on Saturday.
⊖ Clapham Common
🚌 60, 88, 137A
No ♿
£

MGM Hammersmith

King Street, W6 (0181 748 0557)

MGM Hammersmith has a Young Lion Kids Club that puts on films for children and accompanying adults each Saturday morning.

⊖ Hammersmith

🚌 27, 190, 267, 391

No ♿

£

MGM Putney

Putney High Street, SW15 (0181 788 3003)

The Young Lions Kids Club presents films for children every Saturday morning.

⊖ East Putney, Putney Bridge

🚌 14, 39, 74, 85, 93, 270

No ♿

£

National Film Theatre

South Bank, SE1 (0171 928 3232)

The National Film Theatre regularly puts on films for children, particularly during school holidays. Times and dates vary.

⊖/🚆 Waterloo

🚌 26, 68, 171, 171A, 188, 211

♿

£

Phoenix Cinema

High Road, Finchley, N2 (0181 883 2233)
The Saturday Kids Club shows a range of classic and new children's films every week.
⊖ East Finchley
🚌 263
No ♿
£

Rio Dalston

107 Kingsland High Street, Hackney, E8 (0171 249 2722)
On Saturday morning there is a popular children's feature presentation, organized as part of the cinema's Saturday Morning Picture Club scheme. If a child is very keen on the movies, it is worth joining the club (for a small membership fee). In return, there are generous incentives – for example, if you watch four films, the fifth is free.
🚆 Dalston Kingsland
🚌 67, 149
No ♿
£

Riverside Studios

Crisp Road, W6 (0181 741 2251)
Films for the discerning child are shown here on Saturday afternoons, with particular emphasis on foreign movies.
⊖ Hammersmith
🚌 33, 72, 190, 211, 220, 295
♿
£

Circus entertainment

If you want a more traditional laugh – and entertainment for the whole family – keep an eye out for the circus.

The circus comes to town regularly at such places as Richmond, Clapham and Streatham on spring and August bank holidays, but the best way to find out about forthcoming shows is to phone Circusline on 01522 681591.

If you can't wait until the Big Top comes to your neighbourhood, you can always go to a show by Circus Space. This avant-garde performance company comprises acrobats, trapeze artists, physical comics and other circus acts.

Circus Space

Coronet Street, Islington, N1 (0171 613 4141)

⊖ Old Street

🚌 55

♿

Performances: alternate Saturdays, 8.30 p.m.

£–££

9
COMEDY

COMEDY IS ON the way up as one of the most popular forms of live entertainment in London. New comedy clubs are springing up every year, while the established venues, such as the Comedy Store, have proved an important birthplace of many of today's established comics.

Many of the venues offer food and a packed evening of stand-up comedy. The improvisation evenings are good fun too.

CENTRAL

Chuckle Club
London School of Economics, Houghton Street, WC2 (0171 476 1672)
Mainstream stand-up comedy every night from 7.45 p.m. to 11.00 p.m. No food is available.
Θ Holborn
🚌 9, 68, 91, 168, 171, 188
♿
£–££

Comedy Store
Haymarket House, Oxendon Street, SW1
(01426 914433: recorded information)
Top-quality comedy six nights a week in a well-established venue.
Θ Piccadilly Circus
🚌 14, 19, 38
♿

Open: Tuesday–Sunday, doors open 6.30 p.m., show 8.00 p.m.; Friday and Saturday, doors open again 11.00 p.m., extra show 12 midnight
££

The Black Horse
6 Rathbone Place, W1 (0171 580 0666)
Resident comedians and guests perform here each Saturday from 8.30 p.m. onwards.
Θ Tottenham Court Road
🚌 7, 8, 10, 25, 55, 73
No ♿
£

Oranje Boom Boom

De Hems Dutch Coffee Bar, Macclesfield Street, W1 (0171 437 2494)

No, this isn't a venue for Dutch comedians, but you will be able to each Dutch food here, while you are entertained by British comedians at the regular Wednesday evening shows (from 8.00 p.m. onwards).

⊖ Leicester Square, Piccadilly Circus

🚌 14, 19, 38

♿

£

EAST

The Comedy Café

66 Rivington Street, EC2 (0171 739 5706)

New comedians perform here on Wednesday and Thursday, with professional comedians topping the bill on Friday and Saturday (from 8.00 p.m.). A selection of Tex-Mex food is available too.

⊖/🚇 Liverpool Street, then bus

🚌 22A, 22B, 26, 35, 47, 48

Limited ♿

££

NORTH

Bound & Gagged

The Fox, 413 Green Lanes, Haringey, N13 (0181 830 5233)

Alternative stand-up comedy is found here on Friday from 8.30 p.m. onwards. You need to be a member to enter (membership available on first visit).

🚇 Palmers Green and Southgate

🚌 W6, 329

No ♿

£–££

Downstairs at the King's Head

2 Crouch End Hill, N8 (0181 340 1028)

Alternative and mainstream comedy takes centre stage here each Saturday and Sunday evening from 7.45 p.m. onwards.

⊖/🚇 Finsbury Park

🚌 41, 91

No ♿

£–££

Jongleurs Camden

Middle Yard, Camden Lock, Chalk Farm Road, Camden Town, NW1 (0171 924 2248)

A sister venue to the Jongleurs comedy club in Battersea (see page 182), Jongleurs Camden offers a similar menu of comedy. There are shows on Friday and Saturday and food is available. You will need to become a member in order to enter – you can join for a moderate fee over the phone when you book tickets. Only one person per party needs to be a member.

⊖ Camden Town, Chalk Farm

🚍 24, 31, 168

&

££

SOUTH

Aztec Comedy Club

The Borderland, 47–49 Westow Street, Crystal Palace, SE19 (0181 771 0885)
Stand-up comedy on Fridays and Sundays. Improvisation shows are given on the first Sunday of each month, from 8.30 p.m. onwards. A Mexican menu is available.

🚇 Crystal Palace

🚍 2, 137A, 157, 358

Limited &

£

Jongleurs at the Cornet

49 Lavender Gardens, Battersea, SW11 (0171 924 2248)
Stand-up comedy on Fridays and Saturdays. Four comedians per night do a show each (from 8.00 p.m. onwards) and pub food is available. See Jongleurs Camden, page 181, for membership information.

⊖ Clapham Common, then bus

🚇 Clapham Junction

🚍 77, 77A, 345

££

Up the Creek

302 Creek Road, Greenwich, SE10 (0181 858 4581)
Mainstream, stand-up comedy is on offer here on Friday, Saturday and Sunday, from 8.00 p.m. onwards.

🚇 Greenwich

🚍 188, 199

&

££

WEST

Acton Banana

The King's Head, 214 High Street, Acton, W3 (0181 673 8904)
Up-and-coming stand-up comedians perform here on Friday and Saturday evening. Pub food is available.

⊖ Acton Town, then bus

🚍 E3, 207, 266

&

£

Canal Café Theatre

The Bridge House, Delamere Terrace, W2 (0171 289 6054)

In the heart of Little Venice, the Canal Café Theatre offers comedy seven nights a week (from 8.00 p.m.). There are regular revues of the best of new comics too. Pub food is available.

⊖ Warwick Avenue

🚌 6, 18, 46

No ♿

£–££

10
OUTDOOR
ENTERTAINMENT

L ONDON IS FAMOUS for its West End theatres and celebrity concerts, but there is also plenty of entertainment – from Shakespeare to symphony concerts – outdoors. Several of the larger parks have purpose-built open-air theatres in which seasons of plays are staged during the summer, while street entertainers offer something a little more off-beat.

Regimental bands give regular performances most days from mid-afternoon to early evening in the royal parks – Greenwich, Hyde, Regent's and St James's. Their repertoire includes plenty of traditional tunes.

Although some forms of outdoor entertainment are free, such as the buskers in Covent Garden and concerts in public parks, there are many others for which a charge is made. Where there are charges, this has been indicated.

Broadgate Arena

Corner of Liverpool Street and Eldon Street, EC2 (0171 588 6565: information)
The centrepiece of the Broadgate Centre, the arena has become a popular artistic and cultural oasis in the heart of the City. A programme of events throughout the year attracts people from all over the metropolis. In the winter the arena is flooded and frozen to become London's only open-air ice rink. From April onwards, the space is used for lunch-time programmes of theatre, dance and music.

⊖/▣ Liverpool Street
🚌 11, 42, 100, 133, 214
♿

Performances: weekday lunch-times
Free

Covent Garden Street Theatre, WC2

Just round the corner from the prestigious but expensive Royal Opera House you can watch all sorts of budding performers for free. From clowns and dancers to musicians and mime artists, the variety is endless. Although the entertainment is officially free, performers are allowed to ask for money and, as this is often their only livelihood, please support them by digging deep into your pockets!

⊖ Covent Garden
🚌 9, 11, 15, 24, 29, 176
♿

Performances: daily
Free, but donations welcome

❖

"Now that
Covent Garden Station
is open on Sundays,
most of my audience
have come by Tube."

COVENT GARDEN

Crystal Palace Park

SE20 (0181 778 7148)

Concerts are given here regularly during July and August – phone for details of each concert and for advance bookings. This park is quite high up so after a concert you can enjoy a spectacular view of the lights of London below.

🚉 Crystal Palace

🚌 157, 176, 227, 312, 227

♿

£

George Inn

77 Borough High Street, SE1 (0171 407 2056)

The George Inn is a beautiful galleried coaching inn which was used regularly by the nineteenth-century writer, Charles Dickens, and has close connections with the Elizabethan playwright, William Shakespeare. Plays are produced occasionally during the summer season. Look out for posters on the gates of the pub, or phone for details. Morris dancers also perform here some evenings and weekends during the summer.

⊖ Borough, London Bridge

🚌 P3, 21, 35, 40, 133

♿ (in courtyard)

Free

Holland Park Theatre

Holland Park, W14 (0171 602 7856: box office; 0171 603 3436: recorded information)

With part of Holland House used as a backdrop and with a 100-square metre (1,100-square foot) canopy over the stage, performances here are impressive theatrical experiences. The theatre offers twelve weeks of the finest opera and dance from June to August – productions include work by established and up-and-coming companies.

On special occasions you can dine afterwards at the nearby Belvedere Restaurant on the other side of the park, although most people prefer to bring a picnic.

⊖ High Street Kensington

🚌 9, 10, 27, 28, 49, 94

♿

Performances: June–mid-August, 7.30 p.m. or 8 p.m. (phone for details)

££

Horniman Gardens

100 London Road, Forest Hill, SE23 (0181 699 8924)

See also page 64

Concerts take place during July and August. During the school holidays there are shows for children on Tuesdays and Thursdays. Phone for details.

🚉 Forest Hill

🚌 P4, 176, 185, 312

♿

Performances: Sundays

Free

Holland Park Theatre

Kenwood Lakeside Concerts

Kenwood House, Hampstead Lane, NW3 (0181 348 1286)
See also page 92
The elegant grounds of Kenwood House provide an imposing backdrop to these popular concerts which attract audiences from all across London. On some evenings the music is accompanied by dazzling displays of fireworks.

⊖ Archway, Golders Green; then bus
🚌 210
♿

Performances: mid-June–early September every Saturday evening (you are advised to book well in advance)

££

Kenwood House

Marble Hill Concerts

Twickenham, Middlesex (0181 892 5115)

See also page 103

Concerts take place in the grounds of this beautiful Palladian villa every Sunday between mid-July and early September. Mostly classical music is played but the last concert of the season is usually a jazz night. Strict parking restrictions are enforced so it is sensible to take public transport, unless you have booked a parking space (limited) within the grounds.

⊖ Richmond, then bus

▣ St Margaret's, Twickenham

🚌 H22, 33, R68, R70, 90, 290

♿

Performances: phone for details

££

Open Air Theatre

Inner Circle, Regent's Park, NW1 (0171 486 2431: box office)

The season alternates between two Shakespearean productions and one other play (either a musical or modern classic) throughout the summer. Food is served before the show and coffee and other refreshments bought during the interval can be taken back to your seat. The bar stays open afterwards until midnight.

⊖ Baker Street, Great Portland Street, Regent's Park

🚌 13, 27, 30, 82, 113, 274

♿

Performances: May–September, Monday–Saturday 7.45 p.m.; matinée Wednesday, Thursday and Saturday, 2.30 p.m.

££

Bubble Theatre Company

Any open space large enough for its 'bubble' tent becomes a temporary home for the Bubble Theatre Company, the only fully mobile theatre company in Britain. The company tours the parks of London every summer, spending about two weeks at each location. Its touring plays are aimed at under-elevens but the company also has two youth theatres, for fourteens to twenty-fives in Southwark and twelves to sixteens in Bexley. 0171 237 4434. See also page 129.

Victoria Embankment Gardens

Villiers Street, WC2 (0171 798 2063/4)

Between the end of May and the first week of August, lunch-time concerts take place daily in these gardens. There is also a short opera season during June and July.

⊖ Charing Cross, Embankment
🚇 Charing Cross
🚌 6, 9, 11, 13, 15, 23
♿

Performances: concerts: May–August, daily, lunch-times; opera season: June–July, three or four nights a week

Free

The Arts & Entertainment Day

Morning: Go to an art gallery or museum. It is best to arrive as soon as they open – they quickly fill up, even on weekdays, and it is much more enjoyable to have the place to yourself.

Lunch-time: Most museums and galleries have excellent restaurants or cafés (see individual entries). For a low-cal alternative, take in a classical concert at one of the lunch-time concert venues (see pages 139–144).

Afternoon: Matinée cinema performances are usually cheaper than evening ones and it is not generally necessary to book in advance – even for the latest release.

Early evening: Attending a private view at a gallery is a very civilized way to start the evening. The way to get your name on the best party lists is to register your details with your favourite galleries – they should put you on their mailing list if you do.

Mid-evening: There is a huge choice of things to do every evening in London from comedy to Chekhov – take your pick from concerts, theatre, dance, opera or comedy.

Late night: To round off your day, unwind at a laid-back jazz club – see pages 144–147 for details.

❖

11
THE
ENTERTAINMENT YEAR

AN ANNUAL CALENDAR OF
ARTS AND ENTERTAINMENT EVENTS

THROUGHOUT THE year dozens of cultural events take place in London but the summer is especially busy. The summer arts season kicks off properly in June with events such as the Summer Exhibition at the Royal Academy and the Grosvenor House Antiques Fair. In July it is the ever-popular Royal Tournament and the start of the Proms season which takes us through to September. Another busy period is over Christmas and New Year, with pantomimes and carol services.

There is plenty to do for the rest of the year too. Antiques and art fairs are held almost every month and there are regular drama and dance festivals throughout the city too. For film buffs, the annual highlight is the National Film Festival in November, while the theatre takes centre stage in July with the bi-annual London International Festival of Theatre.

JANUARY/FEBRUARY

Pantomimes
Oh yes, you will enjoy Britain's favourite Christmas family outing. Pantomimes starring popular celebrities are performed at theatres throughout the London area over Christmas and well into the New Year.

London International Mime Festival

Mime and physical theatre (a modern development of traditional mime) have their annual festival in London each January, where various venues from across the city play host to companies from around the world.

West London Antiques Fair

Kensington Town Hall, W8 (01444 482514: organizers)
The first antiques fair of the year (in January). A vast selection of top dealers come to this, specializing in all types of antiques and works of art, from posters to pine furniture.
⊖ High Street Kensington
🚌 9, 10, 27, 28, 31, 49
♿

The London Contemporary Art Fair

Business Design Centre, Islington, N1 (0171 359 3535)
The huge Design Centre in Islington plays host to work by contemporary artists. All the big London galleries are represented, as well as less pricey out-of-town dealers.
⊖ Angel
🚌 4, 19, 30, 38, 43, 56
♿

World of Drawings and Watercolours Fair

Park Lane Hotel, W1 (0181 995 1488)
Antique and contemporary drawings and watercolours jostle for attention at this fair in January.
⊖ Green Park, Hyde Park Corner
🚌 2, 10, 16, 36, 73, 74
♿

Fine Art & Antiques Fair

Olympia, W14 (0171 224 2219: box office)
The first of three important annual fairs at Olympia where you can buy antique furniture, clocks, silver, jewellery, glass, ceramics and textiles as well as modern works of art. The other fairs are held in June and November.
⊖/🚃 Kensington (Olympia)
🚌 9, 10, 27, 28
♿

MARCH

Chelsea Antiques Fair

Chelsea Old Town Hall, King's Road, SW3 (01444 482514: organizers).
A smallish venue, but always packed with antique goodies.
⊖ Sloane Square
🚌 11, 19, 22, 211
♿

British Antique Dealers' Association Fair

Duke of York Headquarters, King's Road, SW3 (0171 589 4128)

One of the top antiques fairs of the year.

⊖ Sloane Square

🚌 11, 19, 22, 211

♿

SPRING BECKONS YOU

UNDERGROUND

APRIL

Spring Craft Fair

Alexandra Palace, N22 (0181 366 3153)

Crafts made all over Britain are displayed for sale here.

🚆 Alexandra Palace

🚌 W3, 84A

♿

MAY

Punch and Judy Festival

St Paul's Churchyard, Covent Garden, WC2

An annual Punch and Judy Festival is held on the Sunday closest to 9 May to commemorate the date in 1662 when Samuel Pepys watched the first recorded Punch and Judy show.

⊖ Covent Garden

🚌 6, 9, 11, 24, 29, 176

♿

Bank Holiday Music Events at the Barbican

Barbican Centre Foyer, Silk Street, EC2 (0171 638 8891)

Themed music events, including folk and jazz, are held at the Barbican on both May bank holidays. Two days of foyer and concert events covering modern and traditional jazz are held during the May Day weekend.

⊖ Barbican

🚌 4, 56

♿

JUNE

Royal Academy Summer Exhibition

Royal Academy of Arts, Burlington House, Piccadilly, W1 (0171 439 7438)

See also page 25

The Summer Exhibition lasts from June to August and is the largest contemporary art exhibition in the world, drawing together some of the finest examples of work by living artists. Painters, sculptors, printmakers and architects, some of whom have never exhibited before, are given the opportunity to show their work alongside that of established artists. Many of the works are for sale.

Royal Academy Summer Exhibition

⊖ Green Park, Piccadilly Circus
🚌 9, 14, 19, 22, 38
♿

Greenwich Festival

Greenwich
A host of arts events and activities takes place in Greenwich over one weekend every June. They include jazz, street theatre, a boat show and art exhibitions.
🚃 Greenwich
🚌 177, 180, 188, 199, 286
Limited ♿

Open-air theatre and concerts

A summer season of theatre, concerts and opera in several venues throughout London begins in June and lasts until mid-September.
♿

Grosvenor House Art & Antiques Fair

Grosvenor House, Park Lane, W1 (0171 499 6363)
The grandest of London's annual art and antiques fairs.
⊖ Marble Arch
🚌 2, 10, 16, 36, 73, 74
♿

❖

Chelsea Festival

(0171 824 8219)

For one week in June, Chelsea comes alive with dozens of festival concerts, exhibitions and performances.

⊖ Sloane Square

🚌 11, 19, 22, 211

Limited ♿

Fine Art & Antiques Fair

Olympia, W14 (0171 224 2219: box office)

See page 199

⊖ Kensington (Olympia)

🚌 9, 10, 27, 391

♿

London International Festival of Theatre

(0181 335 0508)

On alternate years over the period of a month, from mid-June to mid-July, over twenty international companies together with British artists converge on venues in London from the Royal Court Theatre to the ICA. All types of theatre are represented, including dance, musicals, performance art, circus and children's theatre.

Limited ♿

Hampton Court Palace Music Festival

Hampton Court Road, Hampton, Middlesex (0171 344 4444: box office)

See also page 97

Hampton Court was designed in part to be a setting for the most magnificent music and entertainments and the annual Hampton Court Palace Music Festival aims to re-create some of the sights, sounds and sensations which graced its court-yards and gardens in Tudor times. Such top international artists as Kiri Te Kanawa perform here regularly and the festival also includes opera galas and classical concerts.

🚃 Hampton Court

🚌 R68, 111, 216, 411, 416

Limited ♿

City of London Festival

(0171 377 0540)

A range of choral, orchestral and chamber music is performed at venues across the City in late June and early July. There is also a programme of other events, including talks and architectural walks, together with free lunch-time concerts and street theatre.

⊖ Bank, Mansion House, St Paul's

🚌 4, 8, 11, 25, 501

Limited ♿

Henry Wood Promenade Concerts

Royal Albert Hall, Kensington Gore, SW7 (0171 589 8212)

See also page 140

A lively series of classical concerts are held here every evening from mid-July to the end of September. You can either sit down, which is more comfortable, or 'prom' (stand) in the area in front of the orchestra, which is more fun. Full details are in the Prom Guide, available from early May. Subject to availability, up to two seats per applicant for the last night are allocated to those who apply at the same time for at least five other concerts in the season. Season tickets are good value for money.

⊖ Knightsbridge, South Kensington

🚌 9, 10, 52

♿

THE
PROMENADE CONCERTS
BY UNDERGROUND
TO OXFORD CIRCUS

The Royal Tournament

Earls Court Exhibition Centre, SW5 (0171 373 8141)

With a cast of over 2,000, this action-packed military spectacle is an essential part of the summer season. Armed and exciting, the shows have something for all ages, from marching bands to the Royal Navy Field Gun Competition and re-enactments of military history. Tickets are available from the beginning of January.

⊖ Earls Court

🚌 C1, 31, 74

♿

Almeida Theatre Festival of Contemporary Opera
Almeida Theatre, Almeida Street, N1 (0171 226 7432)
See also page 126
A season of contemporary opera.
⊖ Angel, Highbury & Islington
▦ Highbury & Islington
🚌 4, 19, 30, 43
♿

Capital Radio
A season of weekend road shows begins in July and continues until September. Shows take place in outdoor venues, such as large local parks and commons. Tune in for details.

Children's Festival at the Barbican
Barbican Centre, Silk Street, EC2 (0171 638 4141)
See also page 140
An annual themed event with hundreds of activities and an array of entertainment, including shows and games.

❖

West London Antiques Fair

Kensington Town Hall, W8 (01444 482514: organizers)

While the rest of the art world takes it holiday, this fair offers the chance to buy some antiques.

⊖ High Street Kensington

🚌 9, 10, 27, 28, 31, 49

♿

Notting Hill Carnival

W11

Every August bank holiday since 1965, Notting Hill has been the scene of London's largest and most popular carnival. Over 100 colourful floats, bands and dancers wind their way through the crowded streets, filling the air with music from South America, Africa, the Caribbean and India, not forgetting the incessant screech of the onlookers' whistles. This heady cocktail of noise and colour is further jazzed up with sound systems sited along the route, producing their own variations of funk, reggae, hip-hop and soul music, while stalls sell exotic foods, as well as arts and crafts.

The children's day is usually held on the Sunday, with the main carnival taking place on Monday. A word of warning, though, the area is always extremely busy and provides easy pickings for thieves, so hold on to your money and leave any valuables at home.

⊖ Notting Hill Gate and Ladbroke Grove are closed during the carnival, so use nearby Holland Park or Westbourne Park

🚌 buses are usually diverted from normal routes

♿

Open: early afternoon to early evening for the parades

Chelsea Antiques Fair

Chelsea Old Town Hall, King's Road, SW3 (01444 482514: organizers)

See page 191

⊖ Sloane Square

🚌 11, 19, 22, 211

♿

Covent Garden Festival of Street Theatre

Covent Garden Piazza, Covent Garden, WC2 (0171 836 9136)
Every September a festival of street theatre is held to celebrate the work of all types of performers, from jugglers to dancers.
Θ Covent Garden
🚌 6, 9, 111, 24, 29, 176
♿

The Last Night of the Proms

Royal Albert Hall, Kensington Gore, SW7 (0171 589 8212)
The most popular classical music event of the year. See page 195 for information on how to obtain tickets.
Θ Knightsbridge, South Kensington
🚌 9, 10, 52
♿

OCTOBER

Dance Umbrella Dance Festival

In association with *Time Out*, Dance Umbrella sponsor the annual London Dance and Performance Awards for the best in new dance performance each October.

Royal Court Young Writers' Festival

Royal Court Theatre, Sloane Square, SW1 (0181 960 4641: information)
A bi-annual festival of work by young writers (between the ages of eight and twenty-three) gets the spotlight at the Royal Court Theatre, the home of new writing. There are four main productions, complemented by shorter, five-minute-long curtain raisers by younger children.
Θ Sloane Square
🚌 C1, 11, 19, 22, 211
♿

NOVEMBER

Turner Prize

Tate Gallery, SW1 (0171 887 8000)
See also page 14
The purpose of the Turner Prize, according to the Tate, is to bring new development in the visual arts to the attention of people who are interested in modern culture, but who do not regularly visit commercial and smaller galleries, where 'young' artists (under fifty years old) are represented. The works of the shortlisted artists and the winner are on view throughout November each year. You can catch the prize-giving on Channel 4, which broadcasts the ceremony live from the Tate each year.
Θ Pimlico
🚌 2, C10, 36, 77A, 88, 185
♿

London Film Festival

National Film Theatre and other venues (0171 928 3232)

A film buff's dream – over two weeks of top-quality films from around the world on show at cinemas throughout London each November. This is a chance to see premieres of new films, the best overseas films and the work of new writers and directors.
Limited ♿

London International Jazz Festival

Serious, Windsor House, 83 Kingsway, WC2 (0171 405 5974: recorded information/ leaflet requests)

The largest jazz festival in London, with hundreds of performances held in numerous venues for ten days.

⊖ Holborn
🚌 68, 91, 168, 171, 188
Limited ♿

Fine Art & Antiques Fair

Olympia, W14 (0171 244 2219: box office)

See page 194
⊖/🚉 Kensington (Olympia)
🚌 9, 10, 27, 28
♿

DECEMBER

Carol Concerts

Concerts are given throughout London, including Trafalgar Square, where there is carol singing every evening from the second week of December to Christmas Eve between 4.00 p.m. and 10.00 p.m. in aid of charities. To attend services at larger venues, such as Westminster Abbey and the Royal Albert Hall, you will need to buy tickets in advance. Full details of carol services can be found in December's listings magazines.

There are also regular performances of seasonal choral works, such as Handel's 'Messiah'.

❖

ADDITIONAL INFORMATION

TOURIST INFORMATION CENTRES RUN BY THE LONDON TOURIST BOARD

Heathrow Terminals 1,2,3
Underground Station Concourse, Heathrow Airport
Open: 8.00 a.m.– 6.00 p.m.

Liverpool Street Underground Station
EC2M 7PN
Open: Monday 8.15 a.m.–7.00 p.m.; Tuesday–Saturday, 8.30 a.m.– 4.45 p.m.

Selfridges
Oxford Street, W1A 1AB (Basement Services Arcade)
Open: during store hours

Victoria Station Forecourt
SW1 5ND
Open: 8.00 a.m.–7.00 p.m.

OTHER TOURIST INFORMATION CENTRES

British Travel Centre
12 Regent Street, SW1Y 4PQ (0181 846 9000)
Open: Monday–Friday, 9.00 a.m.–6.30 p.m.; Saturday and Sunday, 10.00 a.m.– 4.00 p.m.;
May–September, Saturday, 9.00 a.m.–5.00 p.m.; personal callers only

Croydon Tourist Information Centre
Katharine Street, Croydon, CR9 1ET (0181 253 1009)
Open: Monday, Tuesday, Wednesday and Friday, 9.00 a.m.– 6.00 p.m.;
Saturday, 9.00 a.m.–5.00 p.m.; Sunday, 12.00–5.00 p.m.

Discover Islington
Visitor Information Centre, 44 Duncan Street, N1 8BL (0171 278 8787)
Open: Monday, 2.00 a.m.–5.00 p.m.; Tuesday–Saturday, 10.00 a.m.–5.00 p.m.

❖

Greenwich Tourist Information Centre

46 Greenwich Church Street, SE10 9BL (0181 858 6376)
Open: 10.15 a.m.– 4.45p.m.

Harrow Tourist Information Centre

Civic Centre, Station Road, Harrow, HA1 2UJ (0181 424 1103)
Open: Monday–Friday, 9.00 a.m.–5.00 p.m.

Hillingdon Tourist Information Centre

Central Library, 14 High Street, Uxbridge, UB8 1HD (01895 250 706)
Open: Monday, Tuesday and Thursday, 9.30 a.m.–8.00 p.m.; Wednesday and Friday,
9.30 a.m.– 5.30 p.m.; Saturday, 9.30 a.m.– 4.00 p.m.

Hounslow Tourist Information Centre

24 The Treaty Centre, Hounslow High Street, Hounslow, TW3 1ES (0181 572 8279)
Open: Monday, Wednesday, Friday and Saturday, 9.30 a.m. –5.30 p.m.; Tuesday and
Thursday, 9.30 a.m.–8.00 p.m.

Lewisham Tourist Information Centre

Lewisham Library, 366 Lewisham High Street, SE13 6LG (0181 297 9677)
Open: Monday, 10.00 a.m. –5.00 p.m.; Tuesday and Thursday, 9.00 a.m.–8.00 p.m.;
Wednesday, Friday and Saturday, 9.00 a.m.–5.00 p.m.

London Docklands Development Corporation

Visitors' Centre, 3 Limeharbour, E14 9TJ (0171 512 3000)
Open: Monday–Friday, 9.00 a.m.–6.00 p.m.; Saturday and Sunday, 9.30 a.m.– 5.00 p.m.

Redbridge Tourist Information Centre

Town Hall, High Road, Ilford, Essex IG1 1DD (0181 478 3020)
Open: Monday–Friday, 8.30 a.m.–5.00 p.m.

Richmond Tourist Information Centre

Old Town Hall, Whittaker Avenue, Richmond, TW9 1TP (0181 940 9125)
Open: Monday–Friday, 10.00 a.m.– 6.00 p.m.; Saturday, 10.00 a.m.–5.00 p.m.;
May–October, Sunday, 10.15 a.m.–4.15 p.m.

Twickenham Tourist Information Centre

The Atrium, Civic Centre, York Street, Twickenham, TW1 3BZ (0181 891 7272)
Open: Monday–Friday, 9.00 a.m.–5.15 p.m.

❖

INDEX

Acton Banana 182
Adam, Robert 104, 105
Adelphi Theatre 111–13
Albert Hall 140–1
Albert Memorial 140
Albery Theatre 113
Aldwych Theatre 113
Alexander Fleming Laboratory
    Museum 56–7
All Hallows-by-the-Tower Undercroft
    Museum 40
Allingham, Helen 52
Almeida Theatre 126, 164
  Festival of Contemporary Opera 196
alternative theatres 125–33
Ambassadors Theatre 113
Angerstein, John Julius 11
antiques fairs 191–9
antiquities 35–6
Apollo Theatre 114
Apollo Victoria 115
Apsley House 84–5
archaeology museums 40–1
Architectural Association 15–16
architectural drawings 17–18
Architectural Study Centre 94
Architecture Foundation 24
architecture museums 41
arms and armour 20
Army Museum 62
Arsenal Museum 81
Art Nouveau Gallery 28
Ashcroft Theatre 128, 160
Associate Artist scheme 11
Astoria 148
Aztec Comedy Club 182

BAC (Battersea Arts Centre) 30, 128,
    135
backstage tours 138
ballet 154–61
Bank of England Museum 41
Bank Holiday Music Events at the
    Barbican 192
banking museums 41
Bankside Gallery 30
Banqueting House 85
Barbican Centre
  Children's Festival 196
  cinemas 171
  music events 140, 192
  Splodge Club 176
  The Pit 109–10
  Theatre 109–10

Barnett, Canon Augustus Samuel 28
Battersea Arts Centre (BAC) 30, 128,
    135
Baylis, Lilian 158, 160, 162
'Beefeaters' 89
Belfast, HMS 61
Ben Uri Art Gallery 24
Benton Fletcher Collection 70
Bethnal Green Museum of Childhood
    45
Bexley Museum 53
Big Ben 87
Black Cultural Archives and Museum
    64
Black Horse 148, 180
Blandford Collection 72
Blue Note 146
booking theatre tickets 110
Booth, General William 80
Borderline 148
Boston Manor 94–5
Bottom Line 152
Bound & Gagged 181
Bramah Tea and Coffee Museum 78
Break for the Border 148–9
Brent Town Hall 52
British Antique Dealers' Association
    Fair 192
British Council Collection 16
British Library 35
British Museum 34–7
Brixton Academy 151
Brixton Shaw Theatre 128–9
Broadgate Arena 159, 184
Bromley Museum 54
Brooking Collection 41
Bruce Castle 53
Brunel Exhibition Rotherhithe 74
BT Museum 74
Bubble Theatre Company 189
Buckingham Palace 85–7
Bull & Gate 150
Bulls Head 147
Burgh House 91
Burlington Gardens 25
Burlington House 26
Burlington, Lord 95, 96
buses 4
Bush Theatre 133–4

Cabinet War Rooms 67
Cambridge Theatre 115
Camden Arts Centre 28–9
Camden Palace 150

Canal Café Theatre 183
Capital Radio 196
Carlyle's House 95
carol concerts 199
Cartoon Art museum 27
Ceremonial Dress Collection 100–1
Chambers, Sir William 104
Charles Darwin Memorial Museum 74–5
Chelsea Antiques Fair 191, 197
Chelsea Cinema 174
Chelsea Festival 194
Child, Sir Francis 104
Childhood Museum (Bethnal Green) 45
children's cinema 176–8
Children's Festival at the Barbican 196
children's theatre 135–7
Chinese art 44
Chinese ceramics 44
Chisenhale Dance Space 159
Chiswick House 95–6
Chuckle Club 180
cinema
    children's 176–8
    current releases 166–7
    film classifications 165
    late-night 175
    London Film Festival 165, 199
    repertory cinemas 169–76
Circus Space 179
circuses 179
City of London Festival 194
Clapham Picture House 173, 176
classical music 139–43
Club Azul 161
coins 35, 41
comedy 178, 180–3
Comedy Café 181
Comedy Store 180
Comedy Theatre 115
concerts see music
Conran, Sir Terence 43
Contemporary Art Fair 191
Coombe Cliff 64
Coronet 174
Corporation of London Permanent Collection 21
costume museums 39, 42, 101
Cottesloe, Lord 110
Counterpoint Theatre 128–9
Court Dress Collection 101
Courtauld Gallery 16–17
Courthouse, The 54
Covent Garden Street Theatre 184, 198
Coward, Noel 119
craft fairs 192
craft museums 42–3
Crafts Council 42–3

cricket museum 81–2
Criterion Theatre 115
Croydon Palace 93
Crystal Palace 37
Crystal Palace Park 186
Cuming Museum 54–5
Curzon Cinemas 169
Cutty Sark 59
Dance Umbrella Dance Festival 198
dance venues 154–61
Darwin, Charles 74–5
decorative arts 6, 34–45
    Japanese 35
Desenfans, Noel 22
Design Museum 43
Dickens, Charles 186
Dickens House 67–8
Diocesan Treasury in the Crypt of St Paul's Cathedral 42
dolls 45–6
domestic interior museums 43–4
Dominion Theatre 116
Donmar Warehouse 124
Dover Street Wine Bar 149
Downe House 75
Downstairs at the King's Head 181
Dr Johnson's House 68
Drill Hall Theatre 124
Drury Lane 135
Dublin Castle 150
Duchess Theatre 116
Duke of York's Theatre 116
Dulwich Picture Gallery 22
Dungeon 78
'Dutch House' 101

Egyptian antiquities 35, 37
Egyptian archaeology 40
Empire 166
English National Ballet 154
Everyman Cinema 172
exhibition spaces 25–33

Fairfield Hall 128
Fan Museum 42
Faraday, Michael 58
Fenton House 70, 91
film classifications 165
Filthy MacNasty's & the Whiskey Café 150
Fine Art & Antiques Fair 191, 194, 199
fine arts 6, 10–33
    exhibition spaces 25–33
    national collections 10–15
    permanent collections 15–23
    public galleries 25–33
Fishmongers' Hall 103
Flamsteed, John 63

Fleming, Alexander 56–7
Florence Nightingale Museum 57
Fortrey, Samuel 101
Fortune Theatre 116
Forty Hall 92
Freud Museum 57–8

Garden History Museum 50
garden museums 50
Garrick Theatre 117
Gas Museum 75
Gate Cinema 174
Gate, The 132
Geffrye Museum 43–4
George Inn 186
Gibbs, James 23
Gielgud Theatre 117
Glass Blowing Workshop 32
Glasshouse 32
Globe Theatre 73
Goethe Institute 31
Goldsmiths' Hall 103
Goode, Ron 55
Grand, The 151–2
Grand Tour 20
Grange Museum of Community
    History 52
Great Exhibition 37, 38
Greenwich Borough Museum 55
Greenwich Festival 193
Greenwich Theatre 129
Grosvenor House Art & Antiques Fair
    193
Guards Museum 60

Haberdashers' Hall 103
Hackney Empire 126, 160, 164
Hackney Museum 51
Half Moon, Putney 152
Hall Place 53
Ham House 96–7
Hampstead Museum 52–3
Hampstead Theatre 126–7
Hampton Court Palace 97–100
    Music Festival 194
Handel, Georg 138
Haringey Museum and Archive Service
    53
Harlequinade 135
Harrow School Old Speech Room
    Gallery 21
Haymarket Theatre Royal 117
Hayward Gallery on the South Bank 31
Henry Wood Promenade Concerts 195
Her Majesty's Theatre 118
heritage museums 50
Hill, Sir Benjamin 87
Hogarth's House 100
Holland Park Theatre 186

Holmes, Sherlock 69
Horniman Gardens 186
Horniman Museum 64
Houses of Parliament 87
Hunt, Leigh 68

ICA
    cinema 169
    dance 154
    fine art gallery 25
    theatre 125
Imperial War Museum 61, 173
Institut Français 175
Ionides Collection 23
Italian Night Scenes 135

Japanese decorative arts 35
Jazz Café 146
jazz venues 144–7, 199
Jewish Museum 64–5
Johnson, Dr Samuel 68
Jones, Inigo 62
Jongleurs at the Cornet 182
Jongleurs Camden 181–2
juvenile drama 46

Keats House 68–9
Kensington Palace State Apartments
    100–1
Kenwood House 92
Kenwood Lakeside Concerts 187
Kew Bridge Steam Museum 75
Kew Gardens Gallery 32
Kew Palace 101
King's Head 152
    Downstairs at the King's Head 181
Kings Head Theatre Club 134
Kingston Museum 56
Kneller, Sir Godfrey 12

LA2 (London Astoria Two) 149
Labatt's Apollo 132, 152
Lambeth Palace and Library 93
Last Night of the Proms 198
late-night cinema 175
Lauderdale House Community Arts
    Centre 29
Leighton House 101–2
Lewisham Studio Theatre 161
Liberty, Arthur 55
Lilian Baylis Theatre 160
Linley Sambourne House 102–3
Little Marionette Theatre 135–6
Livery Companies' Halls 103
local history museums 51–6
London Astoria Two (LA2) 149
London Bubble Theatre 129
London Coliseum 155, 162
London Contemporary Art Fair 191

London Dungeon 78
London Film Festival 165, 199
London Gas Museum 75
London Glass Blowing Workshop 32
London International Festival of
    Theatre 194
London International Jazz Festival 199
London International Mime Festival
    191
London Palladium 118
London Planetarium 75–6
London Symphony Orchestra 139, 140
London Toy and Model Museum 45
London Transport Museum 83
London White Card 47
Lubbock, John 54
Lumiere 169
Lyric Hammersmith 132
Lyric Theatre 118
Lyttelton, Oliver 110

Madame Tussaud's 79
major museums 34–9, 47–9
Man in the Moon, The 134
Marble Hill Concerts 188
Marble Hill House 103
Marianne North Gallery 22–3
Maritime Museum 62–3
maritime museums 59–63
Marquee 149
Martinware Pottery Collection 44, 56
MCC Museum 81–2
Mean Fiddler 151
medals 35
medical science museums 56–9
Mermaid Theatre 126
Methodism Museum 69–70
Metro 170
MGM Cinemas 166
MGM Hammersmith 177
MGM Hampstead 172
MGM Putney 177
MGM Swiss Centre 170
Michael Faraday's Laboratory and
    Museum 58
Micro Gallery 11
military museums 59–63
Military School of Music 72
mime 137–8, 191
Minema 170
MOMI (Museum of the Moving
    Image) 71
Morris, William 55, 90–1
Movingstage Marionette Company 136
Mozart, Wolfgang 139
multi-culture museums 64–7
Museum of Garden History 50
Museum of Instruments 70
Museum of London 65–6, 172

Museum of Mankind 66
Museum of Methodism 69–70
Museum of the Moving Image
    (MOMI) 71
Museum of Richmond 56
Museum of Rugby 82
museums
    archaeology 40–1
    architecture 41
    coins and banking 41
    costumes 39, 42, 101
    crafts 42–3
    design 43
    domestic interiors 43–4
    gardens 50
    heritage 50
    local history 51–6
    major museums 34–9, 47–9
    maritime 59–63
    medical science 56–9
    military 59–63
    multi-culture 64–7
    people, politics and religion 67–70
    performing arts 70–3
    pottery and porcelain 44
    science and technology 74–7
    social history 78–80
    South Kensington 37
    specialist decorative arts 40–1
    sport 81–2
    textiles 42
    toys 45–6
    transport 83
music 6–7, 139–53
    carol concerts 199
    city churches 143–4
    classical 139–43
    jazz 144–7, 199
    museums 70–3
    open-air concerts 186–9, 193
    pop 148–53
    Promenade Concerts 195, 198
    regimental bands 184

Narwhal Inuit Art Gallery 32–3
National Army Museum 62
National Collection of watercolours 38
National Film Theatre 173, 177
national fine art collections 10–15
National Gallery 10–12
National Maritime Museum 62–3
National Museum of Cartoon Art 27
National Portrait Gallery 12–13
National Postal Museum 79
National Studio 108
National Theatre 108–9, 110–11, 138
Natural History Museum 47–8
Naval College 94
New End Theatre 127

New London Theatre 118
Nightingale, Florence 57
North, Marianne 22–3
North Woolwich Old Station Museum 83–4
Notting Hill Carnival 197

Observatory 62–3
Odeon Cinemas 166–7
Old Bull Arts Centre 27, 160
Old Operating Theatre, Museum and Herb Garret 58
Old Red Lion Theatre 134
Old Vic 129
O'Leary Gallery 51
Olivier, Sir Laurence 108, 110
Olympia Fine Art & Antiques Fair 191, 194, 199
100 Club 148
Open Air Theatre 188
open-air concerts 186–9, 193
open-air theatre 193
opera 162–4, 196
Oral History Archive 65
Orange 153
Orange Tree Theatre 134
Oranje Boom Boom 181
Orleans House Gallery 23
Osterley Park 104

Palace Theatre 119
Palace of Westminster 87
Palladium 118
pantomime 111, 135, 190
Paton Collection 23
Percival David Foundation of Chinese Art 44
performing arts museums 70–3
permanent fine art collections 15–23
Petrie Museum of Egyptian Archaeology 40
Philharmonic Orchestra 139
Phoenix Cinema 173, 178
Phoenix Theatre 119
Photographers' Gallery 25
Piccadilly Theatre 120
Pit, The 109–10
Pitshanger Manor Museum 104
Pizza Express 144
Pizza on the Park 145
Place, The 155
Planetarium 75–6
Platforms 108
Players' Theatre 125
Playhouse Theatre 120
Plaza 167
Polar Bear 145
Polish Institute 66–7

Polka Theatre for Children 136
Pollock's Toy Museum 45–6
pop venues 148–53
Postal Museum 79
pottery and porcelain museums 44
Prince Charles cinema 170
Prince Edward Theatre 120
Prince of Wales Theatre 121
Promenade Concerts 195, 198
pub theatres 133–4
public galleries 25–33
Pumphouse Educational Museum 55
Punch and Judy Festival 192
Puppet Centre 71, 135
puppet theatre 111
Puppet Theatre Barge 136
Purcell Room 142

Queen Elizabeth Hall 142, 155
Queen's Gallery 17
Queen's Theatre 121

RAF Museum 63
Ragged School Museum 80
rail travel 5
Ranger's House 93–4
Raphael Cartoons 39
regimental bands 184
Renoir cinema 171
repertory cinemas 169–76
Rhythmic, The 146
Richmond Filmhouse 175
Richmond Museum 56
Rio Dalston 172, 178
Ritzy 174
Riverside Studios 132, 161, 175, 178
Rock Circus 71
Rock Garden 149
Roman Bath 88
Ronnie Scott's Club 145
Rotherhithe Heritage Museum 55
Royal Academy of Arts 25–6
Royal Academy Summer Exhibition 192–3
Royal Albert Hall 140–1
Royal Ballet Company 154, 158
Royal Ceremonial Dress Collection 100–1
Royal Collection 17
Royal College of Music 23
Royal College of Physicians 21
Royal Court Theatre 133
Royal Court Young Writers' Festival 198
Royal Festival Hall 142, 155
Royal Hospital, Chelsea 104–5
Royal Institute of British Architects 17–18
Royal Military School of Music 72

Royal National Theatre 108–9, 110–11, 138
Royal Naval College 94
Royal Observatory 62–3
Royal Opera House 158, 163
   archives 72
Royal Shakespeare Company 108, 109
Royal Society of Painter-Printmakers 30
Royal Tournament, The 195
Royal Watercolour Society 24, 30
Rugby Museum 82

Saatchi Gallery 29–30
Sadler's Wells Theatre 158, 159
Sainsbury Wing 11
St Anne and St Agnes 143
St Bride's church 144
St Bride's Crypt Exhibition 40–1
St James's church 142
St John's church 27, 142–3
St Martin-in-the-Fields 143
St Martin's Theatre 122
St Mary-le-Bow 144
St Paul's Cathedral 42
Salvation Army Heritage Centre 80
Sambourne, Linley 102–3
Savoy Theatre 121
Science Museum 49
science and technology museums 49, 74–7
Screen on Baker Street 176
Screen on the Green 176
Screen on the Hill 176
season tickets 5
Serpentine Gallery 33
Shaftesbury Theatre 121
Shakespeare's Globe Exhibition 73
Shepherd's Bush Empire 153
Sherlock Holmes Museum 69
Showroom, The 27–8
Sikorski Museum 66–7
Sir John Soane's Museum 88
606 Club 147
Skinners' Hall 103
Soane, Sir John 20, 22, 41, 88, 104
social history museums 78–80
South Kensington museums 37
South London Art Gallery 31
Southwark Playhouse 131
specialist decorative arts museums 40–1
Splodge Club 176
sport museums 81–2
Spring Craft Fair 192
Stanislas Augustus II, king of Poland 22
Steam Museum 75
Strand Theatre 122
Suffolk Collection 94
Sutton House 90
Syon House 105

Tate Gallery 13–15
tea museums 78, 80
teddy bears 45–6
tennis museum 82
textile museums 42
theatre 7, 108–38
   alternative 125–33
   backstage tours 138
   children's 135–7
   juvenile drama 46
   local 125–33
   London International Festival of Theatre 194
   mime 137–8, 191
   museums 70–3
   open-air 193
   pantomime 111, 135, 190
   pub theatres 133–4
   puppet theatre 111
   tickets 109, 110
   West End 111–24
Theatre Museum 73
Theatre Royal 122
Theatro Technis 127
Ticketmaster 110
Tiffin 153
tourist information centres 200–1
Tower Bridge Museum 76
Tower of London 88–9
Townsend, C.H. 28
Toy and Model Museum 45
toy museums 45–6
toy theatres 46
Tradescant Garden 50
Transport Museum 83
transport museums 83
travel information 5
Travelcards 4, 5
Tricycle Theatre 128, 137
Turner Collection 14
Turner Prize 198
Twelve Bar Club 150
Twinings in the Strand 80

UCI Whiteleys 167
underground trains 4, 5
Unicorn Theatre 137
University College Art Collection 18–19
University of London 16
Up the Creek 182

Valence House Museum 51
Vaudeville Theatre 123
Vestry House Museum 51–2
Victoria & Albert Museum 37–9
Victoria Embankment Gardens 189
Victoria Palace Theatre 123
Vortex, The 147

❖

Wallace Collection 19–20
Wandle Industrial Museum 55
Warner West End 167
watercolours collection 38
Waterloo Gallery 85
Waterman's Arts Centre 133, 137
Wellcome Trust 59
Wellington, Duke of 84–5
Wembley Arena 151
Wembley Stadium 151
Wesley's Chapel 69
West End theatres 111–24
West London Antiques Fair 191, 197
Westminster Abbey Museum 50
Westminster Theatre 123
White Cards 47

Whitechapel Gallery 28
Whitehall Theatre 123
Wigmore Hall 143
Willesden Green Library Centre 52
William Morris Gallery 90–1
Wimbledon Lawn Tennis Museum 82
Wimbledon Windmill Museum 77
Windmill Museum 77
Wood, Henry 195
World of Drawings and Watercolours
    Fair 191
Wren, Sir Christopher 42, 50, 63
Wyndham's Theatre 124

Yeoman Warders 89
Young Vic Theatre 131, 164

AUTHOR'S ACKNOWLEDGEMENTS

Thank you to everyone who helped me with this book. I would particularly like to acknowledge the assistance of the following people and organizations: Graham Wiffen at the London Arts Board, the Arts Council, the press offices of London's councils, London Tourist Board, the Tate Gallery, the National Gallery, National Portrait Gallery, the Victoria & Albert Museum, Buckingham Palace, the National Trust, English Heritage, the Barbican Centre, the South Bank Centre, the Royal Opera House, Sadler's Wells, English National Ballet, English National Opera, and Mime Action Group

I am also very grateful to Charlotte Howard and Emily Wright for all their help in planning this book. I would also like to thank all those who helped me when researching for this book, especially Victoria Cooper, Nicolette White and Adrian Gibbs. Finally, I would like to thank Simon and my mother for their support.

PHOTOGRAPH ACKNOWLEDGEMENTS

Photographs courtesy of:
Copyright **British Museum** 34; **Capital Pictures** 177; **Ed Mervish Enterprises Ltd/John Walsom** 130; **English Heritage Photo Library** 188; **Tim Flach** 162; Crown copyright **Historic Royal Palaces** 98-9; **Leighton House Museum & Art Gallery** 102; **Kirsty McLaren** 106-7, 114, 119; **The Maritime Trust** 60; **National Gallery** 8-9, 10; **National Trust Photographic Library/Bill Batten** 96; Copyright **Natural History Museum, London** 48; **Redferns/David Redfern** 145; **John W Rogers** 187; **Royal Academy of Arts, London** 26, Stephen White 193; **The Saatchi Collection** 29; **The Samuel Courtauld Collection** 16; Copyright **Science Museum, London** 49; **Trustees of the William Morris Gallery** 91; **Victoria & Albert Museum, London** 38; **The Wallace Collection** 19; **Ward Lock** 86, 108, 141, 156-7, 158, 171.